THE
DIVORCE
COLONY

THE DIVORCE COLONY

HOW WOMEN REVOLUTIONIZED MARRIAGE *and*
FOUND FREEDOM *on the* AMERICAN FRONTIER

APRIL WHITE

hachette
BOOKS

NEW YORK

Cover design by Kimberly Glyder

Cover illustrations: ripped paper © Picsfive/Shutterstock; woman © lynea/Shutterstock; building photographs courtesy of Siouxland Heritage Museums; photograph of views of Sioux Falls and vicinity [Between 1900 and 1910] retrieved from the Library of Congress

Hachette Books
Hachette Book Group
1290 Avenue of the Americas
New York, NY 10104
HachetteBooks.com
Twitter.com/HachetteBooks
Instagram.com/HachetteBooks

First Edition: June 2022

Published by Hachette Books, an imprint of Perseus Books, LLC, a subsidiary of Hachette Book Group, Inc. The Hachette Books name and logo is a trademark of the Hachette Book Group.

The Hachette Speakers Bureau provides a wide range of authors for speaking events. To find out more, go to www.hachettespeakersbureau.com or call (866) 376-6591.

The publisher is not responsible for websites (or their content) that are not owned by the publisher.

Photograph of the Cataract House Hotel, reproduced by permission of the Siouxland Heritage Museums, Sioux Falls, SD. Photograph of Maggie, courtesy of Library of Congress, Prints & Photographs Division. Photograph of Mary, courtesy of Special Collections, Fine Arts Library, Harvard University. Photograph of Blanche by Wallace Scott, public domain. Photograph of Flora, reprinted with permission of Cleveland Colby Colgate Archives, Colby-Sawyer College. Photograph of Minnehaha County Courthouse, reproduced by permission of the Siouxland Heritage Museums, Sioux Falls, SD.

Print book interior design by Marie Mundaca.

Library of Congress Cataloging-in-Publication Data
Names: White, April, author.
Title: The divorce colony : how women revolutionized marriage and found
    freedom on the American frontier / April White.
Description: First edition. | New York : Hachette Books, 2022. | Includes
    bibliographical references and index.
Identifiers: LCCN 2021049519 | ISBN 9780306827662 (hardcover) |
    ISBN 9780306827686 (ebook)
Subjects: LCSH: Divorce—South Dakota—Sioux Falls—History—19th century. |
    Divorce—Law and legislation—South Dakota—Sioux Falls. | Divorced
    women—United States—Biography. | Married women—Legal status, laws, etc.—
    United States. | Women—United States—Social conditions. | Sioux
    Falls (S.D.)—History. | United States—Social conditions—1865–1918.
Classification: LCC HQ836.S5 W45 2022 | DDC
    306.89/309783371—dc23/eng/20211028
LC record available at https://lccn.loc.gov/2021049519

ISBNs: 9780306827662 (hardcover), 9780306827686 (ebook)

Printed in the United States of America

LSC-C

Printing 1, 2022

Three centuries ago,
Many pilgrims sailed, you know,
To find a home in Freedom's holy land;
Nearly all of them were men,
(How things have changed since then!)
Now the women sail out West to beat the band.

The colonies they build
Are a sort of woman's guild;
And the C's they have to brave are only these:
Counselors and Courts; And yet—
The freedom that they get
Is the same; it is to worship as they please.

—CHARLES ELMER HOLMES,
Sioux Falls, 1905

Contents

Contents

PART IV: FLORA

IS MARRIAGE A FAILURE?

The Cataract House Hotel in the 1890s.

FROM NEW YORK, the journey took four days. The North Shore Limited departed from Grand Central Depot on Forty-Second Street in Manhattan each afternoon at 4:50 p.m. It was not the fastest train to Chicago; that superlative was reserved for the New York and Chicago Limited, which reached the newly crowned "Second City" fifteen minutes quicker. But in the summer of 1891, the North

Shore Limited was considered the most luxurious of the passenger cars that hurtled west from New York City.

A swirl of steam and soot enveloped waiting passengers. Crowds thronged the depot's platforms. It was a democratic sort of chaos. The cacophony and oppressive heat were the same for the woman who had packed up her meager possessions in a tenement on the Lower East Side and the one who had directed her maid to prepare her trunks in the parlor of a Fifth Avenue mansion. Once a monument to innovation, Grand Central Depot was a prematurely aging marvel; the train shed—two hundred feet wide and six hundred feet long, with a glass ceiling arching one hundred feet above—had been the largest in the world when it opened just two decades earlier. But it was not large enough to meet the demands of a restless city barreling toward a new century. Millions now passed through the depot every year.

The well-to-do among the passengers booked tickets for a Wagner Palace Car, a serene mahogany and brocade escape from the overflowing second-class accommodations and dismal third-class option. A woman of means traveling alone booked four seats across two upholstered benches. It was an expensive but necessary signal of her propriety. As the North Shore Limited pulled out of the station, heading north toward Albany before turning west to Buffalo, the woman could use the extra space to accommodate her wide traveling skirt and her hat, wrapped carefully in a thick veil to protect it from the cinders floating through the windows. When night fell and the porters transformed the car into a rolling hotel— the benches reconfigured to form the lower berths, and the ornate ceiling compartments opened to reveal the upper ones—the woman would have complete privacy behind her heavy sleeping curtains.

As the sun rose on the morning of the second day, the North Shore Limited approached the International Suspension Bridge spanning the American-Canadian border. Barely visible in the new morning light and overwhelmed by the sounds of the engine was Niagara Falls, less than three miles away. The magnificent cataract was a highlight of the trip, as was the bridge itself. Since it opened in 1855, this feat of engineering had drawn such daredevils as Maria Spelterini, a young Italian acrobat who stretched a tightrope parallel to the tracks and made the same journey across the river blindfolded and then again with her hands and feet manacled. And it had drawn those far braver: In the years before the Civil War, the bridge was a beacon for the enslaved. To reach its midpoint— the international borderline—was to be free.

The North Shore Limited continued on, skirting the northern edge of Lake Erie and the southern shoreline of Lake Michigan, and before sunset on the second day, the train arrived in Chicago. It was not unusual to see a lady disembark alone in Great Central Depot, a fire-scarred structure that could not rival its grand New York counterpart. The railroad advertised the North Shore Limited to unaccompanied woman travelers. It arrived "in ample time for one to reach her destination by daylight." But for a few aboard, that destination was still further west.

A trek across the breadth of Illinois and Iowa first required an overnight stay in Chicago. The next afternoon the Illinois Central got underway, speeding across the prairie toward the setting sun. Its sleeper cars had all the material comforts of those that ferried passengers between New York and Chicago, but here a woman alone raised eyebrows. A modest traveling dress, clean hat, and tightly pinned sleeping curtains were no guard against the curiosities and judgments of her fellow passengers.

As the train approached its final destination in the early hours of the fourth day, those on board became watchful, casting sidelong glances at any unfamiliar woman not accompanied by her husband. For her, there could be only one reason to undertake this fifteen-hundred-mile trip: she had come for a divorce.

⁓❧⁓

DIVORCE WAS NOT a new phenomenon in the last years of the nineteenth century. For as long as there has been marriage, there has been a debate over its dissolution: Who has the right to end a relationship? When, why, and how? In most countries and cultures, the institution has been deemed too integral to society to leave the decision to separate up to the spouses alone. And yet ending a marriage has always been an option for some.

Throughout much of history, that choice was the domain of the wealthy man, who had the income and influence to shape, circumvent, or simply ignore the laws of the church or the state. Many men could walk away from their wives and still remain secure in their fortunes, their places in society, and the legitimacy of their children. Women, who for centuries lacked economic independence and social standing outside marriage in most cultures, rarely had that luxury. They needed the government sanction that was often just out of reach.

Such was the story in the United States. In the earliest days of the nation, the legal dissolution of a marriage came under the purview of state legislatures. An unhappy spouse was forced to lobby the government assembly for a private bill of divorce, an opaque process accessible only to a few. But slowly, over the course of the early 1800s, jurisdiction over marriage had moved to the courts. The legislator's vote gave way to the determination of a judge, who weighed evidence in an adversarial process. Either wife or husband could initiate a suit for divorce, accusing the other of a breach of the marital contract.

This transition from the legislature to the courts had not been intended to give more women the ability to end their marriages, but it had that effect—in some places. The United States was a hodgepodge of state laws on the topic. South Carolina had no provisions at all for divorce, except during a controversial six-year window in the 1870s, when a mere 157 petitions were granted on charges of adultery and desertion. New York was only slightly less strict, severing the marriage bond only with proof of adultery. Further west, however, were new states and territories with more lenient laws. Those who could afford to make the trip—an expensive proposition—could find refuge on the frontier and release from their marriages on their own terms.

The most permissive divorce statutes in the United States had long existed at the edges of the settled country, where the land and the laws had not yet been tamed. Those same places often had short residency requirements before a settler fell under the jurisdiction of its courts. This was a simple acknowledgment of the itinerant nature of pioneer life, but it was also an opportunity for divorce seekers. In the 1840s and 1850s, Ohio and Indiana were popular destinations for divorce, before their residency requirements were lengthened. In the 1860s Illinois earned a reputation for quickly severing marriages, and Iowa gained similar fame in the 1870s and 1880s.

These "migratory divorces" enflamed a country already worried about a growing epidemic of broken marriages. In 1889, the newly formed Bureau of Labor put a number on those fears, counting 328,716 divorces between 1867 and 1886, far more than anyone had anticipated. Even more alarming to many, there were more than twice the number of divorces in the mid-1880s as there had been in the mid-1860s. Newspapers nationwide heralded the finding with ominous headlines asking, "Is Marriage a Failure?"

For most of the next two decades, the effort to limit access to divorce allied the country's clergy, large swaths of its political and judicial classes, and many of its social leaders. For them, at this moment of rapid social and economic change, the stakes of the divorce debate were no less than the future of the American family, the very building block of the country itself. They would attack this scourge with religious condemnation, legal obstacles and expense, new legislative restrictions, and the threat of ostracism.

On the other side of this battle were those who did not want a fight. They wanted nothing more than release from their marriages. Some had tales of abuse, infidelity, and desertion. Some were just unhappy and saw, for the first time, an escape route. They had, at least in some states, the law on their side, but that could change in the face of vocal opposition to divorce. They had few champions and little political power of their own. In the last half of the nineteenth century, most divorce seekers—nearly two out of every three—were women.

⌒∞⌒

WHEN THE BUREAU of Labor counted American divorces in the late 1880s, the territory of Dakota had the dubious honor of posting the biggest increase: 6,691 percent more had been granted there in the mid-1880s than in the years just after the Civil War.

The statisticians were quick to offer an innocent reason for this stunning finding: Dakota's population had grown exponentially during that time, if not quite enough to fully account for the rise. But those who feared divorce did not want a mathematical equation. They wanted a scapegoat for the rampant immorality the study had revealed. The country turned its eyes west and then focused on one upstart city on the frontier. At the turn of the century, Sioux Falls, South Dakota, became the unexpected epicenter of the country's divorce crisis.

In the small western city at the bend of the Big Sioux River, migratory divorce roiled the community. The opposition assembled. An outspoken bishop, a by-the-book judge, an ambitious senator, and a disapproving public seemed poised to limit—or even eliminate—the availability of divorce. But, to their surprise, the threat did not deter arriving divorce seekers.

The women who traveled to Sioux Falls from around the country and the world—for it was the women who caused the most public consternation—were not activists. For each of them, the decision to end her marriage was a private one. But what might have been a quiet act of personal empowerment and self-determination became, in the glare of the national spotlight, a radical political act. Though married women had secured the right to own property only a generation earlier and the right to the vote was still a distant dream, these divorcees collectively forced the issue into the national conversation, into the country's churches, its courts, its legislatures, and its pinnacle of power: the White House.

These divorce seekers were not representative of the legions of unhappy spouses in the country. Most were among the social elite of the fading Gilded Age, white women of some means. For them, the obstacles to divorce were high, but with time, money, and no small measure of bravery, they were surmountable. The challenges those without financial resources faced were more formidable, especially for Black women in the South, most of whom did not even have a legally recognized right to marry until after the Civil War.

The women who made Sioux Falls their temporary home were not perfect test cases. These women, the men they had married, and the men who would determine their fates led messy lives. Their personal foibles, failed romances, and hopes for the future filled the country's newspapers. The public could not look away from Sioux Falls and the Cataract House, the storied hotel where many of the women stayed while awaiting their freedom. But it was not the divorce crisis itself that so captivated most of the country; it was the love triangles, the false identities, the poisonings, and the sensational trials.

An unlucky few among the divorce seekers—Maggie De Stuers, Mary Nevins Blaine, Blanche Molineux, and Flora Bigelow Dodge— became celebrities, known both at home and abroad, by their husbands' last names, for their failed marriages. These four did not desire the attention; they were thrust center stage by the men who opposed them and the religious, political, legal, and social impediments they faced. The infamy scarred each of them, but in their notoriety, these women and those who joined them in Sioux Falls forever reshaped the country's attitude toward divorce. They themselves—not the clergy, the judiciary, elected officials, their nosy neighbors, or even their families—would set the terms of their most intimate relationships.

The evolution of marriage in the United States is a history told in lofty and heroic terms, the expansion of the institution and its attendant benefits heralded as civil rights victories. Divorce is rarely celebrated in the same way, but the two are inextricable. The divorce seekers in Sioux Falls more than a century ago saw this clearly: to be free to choose whom to love and how to live is to be free both to marry and to divorce.

··· **PART ONE** ···

MAGGIE

Chapter One

A THRIVING AND INTERESTING PLACE

B ARONESS MARGARET Laura Astor De Stuers arrived at the end
of the line on the first day of June 1891. Rain poured down outside the soot-streaked windows as the Illinois Central pulled into a depot
on the east bank of the Big Sioux River. For five hundred miles, each
station stop she could glimpse from her berth had been more bedrag-
gled than the one before, but Sioux Falls was a surprise. The elaborately
gabled terminal was a promising introduction to the yet-unseen city: it
was small but beautiful, even elegant. In the murky morning light, the
depot's sturdy stone walls were a peculiar periwinkle color unique to the
Sioux quartzite quarried nearby.

For Maggie, as she had been known for most of her life, the journey
to Sioux Falls had begun sixteen years earlier, on April 20, 1875, in the
grand drawing room of her family home at Madison Avenue and Thirty-
Fourth Street in Manhattan. There, in front of a coterie of the city's most
powerful and affluent, twenty-two-year-old Maggie Carey had pledged
herself to Baron Alphonse Lambert Eugene De Stuers, a thirty-four-
year-old Dutch diplomat serving as chargé d'affaires to Washington,

DC. An Episcopal minister, representing Maggie's faith, and a Catholic priest, representing her betrothed's, presided over the union. There had been no shortage of nuptials to occupy New York society that clear and chilly spring week, but Maggie's wedding, one newspaper opined, "in point of elegance and importance deserves to rank foremost of the many that have occurred."

It was newly fashionable in the 1870s in New York to marry a titled European, but the importance of the event was due almost entirely to Maggie's own lineage. She was already American royalty, a descendant of the first John Jacob Astor, who had immigrated to the United States after the Revolutionary War and established himself as a leading fur trader and a real estate mogul. Her mother, Alida, was the youngest daughter of his son William Backhouse Astor Sr. and Margaret Armstrong, and the sister of William Backhouse Jr. and John Jacob III. Maggie's father, John Carey, had been a classmate of John Jacob's at Columbia College and, after marrying Alida, had become a confidant of William's. Long the wealthiest family in the city, the Astors owned New York, and John Carey managed much of it.

The now numerous branches of the Astor family dominated the New York social scene too. Most of the Careys—including Maggie's two younger brothers—were more reticent than their other relations, but not Maggie. She "lit up any room where she entered," observed a fellow socialite. She was glittering, dramatic, extravagant. She was not beautiful, but she was always described that way. Her high spirits earned her appearance adjectives like "magnificent," while her large fortune ensured she was also considered "refined," "graceful," and "aristocratic." She had made her entrance into society at a brilliant private ball hosted by her aunt Augusta, the wife of John Jacob III, and she had made a good marriage, a strategic alliance of money and influence across two continents.

He is "the nicest foreigner I have ever met," Sallie Delano raved about the Baron. Sallie was one of Maggie's cousins and had been among her closest friends since childhood. On the day of the wedding, Sallie wore a delicate dress of bright red tulle and took her place along-side the other bridesmaids. The event was a who's who of the country's best-known clans: Astor, Delano, Rutherford, Rhinelander. The Baron could not match those bank accounts, but he was prosperous and had professional promise, and he hailed from a well-connected family. For generations, the De Stuers had been Dutch politicians and military officers; Alphonse's father had commanded the Royal Dutch East Indies Army. The Beyens, his mother's family, were Belgian lawyers and diplomats. The Baron had once been dashing, with piercing pale eyes, an elegant Roman nose, dark hair that curled at his temples, and a carefully coiffed goatee, but he had long since settled into the mold of an upper-crust bureaucrat. Maggie's groom, twelve years her senior, was now mostly bald, his nose widening and his beard bushy beneath a walrus mustache. He was known to wear a monocle.

Maggie's life with the Baron promised to be much as her childhood had been. In marriage, she would again flit between New York and chic European capitals, moving among their most distinguished citizens, and she would retreat each summer to the spa towns of Germany, or the vineyards of France, or the mansions of Newport to enjoy the same society in cooler climes. A few weeks after their wedding, Maggie and the Baron had set sail for a new home in Europe.

Now Maggie found herself in unknown territory. She was on the edge of the American frontier, with her maid, her private secretary, and her dog, Tweedle; her husband and their three children were in Paris, more than four thousand miles away.

⧫

IT WASN'T UNTIL the Illinois Central pulled out of the station that Maggie's new home became visible from the platform.

On the northern edge of downtown, a quartzite clock tower rose 165 feet into the Dakota sky—the new Minnehaha County Courthouse. On that day in 1891, the building was almost complete. Just a few weeks earlier, a lightning rod had been placed atop the steep slate roof of the city's tallest tower, but a nine-foot round hole remained in each of its four sides. The clock was still missing. When the building was finished, architect Wallace L. Dow said, it would be the largest courthouse between Chicago and Denver.

Dow had built much of Sioux Falls, carving a new city from the same stone that formed its namesake waterfall. Its heft and the architect's artistry gave the city a sense of permanence that belied its youth; it had been incorporated as a village just fifteen years earlier. For more than a century prior, the prairie had been the bison hunting grounds of the nomadic Sioux tribes—as white travelers knew the Lakota, Dakota, and Nakota people—and throughout the early 1800s, the falls had served as a meeting point for the tribes and itinerant fur traders. Among those vying for the luxurious bison hides and beaver pelts were representatives of the American Fur Company, founded by the original John Jacob Astor. Maggie's family had grown fat off the region in the first half of the nineteenth century, its fashionable furs earning a premium in New York and London.

White settlers first arrived in the late 1850s, drawn to this place by descriptions of its falls. The cataract was "great and picturesque," army captain James Allen had written in his journal in 1844. "The rock in the course and on the borders of the stream is split, broken and piled up in the most irregular and fantastic shapes, and presents deep and frightful chasms." The United States laid claim to the land, establishing the Dakota Territory in 1861, but the Lakota and Dakota people did not cede their home willingly to the newcomers. During the Dakota War of 1862, the settlement on the banks of the Big Sioux River was abandoned, and when settlers returned to its ruins in 1865, it was to establish the site as a small military outpost. After several years of relative peace and prosperous harvests, though, the fort was shuttered, and a town again began to grow. By the early 1870s, Sioux Falls had become a destination for optimistic arrivals from the East, the farmers, businessmen, and hustlers who had shaped the city Maggie saw before her. The great and picturesque falls—never quite as dramatic as Allen and other explorers had depicted them to be—had been harnessed to polish Sioux quartzite, grind grain into flour, and power the city of ten thousand.

To the south of the Illinois Central depot, a stone cross was barely visible against the stormy gray sky: St. Augusta Cathedral, the home church of Episcopal bishop William Hobart Hare. The bishop was a stranger to Maggie, but in this unknown place, his church was a welcome sight. The cathedral was named in honor of her aunt Augusta, the woman who had thrown such a spectacular party for Maggie's debut. Augusta had been a friend to the bishop, generously supporting his work among the Sioux. After she died, her husband, John Jacob, donated more than $25,000 to construct the imposing building. The church had been completed two years earlier, but a proposed campanile that would have rivaled the courthouse tower in stature was never built, and the congregation was still fundraising for stained glass windows. Maggie remembered her uncle showing her pictures of Sioux Falls shortly before his death in early 1890. "This gave me the first idea of coming here," Maggie told those who asked.

John Jacob had described the city as a "thriving and interesting place" and encouraged Maggie to travel there someday to see the memorial he had built to his wife. But as Maggie's fellow passengers on the Illinois Central had surely concluded, that was not what had lured her to Sioux Falls. The city had another attraction, which Maggie had read about in a guide she had discreetly procured from a Parisian bookseller: the laxest divorce laws in the United States. Maggie needed only to live in the new state of South Dakota for ninety days to be considered a resident and come under the jurisdiction of its courts. On the ninety-first day, she could file a petition to end her marriage.

❦

HORSE-DRAWN CARRIAGES ferried the Illinois Central passengers across the Eighth Street bridge to downtown Sioux Falls. Weighed down by travel trunks, their wheels sank into the muddy streets, which, just a few days earlier, were so dry and dusty that the business owners along the route were agitating for regular sprinkling. Maggie's destination was the Cataract House Hotel, a little more than a quarter mile away. From the depot, only the top of the hotel's observation tower had been visible, but once the carriage turned onto Phillips Avenue, the Cataract dominated the landscape. The hotel—in various incarnations, each bigger than the last—had served western travelers since 1871, seven years before the first railroad arrived in Sioux Falls. In the decades since, the establishment had become so central to civic life that the city's address system started at its doors at Ninth and Phillips. In 1889, the townspeople celebrated South Dakota's statehood in its lobby. The current brick building was another Wallace L. Dow creation; he had recently added a fourth floor to the busy hotel with a sloping steel-shingled roof and dormers that suggested the Parisian skyline Maggie had left behind. The Cataract was "the great rendezvous," wrote the *Argus-Leader*, which competed with the *Sioux Falls Press* for scoops and hotel advertisements. "It is generally just about headquarters for everything."

For decades, the Corson brothers, Harry and Henry, had presided over the hotel Harry had originally established. Little that happened in the Cataract escaped the duo's notice. The aging brothers had differing political views—Henry was a staunch Republican, Harry a stalwart Democrat—but they were in agreement when it came to making money. They both stood against prohibition, which was the law of the land in South Dakota, and were both vocal in their support of the shops and services growing up around the hotel. Most importantly, they did not care what errands brought guests to Sioux Falls, as long as the guests could pay. The Cataract was the city's nicest hotel, Dakota's rival to the best destinations in Boston, New York, and Chicago, which boasted sumptuously appointed parlors, elaborate dinner menus overflowing with fresh seafood and fruits year-round, and a constant swirl of social events. It was also the priciest: a room with steam heating, electric bells, and elevator service cost $2.50 a day, 25 percent more than other lodging options in the city, though a fraction of the cost of a room at New York's top accommodations. In the summer of 1891, that mercenary hospitality, paired with South Dakota's liberal laws and Sioux Fall's five railroad lines, made the Cataract the city's headquarters for divorce seekers.

When Maggie passed through the arched entranceway to the Cataract House that June day, she joined a small but growing contingent of others with the same intentions. The phrase "going to Sioux Falls" was already on its way to becoming a euphemism for divorce among Eastern elites, and the hotel ledger where Maggie's name would be recorded read like the courthouse docket. Edward Pollock was here, sent from New York by his father with instructions to sever his ties to the household maid with as much secrecy as he had maintained when marrying her. Florence Cuthbertson was here too. The pretty twenty-three-old from Chicago was awaiting release from her second husband. Eva Lynch-Blosse had journeyed from London for the decree she had twice tried—and failed—to obtain in England. She was only two weeks away from a hearing to determine if she would be freed from her husband, a man "of good family, but bad habits," another guest observed. Before Maggie arrived, the most recognizable of the divorce seekers at the Cataract was Mary Nevins Blaine, the young, unhappy wife of Jamie Blaine. Her father-in-law was Secretary of State James G. Blaine, a likely 1892 presidential candidate.

Maggie and her maid, Mary Van den Heuvel, who had been with her for most of her marriage, booked a suite of four rooms on the top floor of the Cataract House. Her private secretary, William Elliot, took two at the other end of the hallway. Maggie's parlor filled a prime corner of the hotel, with windows facing south toward St. Augusta and east to the Edmison-Jameson Block, home to nearly a quarter of the city's thirty-eight law firms. In peaceful moments, the roar of the falls, a mile away, could be heard. Maggie set about redecorating her suite, ordering new furniture, a bigger bathtub, and a piano.

And then she waited.

Chapter Two

IN GOOD FAITH

T HIS WAS not the first time Maggie had tried to leave her husband. In June 1889, she departed from the home she shared with the Baron in Paris to pass the summer months in Newport. Her extended family had long owned majestic mansions in the Rhode Island resort town, and Maggie had spent the summer season there often as a child. Even then there had been whispers about the wives who did not return to the city with the arrival of fall.

By the mid-1800s, the United States' patchwork of divorce laws had given rise to a legally debatable phenomenon, available only to those who could afford the expense: to end a marriage, one spouse would travel to a jurisdiction with fewer restrictions and live there for as long as necessary to obtain a divorce. Manhattan's elite, many of whom made Newport their summer playground, had been known to take advantage of this legal loophole. New York allowed "absolute divorce"—the dissolution of the marriage contract—only for adultery. Maggie had many complaints against her husband, but his fidelity was not one of them. There was another, rarely used option in New York and other states with strict statutes: a "limited divorce." Also known as a "divorce of bed and board," a limited divorce—available for cruelty, abandonment, and neglect in New York—permitted husband and wife to live separate lives, but they remained legally married and therefore could not take other spouses. It was not an attractive choice, especially for women who did not have a share of the Astor riches to support themselves.

In Rhode Island, an absolute divorce required 365 days residency and a claim of one or more of ten offenses, among them adultery, extreme cruelty, neglect, and other "wickedness." These provisions were not notably permissive, except when compared to those of neighboring New York, but Newport certainly wasn't a bad place to pass a year.

Maggie had not revealed her intention to divorce her husband before she crossed the Atlantic in the first-class cabins of the SS *La Bretagne* in the company of her eleven-year-old daughter, Margot, and Margot's governess, Agnes Whiteside. After docking in New York City, the group traveled on to Rokeby, a sprawling Hudson Valley estate that had been in the Astor family for decades. Maggie's brother Arthur was in residence at the forty-three-room home, which overlooked a vast lawn and the width of the Hudson River, but Maggie did not visit for long. Leaving her daughter and Agnes behind, she continued on to Newport, where the social season was in full swing. *The* Mrs. Astor—Maggie's aunt Lina— had arrived weeks earlier in the first days of July to oversee the addition of an elegant ballroom at her cliffside mansion, one large enough to host all of "the Four Hundred," as preeminent families of New York society had recently been dubbed by tastemaker Ward McAllister. Maggie had missed the first throw-in on the polo fields and the debut dance at the Casino, but her presence itself was treated as an event, and there was still the opening of the opera house to look forward to, as well as the grand ball at the Ochre Point home of the Van Alens, also relatives of Maggie's. Maggie rented a charming clapboard cottage with a wide front porch from the Jays, still more Astor relations, and she was often seen in the company of her unmarried cousin Marion Langdon. Even in this unusually rainy year, August days in Newport were a succession of luncheons, receptions, lawn parties, dinners, and dances. As the weather grew colder, though, the grand houses were closed up, and the invitations dwindled. The steamers and trains returning to New York overflowed with passengers, but Maggie was not among them.

For a time, Maggie held the whispers about her extended stay in Newport at bay with a doctor's note. "It is my opinion that it is impossible that she should return to Paris and live the existence she has been living without a strong probability of a breakdown in her mental and physical health," wrote Dr. Silas Weir Mitchell, a Philadelphia physician who specialized in the treatment of neurasthenia. It was a distinctly American condition when it was named in the 1880s, and the diagnosis was often a point of some pride among the nation's elite. Neurasthenia was the disease of modern life, afflicting those with busy schedules and pressing social demands. Indigestion, headaches, fatigue, and even depression could all be explained away by exhausted nerves.

Maggie needed rest, the doctor insisted. The cure Mitchell had developed for neurasthenia was so strict that the patient, banished to her bed for weeks or even months, was expected to ask permission to sit up or turn over. He recommended that Maggie remain in Newport for several months for treatment. The doctor's orders provided a convenient excuse for her, but the diagnosis did not come as a surprise to anyone. Maggie had suffered for years from what her doctors diagnosed as nervous afflictions, and she was prone to faints and bouts of depression. These symptoms were usually dismissed with a shrug. Her friends all agreed, one newspaper reported, "that there always had been an eccentric streak in the Astor family."

But Maggie had sought out the diagnosis as part of her ruse. In the early fall, her brother Arthur's surprise wedding to her children's governess, Agnes, had been reason enough to delay her return to the Baron in Paris. But as the weeks progressed, she had cause to fear her affectionate letters would not be enough to quell any suspicions her husband might have about her absence. He was not the trusting sort. "Thousands and thousands of loving messages from your loving M," she scrawled at the end of a letter in October 1889, with no guarantee the declaration would satisfy her husband. Maggie still had some nine months before she would gain residency in Rhode Island and with it, she hoped, the right to sue for a divorce. A doctor's orders might delay the Baron's questions.

Lina Astor would not be so easily put off. Maggie's aunt, the wife of William Backhouse Astor Jr. and the queen of New York society in the 1880s, had sussed out the true reasons for Maggie's residency, and she refused to tolerate a scandal in the family. Her own marriage did not seem to be a happy one. William lived a life largely apart from his wife's. He was rarely in attendance at her exclusive balls, and there were persistent stories of his drunkenness and infidelity. Thirty-six years as a society wife had given Lina much practice at turning a blind eye to a husband's improper behavior, a necessary social skill she felt her niece would do well to learn. Maggie's divorce would not be the first in the Astor family, but it would mar Lina's reign as matriarch.

The distinction of being the first Astor to leave her husband belonged to the late Magdalen, Maggie's great-aunt, who had the benefit of experiencing marital strife before the family rose to such social prominence. With the help of her father, the original John Jacob Astor, Magdalen divorced her first husband, Adrian Bentzon, in 1819 after twelve years of marriage strained by the death of two children and Adrian's abandonment and adultery. Her family did not remember her fondly—"a maniac," wrote one cousin—and Magdalen's unsuccessful union left an unhappy legacy: When Maggie's grandfather, William Backhouse Astor Sr., married her grandmother, Margaret, the new bride was forced to sign away her rights to a percentage of the Astor fortune. The Astor daughters also found themselves cut loose from the family fortune—albeit with a hefty settlement—upon their marriages, lest their husbands abscond with a portion of the Astor bank account.

It was the family's good name Lina was concerned with losing when she sailed for France in early March 1890, shortly after the death of her brother-in-law John Jacob III. Lina made a trip to the continent annually, but this time she was on a mission that could not be delayed: she was determined to meet with the Baron and negotiate a reconciliation between Maggie and her husband. In Newport, Maggie secured a two-year lease on a larger home in early March, but within a month she had acquiesced to her aunt's wishes. The house was up for rent, and Maggie was bound for Europe to reunite with her husband. In forestalling the divorce, one society observer wrote, Lina had "vindicated her reputation as a social diplomat"—until Maggie's presence in Sioux Falls became known fifteen months later.

On the morning of July 14, 1891, the news broke above the fold on the front page of the *New York World*. The *Boston Globe* and the *Chicago Herald* also printed the story that day. The Four Hundred were atwitter with the revelation. Maggie De Stuers had joined the "divorce colony," as the newspapers now called those gathered at the Cataract House.

Dakota's first divorce law, written in 1864, provided liberal causes for ending a marriage—including a catchall for occasions "when it shall be made fully to appear that from any other reason or cause existing, the parties cannot live in peace and happiness together, and that their welfare requires a separation"—and a one-year residency requirement for most who had not been married in the territory, a provision as strict as those in most eastern states. In 1867, the territorial legislature limited the causes for divorce but reduced the residency requirement to ninety days. The change had not been designed to encourage migratory divorce; a ninety-day stay also earned one voting privileges and other legal rights. But arriving divorce seekers did not concern themselves with the intention of the law, only the opportunities it afforded.

"Now that a niece of William Astor has joined the Divorce Colony in Sioux Falls," one paper wrote when Maggie was discovered, "the South Dakota style of severing matrimonial bonds may become more popular than heretofore. The amazing elasticity of the complaisant South Dakota divorce laws has up to this time escaped the attention of all but a few."

In Good Faith

❧❦❧

WITH ATTENTION FOCUSED on Maggie, Mary Nevins Blaine, and their ilk, many divorce seekers without notable family names had the good fortune of escaping the notice of the press in the summer of 1891. Among them, for a while, was a man named Benjamin Mann. Benjamin could trace his ancestors back to the earliest settlers of Doylestown, a village north of Philadelphia, but the Manns were not a wealthy family. They were soldiers and laborers. A veteran of the Civil War, Benjamin had been a plasterer for most of his life; he was now nearing his sixty-second birthday. He had married Phoebe Eastlack at the Eleventh Street Methodist Episcopal Church in South Philadelphia in the spring of 1850, and after more than forty years of marriage, Benjamin wanted a divorce.

Judge Frank R. Aikens would decide if Benjamin could end his marriage. Aikens was the arbiter of every divorce filed in Sioux Falls and across more than thirty-five hundred square miles of southeastern South Dakota. He was first appointed as an associate justice of the Supreme Court of the Territory of Dakota in March 1889 over the strong objections of the Sioux Falls bar, whose members had another favorite for the seat, but the lawyer and legislator from Canton, a town twenty miles south, had impressed his detractors during his first term. He had set aside the fiery speeches that marked his career in the territorial legislature, and although he continued to live in Canton with his wife, Margaret, and infant son, he traveled frequently to Sioux Falls to sit on the bench and to socialize. The glad-handing paid off when Aikens, still a dark horse candidate, was elected judge of the Second Judicial Circuit of the new state of South Dakota in the fall of 1889. By 1891, he was a fixture both in the city and at the Cataract, where he frequently stayed.

It was rare to hear criticism of Aikens's judgments from local politicians or other members of the bar. Those who had been dismayed by an early 1890 decision in which Aikens declined to punish a Canton saloonkeeper for selling liquor in violation of South Dakota law were soon forced to admit that the judge had properly navigated the complicated intersection of territorial and state statutes. In doing so, he had alerted the legislature to a worrisome loophole that it soon remedied. Aikens's rulings hewed closely to the law, and attorneys knew him to be a stickler for proper process. Outside the courtroom, though, opinions of the judge were more mixed. Even those who praised his "genial dignity" and fairness on the bench noted Aikens's vanity and youth. The thirty-five-year-old judge was a handsome man, proud of his dark curls, small symmetrical mustache, and expressive eyes, and he was beginning to show, some worried, too much solicitude toward the plight of the divorce colonists flocking to Sioux Falls.

Most divorces were granted without much fuss in Judge Aikens's small office on the second floor of the Minnehaha County Courthouse. Benjamin Mann's petition should have been no different. On the afternoon of Saturday, August 1, a regular workday for the judge, Aikens read the handwritten filing. In it, Benjamin attested to his arrival in Sioux Falls in late February 1891 and recounted an "unbearable" marriage. He accused his wife, Phoebe, of assaulting him with chairs, dishes, and whatever other household weapons she could find within reach. She called him "vile" names and destroyed the tools he used to make a living. She also, Benjamin charged, refused to make him dinner. Finally, in 1880, Phoebe abandoned him.

Phoebe was not represented before the court that day. In his affidavit, Benjamin claimed that he did not know where to find her. Indeed, he said, he did not know if she was dead or alive. Personal service of the legal complaint to the defendant was not required by South Dakota law, only seventy-two days' publication of the court notice. The case would move forward without her.

If Phoebe had been informed of the proceeding, she would likely have told a very different story. There was much Benjamin had left out. In the court papers, he claimed only two of the eleven children Phoebe had borne, though the seven who survived infancy all carried his name—one, in fact, was Benjamin Jr.—and he also neglected to mention that he had tried, and failed, to obtain a divorce in Chicago eighteen years earlier. Since at least 1877, husband and wife had been living apart, but as Phoebe had remained in the family home with the children, it was hard to argue that she had abandoned him. Perhaps their separation was because of the violent streak Benjamin described. Or perhaps it was because Benjamin had married another woman—a Philadelphia schoolteacher named Carry Pray—in 1877. They had moved to the Midwest, where his bigamy would not be discovered. Phoebe, very much alive and still residing in North Philadelphia, called herself a widow.

Judge Aikens didn't know any of this when he issued his ruling. Nonetheless he declared that Benjamin was not entitled to a divorce.

∎

THAT FIRST WEEKEND of August 1891, Maggie was on holiday in Spirit Lake, Iowa, some eighty miles east of Sioux Falls. As was her style, she had reserved a large suite of rooms at the region's best resort. The Hotel Orleans was a favorite destination of Omaha's wealthiest, who arrived on the northbound Burlington in the early weeks of July to spend the season boating and bathing and fishing. In the evenings, the guests gathered on the sweeping veranda for dancing and hands of High Five, and mornings found spent champagne bottles stacked like firewood behind the hotel. If there was any grumbling about the languorous summers at the Orleans, it was that there were not enough handsome men at the resort. For a time, Maggie's private secretary, William, who had accompanied her on the trip, soothed that concern.

While in Spirit Lake, Maggie had not escaped the gossip that had swirled around her for nearly two years, since her residence in Rhode Island, but she was unprepared for the maelstrom she encountered when she returned to Sioux Falls. The name Benjamin Mann was on everyone's lips. Judge Aikens, it was reported, had refused Benjamin's decree for a very specific and worrisome reason: the judge did not believe that Benjamin was a resident of South Dakota "in good faith," as the divorce law required. His affidavit was a fraud upon the state.

Those who professed to know Aikens's personal thoughts on the matter were not surprised by the pronouncement. The weeks since Maggie had first registered at the Cataract had brought an influx of divorce seekers. By one count, the ranks of the colony had swollen to ninety-six. The South Dakota divorce statute had not been written to attract the unhappy to the state for a brief sojourn, and Aikens's friends whispered that the judge was about to put his foot down. He was no longer content to enforce the letter of the law when doing so clearly undermined its spirit. Future plaintiffs, it was suggested, would have to prove their intentions to make Sioux Falls their home with more than just their own sworn statements.

It had been the general understanding among Sioux Falls lawyers that an address at one of the state's hotels or boarding houses was enough to obtain residency. Now the rules were unclear, and it appeared that the stricter requirements would be applied retroactively. Divorce seekers who were counting each day of their three-month wait had not been advised to sequester themselves within South Dakota's borders, and few had made any effort to integrate themselves into the community. The confusion was a boon, at least, for the city's real estate market. Less than two weeks after the Mann decision, Maggie signed a contract to buy a house from P. H. Edmison, one of the first settlers of Sioux Falls. He was asking $12,500 for the house a half mile from the Cataract. Maggie, like several other colonists for whom money was no impediment, was trying to buy bona fide residency, but she had also fallen in love with the mantel over the fireplace in the Edmison home.

The Mann decision earned Aikens acclaim among critics of the divorce statute. He was heralded as a "righteous judge," and some promoted him as a worthy candidate for national office, an antidote to the

Republican senator who had recently suggested "the divorce law was not a bad thing, inasmuch as by reason of it some very desirable citizens have been added to Sioux Falls." Those in the city who were appalled by the growing number of divorce seekers had been waiting for a prominent local leader to rally the citizenry in opposition, despite the money they brought to the community. As the divorce colony flourished, the man Sioux Falls usually turned to for moral leadership was absent. Bishop William Hare had been on a mission trip to Japan since March 1891. The newspapers now counted down the days until his return. Hare's ship sailed from Yokohama, bound for Vancouver, on July 29; he was expected in Sioux Falls by the first of September.

The son of an East Coast clergyman, the fifty-three-year-old bishop had been a pillar of the region for decades. "There is no man in Dakota who will not take off his hat to Bishop Hare," locals were known to say. As a newly ordained priest, he had originally ventured westward from Pennsylvania in the 1860s for the air, searching for a better climate for his young wife, Mary, whose health was rapidly failing. Something Hare witnessed on that trip set the course of his life. On the Fourth of July 1863, from the windows of the family's temporary home in St. Paul, Minnesota, Hare watched as a group of white settlers incited a dozen Sioux to perform a "savage exhibition." "There they stood before the hotel almost naked, and so bedaubed with paint and set off with feathers that they were frightful to look upon," Hare wrote to his Sunday school pupils back in Philadelphia. "At a given signal they began their dance. They pounded the earth with their feet, they crouched to the ground, they leaped and sang and whooped and yelled, occasionally firing their guns into the air, until I was sickened at the indecent sight." He did not blame the Sioux men for the behavior that he did not understand. "They wandered about like sheep without a shepherd," Hare wrote. "No one taught them what was good."

Hare was determined to fill the role of shepherd. He would build the Sioux schools and churches and offer what he believed to be models of proper behavior. In the years after Mary's early death in 1866, Hare turned his attention to mission work, and in 1873 the recently consecrated bishop headed further west, leaving his school-age son, Hobart, in the care of relatives in the East. Hare was to oversee the new Missionary District of Niobrara, which included the Sioux reservations of central Dakota and stretched clear from the Missouri River to the western border of the territory.

After the bishop's dominion was expanded in 1883 to include all of what would become South Dakota, he laid the cornerstone for the All Saints School for Girls in Sioux Falls. With a donation from Augusta Astor, he extended his care to the daughters of missionaries and others who would be taught the skills necessary for any accomplished young woman: the languages, sciences, literature, music, and proper deportment. Bishop Hare made his home at All Saints too, taking two rooms on the upper floor of the quartzite building and eating his meals with the students in the school's dining room. Even after St. Augusta opened its doors, Hare remained the school chaplain. Six mornings a week, when not traveling, he conducted services in the handsome chapel for the school's eighty or so students; on Sunday evenings, the girls gathered in the parlors to sing hymns and listen to stories of Bishop Hare's early days in the Dakota Territory.

The bishop had been outspoken against divorce since those territorial times. It violated God's law, his own sense of propriety, and his protective instincts toward women. "The notions which prevail in this country on the subject of marriage and divorce are lamentably lax," he cautioned six years earlier in an 1885 address before hundreds of believers gathered on the Crow Creek Reservation. "This laxity arises partly from the fact that it is taken for granted that marriages and divorces which are not condemned by the law of the land are therefore justifiable before the bar of conscience—a preposterous assumption."

Other clergy in the city now echoed that message. On the pulpit at St. Michael, the city's Catholic church, Father Leo Ricklin delivered a bitter sermon against the destruction of marriage. At the First Congregationalist Church, Reverend John A. Cruzan warned his parishioners—including several divorce seekers—of Sioux Falls' complicity in the sin. Even the Sioux Falls lawyers growing rich off the city's new residents professed their dismay at the growing divorce colony. "Out of this will come trouble yet," attorney W. H. Stoddard warned.

Chapter Three

JUST ANOTHER

T HE MINNEHAHA COUNTY CLERK of courts office shared the second floor of the new courthouse with Judge Aikens's chambers.
The architectural plans for the building showed a large room with three
windows looking toward the river, but soon after the clerk and his deputy
moved into the space, there was nothing to see but court filings. Desks
overflowed with paper.

In the month since the judge had dismissed Benjamin Mann's case,
sending him back home without a decree, there had been no break in the
workload for the clerk of courts. In a city where law firms outnumbered
doctors, builders, and barbers, there was always something worth suing
over. And the divorce petitions kept coming. Some were filed by locals
seeking the same release that brought unhappy spouses from around the
world to Sioux Falls, others by optimistic divorce colonists who made
their homes hundreds of miles away.

The panic over Judge Aikens's new understanding of the residency
requirement had passed quickly. He had refused Benjamin's request for
a divorce, but not for the reasons those who despised the institution had

hoped. Aikens had always been a stickler for process, and the Mann case file was a mess. The depositions were not complete or properly signed, and Benjamin had made no effort to inform his wife about the proceedings. Aikens's "friends," who had originally spread word of the judge's change of heart, fell silent when Frank Aikens himself announced that he would make no changes to the way the court determined residency. A plaintiff needed only to swear in an affidavit that he or she was a bona fide citizen of the state and had not come solely for a divorce. "This will protect the spirit as well as the letter of the law," the judge said.

The letter of the law was ninety days' residency. Maggie waited ninety-four, perhaps for good measure. Her divorce complaint was filed on the evening of Thursday, September 3, 1891, after the city's newspaper presses had fallen silent for the night. Clerk of courts Albion Thorne processed the document. He found the bound appearance book amid the landslide of pleadings, depositions, and orders that filled the office, and added the newest case to page 177: *Margaret Laura De Stuers v. Alphonso Eugene Lambert De Stuers.*

Thorne looked at the additional space on the page, where he would typically inscribe the names of the attorneys in the case and might add a few notes. The appearance book was meant to be a record of everything that happened in the courthouse. That's what made it a favorite of the newspapermen who came by most days to find a story. Before becoming the clerk of courts nine months earlier, Thorne had held numerous jobs, among them newspaper editor and attorney. In previous cases, Thorne had sided with the reporters, insisting that the appearance book was public record. On this day, though, his sympathies lay with the bar and with Maggie's counsel, W. H. Stoddard. Thorne did not add Stoddard's name to the appearance book; nor did he note the cause of action. When the reporter for the *Argus-Leader* visited the clerk of courts office the next day, he saw only the case caption.

"Cap" Stoddard was not against using the press to polish his own image or prosecute his cases, but for now surprise seemed the better strategy in Maggie's divorce. Though rumors about her marriage were rampant, no one was certain what charges she would bring against her husband, and until those claims became public, the Baron, still in Paris, was unlikely to begin a counteroffensive. Cap advised silence, and he was used to people following his advice. He was a big man, with broad shoulders and a heavy, downturned mustache that made him appear to be frowning in disapproval, but most of Sioux Falls knew him to be a cheerful and big-hearted fellow. He had earned his nickname during the Civil War, enlisting in the Forty-Third New York Infantry and returning home a captain. He then took up law, joining the New York bar in 1868. He traveled west to Sioux Falls in 1883 and had made a name for himself in the South Dakota courts in the years since. Cap was not Maggie's only representation. She had also retained Herbert A. Shipman, a New York attorney who had previously represented William Elliot. But the role of cocounsel was lucrative. Maggie was reportedly paying Cap $2,500 for his efforts.

After Maggie's case was filed, the law required that the defendant be notified of the proceedings against him, either in person or through publication in the newspaper. The Baron was served in Paris on a Saturday three weeks later, and when the Sioux Falls courthouse reopened on the following Monday, Maggie's complaint was unsealed. She charged her husband with extreme cruelty. He hurled "ungentlemanly epithets" at her and questioned her faithfulness. He tried to cheat her through fraud and misrepresentation, Maggie charged. His abuse had made her sick and nervous. The Baron, Maggie claimed, had also taken her children. She pleaded for a divorce and custody of Margot, twelve years old, whereabouts unknown. The boys—John and Bertie, ages fifteen and eleven—could survive without their mother, but she worried for her poor girl. The detectives Maggie hired to find her daughter had reported just a few days earlier that Margot was living at a convent in the French countryside, then cabled a second time to say that the Baron had hidden her away again.

The Baron wasted no time preparing for his defense. The day after Maggie's complaint was released to the public, young Sioux Falls attorney J. L. Glover filed notice that he would be representing Maggie's husband. A reporter for the *Argus-Leader* spotted him on his errand. Glover had little to say about the client he had acquired less than forty-eight hours earlier, except that he expected the Baron to travel to Sioux Falls to argue for his marriage.

⌒✺⌒

FANNIE TINKER HAD taken a room at the Cataract House in late September, just before news of Maggie's complaint overtook conversation in its dining room. On her first morning in Sioux Falls, she attended breakfast by herself in the hotel and then returned to her room facing the Edmison-Jameson Block. There was a knock at the door, and Fannie opened it to find a pleasant-looking gentleman, hat in hand. He bowed politely.

"Pardon me, madam," he said, "but I simply wished to say that if you were in need of legal advice I would sug—"

Fannie was stunned. "Oh, but I am not," she stammered. "I thank you."

"I beg your pardon," the man said, "but so many young women come here who fall into the hands of designing lawyers that I merely wished to warn you."

The man had not introduced himself by name, but he was likely one of the very lawyers he claimed to be cautioning Fannie about. A report of a new divorce seeker in town would send members of the bar racing to the Cataract.

"The fact is," Fannie observed with amazement, "it is taken for granted that a stranger coming here alone comes for no other purpose than to obtain a divorce."

She began to wonder about her experience at breakfast. The diners seated under the vaulted ceiling of the Cataract's vast dining room had stared at her. At the time she feared that her hat was crooked or her curls awry. It was only several days later that someone explained the odd behavior. They thought you were "another," a woman told Fannie—shorthand for "another divorce colonist."

Fannie was not in Sioux Falls for a divorce. Her mission was potentially much more dangerous for the town's reputation. Fannie was a reporter for the *New York World*, sent to infiltrate the . . . "traveling contingent." "I was going to say divorce colony," Fannie admitted, "but heaven forbid that I should, for it is like pressing on an exposed nerve to refer to the settlement here in that way."

After the initial confusion, Fannie was open about her assignment, but many divorce seekers were welcoming nonetheless. Fannie seemed like one of them. At forty-five, she was a bit older than many members of the colony, but she had grown up comfortably in a respected Indiana family, was well educated, and had earned some measure of celebrity through her writing, both journalistic and fictional. She had been widowed at a young age, she told those who asked, and she had never remarried. She didn't think being a wife precluded one's success, but she admired a woman who struck out on her own path. "I am proud of my sex," she said just before departing for Sioux Falls, "for as years pass by they grow more self-reliant."

That sympathy and her winning smile gained Fannie access to the cottage on Duluth Avenue where Mary Nevins Blaine had moved after the residency scare in August and earned her an invitation to travel to the Santee Sioux reservation near Flandreau forty miles north with John Lester, whose August "disappearance" from his marital home had been the talk of Fannie's Brooklyn neighborhood. She did not, however, secure Maggie's trust; the baroness remained reclusive.

Two weeks later, Fannie left for New York with copious notes and the pictures of colonists she had captured on her Kodak. "It is said the lady will tell a good many stories which will be good reading for New Yorkers, but not especially gratifying to the subjects thereof," the *Argus-Leader* warned. The sensational story was scheduled to be published on Sunday, October 11. That day the *World* mentioned divorce several times, in the context of a suicide, a murder, and a stage play; the young Cora Tanner was starring as a wronged wife in *Will She Divorce Him?*

But there was no mention of Sioux Falls. Fannie's story did not appear the next day either, or the next week.

⚬⟨⟩⚬

MAGGIE HAD LIVED a quiet life in Sioux Falls, even after the papers revealed her family connections and court filings confirmed the reason for her presence. She had ignored every rumor and offered not a single word of defense—nor any of accusation—to Fannie Tinker or to any of the reporters who gathered in the lobby of the Cataract House, competing for the smallest detail about one of the divorce colonists to sell to the newspapers back East. Maggie was of particular interest to the gaggle on the afternoon of Thursday, November 5. J. L. Glover had just been at the courthouse filing a response to Maggie's charges.

The Baron denied everything. According to the newspapers, the filing claimed that Maggie had "manifested the most uneven and irritable temper toward the Baron and their children," a symptom, he said, of her neurasthenia. He asked that her petition for a divorce be denied.

Given the chance, the reporters might have confronted Maggie with some of the Baron's most shocking claims: she had even "insulted the children by declaring that she loathed and hated them because they were the offspring of such a vile and contemptible being as their father." But Maggie, now skilled at avoiding the press, easily slipped through the lobby sometime that evening and boarded a train to Chicago. Nobody noticed she was gone until the next day.

The reporter from the *Chicago Daily Tribune* who approached Maggie in Parlor W of the Palmer House Hotel at the corner of State and Monroe Streets on that Friday afternoon had little reason to think he would be any more successful in his inquiries. Finding the elusive woman hadn't been difficult. The Palmer House, an eight-story edifice built in the faux French style of the Cataract House, was a favorite of Chicago's more notable visitors and a frequent stopover for well-heeled travelers on their way to and from Sioux Falls. The hotel was so opulent that the barber shop floor was tiled with eight hundred silver dollars. Parlor W was decorated almost as sumptuously. Maggie sat at an elegant secretary desk finished with red Moroccan leather so soft it was also a fashionable choice for women's gloves. She wrote with a carved gold pen. Among her correspondence that afternoon was a letter to her lawyer, Cap Stoddard, who was also in town. She was desperate to meet.

At first, the *Tribune* reporter encountered the same reticence that Maggie had shown with every newspaperman. She politely refused to answer the questions he posed to her. She was tired from the long journey from South Dakota, she explained, and she suggested the reporter talk to her private secretary instead. William Elliot had spoken to the correspondents in Sioux Falls on her behalf on the few occasions when their interrogations proved unavoidable. In many ways, he was well suited to the task. William had shown himself to be far more gregarious than Maggie, and he was, the reporter observed that afternoon, a man who understood "the art of being agreeable without being communicative."

Seated in Parlor W, William puffed on a cigarette and considered the reporter's questions. Why was Maggie in Chicago? It wasn't to see Stoddard, William explained. That the Sioux Falls lawyer and his client were both in the same city was just a convenient coincidence. "Mme. De Stuers has come to Chicago for—" William paused. "Well, a change of air. She wants to get some new clothes and to see the opera. She is, of course, much worried over her affairs, and needs a little recreation away from home." That word—"home"—caught the reporter's attention.

"The Baron's answer to her plea for divorce alleges that the Madam isn't a resident of Dakota at all," the reporter challenged William. "Is she?"

"She has lived there about six months, I believe," William said, though he had arrived in Sioux Falls with her a little more than four months earlier. "But I don't want to talk about the case. See the madam's lawyer." Shortly after that, William ended the conversation and exited the parlor.

Maggie had watched the exchange from an upholstered chair nearby. She sat in silence, in a loose gown of green velvet lined in blue satin. Her dark golden hair was brushed back from her round face, which the reporter described as "fresh" with "lines of gentility and prettiness." Now, to the reporter's surprise, Maggie spoke. "The answer that my husband has made to my plea for a divorce is a tissue of falsehoods," she declared.

That afternoon in Chicago was the first time Maggie had spoken openly about anything since the public first discovered her desire to end her marriage in 1889 while she was in Newport. The *Tribune* had printed some fantastic speculation in the intervening years, but an interview would be a real scoop. In the face of her husband's accusations, Maggie seemed determined to set the record straight.

She began describing the typical life of a well-heeled couple in 1870s France. "We lived on there in the height of Parisian society," she said. "But in time we began to drift apart." At first she blamed religious differences, she told the reporter. Then came the arguments about money.

Maggie had always chafed at the Baron's insistence that he manage their finances. "I turned my money over so completely to him that in fact if I wanted a few francs, I had to ask him for them," she said. But she soon came to see his control as something more sinister. In 1881, Maggie's parents had died. First, John succumbed to cancer, and then, three weeks later, Alida died. Her doctors could offer no other explanation than the neurasthenia she suffered from, a relatively unusual cause to be recorded on a death certificate. With their passing, Maggie's annual income grew to a reported $80,000. Her New York properties were worth an astounding $1 million. "It was not long before I saw clearly that the Baron was plotting to get my fortune," Maggie said.

Maggie seemed on the verge of confirming the rumors that had been circulating for months. Her tone was "deliberate," the reporter noted, and her gestures "graceful," even as her story stopped, then skipped ahead almost a decade, from the early 1880s to the spring of 1890. Maggie didn't want to talk about the years in between. The reporter would not be hearing about her first, aborted attempt to get a divorce. He would not be hearing about her family's intervention and their insistence that she return to her husband. But he would get a story.

"One morning the plot came to a head," Maggie said. It was early on Friday, June 13, 1890—barely two months after Maggie had reluctantly returned to Paris from Newport. Maggie was in the boudoir of her elegant new home in "le 16e," an address that doubled as a shorthand for high society in the French capital. She was preparing for her daily promenade along the city's wide boulevards. This day, however, the Baron asked her to forgo her stroll. The sculptor the Baron had commissioned to make a bust of his wife was coming for a sitting. Maggie agreed to the meeting. But as the sculptor worked, her maid, Mary, burst into the room.

"O, madame! There are two strange doctors coming to your boudoir!" she cried.

"I knew in an instant what it meant," Maggie told the reporter. She had not been in attendance at the usual dinners and galas in Paris that spring. She was in mourning for her uncle, she had explained to friends. Meanwhile, the Baron was telling people that Maggie was "mentally unbalanced."

"The idea struck me so ridiculously that I laughed at it," Maggie said. "But my friends assured me that it was true."

The two men who accompanied the Baron into Maggie's room were Dr. Eugene Cheurlot and Dr. Jean-Martin Charcot. Maggie recognized Cheurlot by sight; the Baron had called him previously to treat Maggie's fainting spells and nervous disposition. Maggie had promptly sent him away that time, accusing him of gross ignorance and incompetence. She recognized Charcot by reputation; he would not be so easily dismissed.

Charcot was the chief physician of Hospice de la Salpêtrière. The hospital was not the rat-infested prison for outcast women—the insane, the ill, the poor, the unmarried mothers, and the nonbelievers—it had been a century earlier, but Charcot himself thought the sprawling former warehouse complex along the Seine a "grand asylum of human misery." The five thousand women institutionalized there had become Charcot's research subjects. He identified and named multiple sclerosis, Parkinson's disease, and amyotrophic lateral sclerosis, which became known as Charcot's disease. But it was the neurologist's work on hysteria that made him famous and fearsome. He believed the ancient affliction of the "wandering womb," once thought to be a sign of sorcery and sin, was an inherited neurological disorder, but he could not locate the cause of symptoms as disparate as melancholy, licentiousness, and seizures. In the grand amphitheater of the Hospice de la Salpêtrière, Charcot put his patients on display for colleagues, students, and even tourists; their tremors, tics, and terrors were part education, part entertainment. There was no cure, just a variety of painful treatments. With Charcot's interest in the illness, its incidence in Paris surged. The hospital admitted another woman for study almost every day.

For a half hour, the doctors quizzed Maggie about her health and state of mind. Charcot then delivered his diagnosis: "Well, Madame," he informed Maggie, "you are not insane enough to be sent to a retreat." This was a relief. Hysteria was often diagnosed alongside neurasthenia, and both were thought to be precursors of insanity; Maggie believed her husband's intent was to institutionalize her and take charge of her income. But the doctor continued: "You are not insane enough to be sent to a retreat, but you are sufficiently unbalanced not to be capable of managing your children." The Baron had threatened to take her children before. He had warned her that she would have no recourse. Maggie could not forget his words: "All will say, when a child is taken away from its mother, there must be some charge against her moral character."

"I saw just how things were going," Maggie told the reporter. That night, a year and a half earlier, she fled Paris, but Maggie was not ready to reveal that story either.

The reporter changed the subject as William returned to the parlor.

"What relation is Mr. Elliott [*sic*] to you?" he asked.

"He is my second cousin," Maggie responded. "He has been very good to me." When William realized that Maggie was speaking to the newspaperman, the protectiveness she praised took the form of scolding. He chided her for her indiscretion, but Maggie was uncowed.

"I have only told facts," she said. "I would as soon as not that they be known. I want a divorce and my children."

It was a bold statement for any woman to make, but when the story was published the next day, it was not Maggie's words but William's that caused an uproar. After William had referred the reporter to Maggie's lawyer, the reporter continued peppering him with questions.

"Is the Baron coming over here?" the reporter had asked.

"I shouldn't be surprised if he did. I think he would enjoy the country immensely after a winter sea voyage," William answered.

The reporter then asked William the same thing he would later ask Maggie: Was the private secretary related to the baroness?

"No, my dear fellow, I won't say whether I am a relative of the madam or not," William responded. "But I can say this: If I ever mix up in the case, it will be with a revolver."

Chapter Four

BUDDING HOPE AND
DEAD PASSIONS

"WHAT A GRAND PHANTASMAGORIA, a potpourri of unplaced affections and mixed up matrimonial alliances, it all is!" Fannie Tinker wrote with characteristic melodrama in her dispatch from Sioux Falls. "No one can begin to appreciate the situation unless he is here on the spot. December wed to May, old men's disappointed darlings and young men's slaves, young men with elderly affinities, yet-unrequited love and budding hope and dead passions, all figuring into one fantastic show." Those who bought a copy of the *New York World* on Sunday, November 8, 1891, found—depending on their perspective—a frothy society column or a scathing social critique, delivered with Fannie's usual mix of sincerity and sarcasm.

Fannie's description of Maggie's life in "the land of divorcees" lacked the drama of Maggie's confessions in the *Chicago Daily Tribune*. Most of what she had to say about the baroness was old news, but William's lifestyle offered exactly the type of extravagance that her readers craved. Fannie described his rooms at the Cataract in intimate detail. One served as his parlor and bedroom, decorated in "true bachelor style," and the

33

other was a dressing room and clandestine wine cellar, filled with "wine-cases, demijohns, flasks, and all sorts of beverages and drinkable things, usually to be found in a gentleman's cellar, though very hard to be found in this prohibition town." That and his free-spending ways made Maggie's private secretary a popular figure in the hotel.

Edward Pollock, still awaiting his divorce, had also caught Fannie's keen eye. Edward was very attentive to a young woman from Chicago, she reported alongside the news that Florence Cuthbertson, "a pretty woman from Chicago," was quite enjoying life in Sioux Falls while she counted down the days to her decree. Fannie outed one Robert Buchanan, a furtive member of the colony who had tried to sneak out of New York for a divorce from his second wife, Anna. Prior to marrying the doctor a year earlier, Anna had been a successful brothel madame. And Fannie did not shy from retelling the tragedy that had befallen Essie Snyder. While Essie was biding her time in South Dakota, the man she was to marry after her divorce was murdered in New York in an unrelated love triangle. Over three inky columns, Fannie divulged the secrets of more than a dozen colonists. Only Mary Nevins Blaine was treated with real kindness, lending credence to talk that Mary had traded others' tales for silence about her own marital troubles.

Sioux Falls breathed a sigh of relief when Fannie's story was finally published. A month of back-channel negotiation between the city's legal establishment and the managing editor of the *New York World* had expurgated the most outrageous stories Fannie stumbled upon in her reporting. "The article originally sent contained some very sensational details, which would have been a nine days wonder all over the state," the *Argus-Leader* reported. Fannie was furious about the censorship. "Such horrible tales they told me. I could scarcely believe them," she groused to another reporter. "I could not begin to tell you half of what I heard."

As ready as Fannie had been to expose the private lives of the divorce seekers and those who supported them in Sioux Falls, there was one story she kept to herself: Fannie had more in common with the colonists than she let on. She was not a widow. The man she married in 1872 was currently living in Washington State. More than fifteen years earlier in Cincinnati, Fannie had filed for a divorce from Wilford Tinker. She claimed "gross neglect of duty"—an ambiguous legal catchall that often meant a failure to support aggravated by another claim, such as abandonment—throughout the three years of their marriage. In 1876, at the age of thirty, she had just begun to see success as a writer. She had supported herself since, but no matter how accomplished, she could not risk being labeled a divorcee.

⌒⟨∞⟩⌒

SECRETS DID NOT keep well in Sioux Falls. What the *New York World* was too timid to publish, some of the city's ministers were eager to announce. For several years, the men who preached from Sioux Falls' pulpits had gathered each Monday at 10 a.m. to discuss "matters of current interest." But a few days before Christmas 1891, Reverend William J. Skillman, pastor of the First Reformed Church and editor of the weekly *Sioux Falls Journal*, called the ministers' association together for an emergency meeting at the YMCA, a sturdy but uninspired new brick building that also housed the *Argus-Leader*. The crisis: Judge Frank Aikens.

The outlandish tales could no longer be ignored, Skillman warned those who gathered in the YMCA parlors. Skillman believed the stories spreading through Sioux Falls were "perfectly stenchful and outrageous," a stain on the judge's reputation and on the city's. Aikens was a drunk and a lecher, the reverend railed. He had recently been seen in the company of two divorce colonists drinking a case of champagne. When the bottles were all empty, the trio ventured to a saloon the judge had ordered closed just days earlier and then hired a carriage to drive them to a "house of questionable character." Essie Snyder was said to have leveled an even more damning charge against the man. She had given up her divorce suit—but not because her lover had been murdered.

"If Judge Aikens's hand must be placed upon every woman's skirt before she can get a decree then I'll do without a decree," she reportedly said before leaving Sioux Falls for New York.

And then there was the alleged incident at the Cataract House with Mary Van den Heuvel, Maggie's maid. Skillman had not been present at the hotel, but he had heard that Mary had been walking through its halls one evening that fall when Aikens accosted her and tried to kiss her. The Frenchwoman spoke little English, but she could scream. As the story went, the commotion drew the attention of other boarders, who grabbed the intoxicated man and locked him in a nearby room. When the Corson brothers learned of the incident, they supposedly banished the judge from the building. Skillman was an accomplished scholar, with smartly groomed white hair and wire-rimmed glasses, but Aikens's accuser was also a firebrand with a talent for stirring up passions. When Skillman finished his screed against the judge, one of the other ministers dropped to his knees. "Let us pray, brothers," he pleaded.

For a week, as each celebrated the advent season with his flock, the ministers privately debated the proper course of action against Aikens. Skillman and the majority of those he had invited to the initial meeting believed that the only appropriate response was a public listing of the judge's offenses followed by a swift resignation. Only Reverend Arthur Hastings Grant seemed unconvinced by the allegations. He took it upon himself to investigate their source.

Grant was the newest member of the ministers' association. He had arrived just six months earlier, in July 1891, with the influx of divorce colonists. Like Skillman, Grant was a minister and a journalist. Both had been correspondents for the *New York Evening Post*, which published surprisingly detailed accountings of the Sioux Falls divorce colony. The young Grant—just twenty-six to Skillman's fifty-six years—shepherded the All Souls Unitarian congregation. When the ministers met again, in the last week of 1891, Grant reported that he had uncovered no evidence of wrongdoing on the part of the judge. What the newcomer did not understand was that it did not matter much to the men whether the rumors were true or false. Aikens had already committed several unforgivable sins in the eyes of the gathered clergy: he opposed prohibition, and he supported the divorce colony with every decree he signed.

Grant's All Souls Unitarian was the only ministry in Sioux Falls that did not condemn the divorce seekers. The church had been founded in 1886 by Eliza T. Wilkes, a suffragist and minister who still sometimes presided over the weddings and funerals of her congregants; her husband, William, who sat on the board of trustees, was a local lawyer who occasionally took divorce cases. The couple had a practical view of the colony, in line with the conclusion reached by the National Conference of Unitarian and Other Christian Churches a few months earlier: "It is clear that no remedy for present difficulties is to be sought by an effort to ignore the necessity of divorce, but rather that we are to improve our present conditions by making marriage more sacred." For the rest of the city's ministers, every divorce Aikens granted was a betrayal. That summer, the judge had looked like the city's savior. By reinterpreting the residency clause of the state's divorce law, he could have banished the colony. Instead, he was abetting it.

Bishop Hare urged a compromise among the ministers. The bishop had finally returned to South Dakota from Japan several months earlier, but his personal and professional responsibilities had kept him away from Sioux Falls for much of the autumn. His absence had not lessened his influence in the city, and he spoke now with unchallenged authority: the ministers could not ignore the allegations leveled against the judge; nor, as Grant had shown, could they prove them. Hare had found himself in a similar position more than a decade earlier.

In 1878, Hare disciplined a reverend in his charge who stood accused of "abandoned character"—sexual misconduct and drunkenness—and financial impropriety. The reverend, Samuel D. Hinman, protested his innocence, and some in the church wondered if Hare had punished Hinman because he was a rival. Hare and Hinman disagreed on theological issues and on the best way to minister to the Sioux. In the face of these aspersions on his character, the usually restrained Hare grew increasingly strident in his accusations against Hinman, printing a pamphlet defending his decision. Hinman took the bishop to court for libel. After nine years of legal wrangling, the parties agreed to a settlement, but Hare still felt the humiliation of the affair and worried about the indelible stain on his reputation.

The Hinman affair may have given Hare pause in the Aikens case. Or perhaps he did not share Skillman's bitterness toward the judge because he did not blame the court for the existence of the divorce colony. The responsibility lay with the law and those individuals who took advantage of it in flagrant violation of church teachings. Whatever his exact words in the meeting, Hare's arguments tempered Skillman's ire. Eventually, Skillman acquiesced to a more moderate course of action. The ministers association wrote a private letter to Aikens, cautioning him about the stories that were circulating, but it did not detail the complaints or call for the judge to step down.

"These charges are the result of spiteful feelings toward me," Aikens retorted when the ministers' letter inevitably became public anyway. He called Skillman "a prohibition crank," a tame retort for a man fluent in profanity, and he exhorted the local bar association to come to his defense. Predictably it did, with lawyers who regularly made appearances before the judge offering impassioned defenses of his official conduct. Fewer were willing to publicly defend the judge's private actions. He was a drinker, who, by his own admission, "had been known to take a drop too much," though he swore he had not been intoxicated since he had taken the bench. But, behind the scenes, some of the same forces that had spiked Fannie Tinker's exclusive worked to rehabilitate the judge's image. The editor of the *Sioux Falls Press* eventually confessed to manufacturing some of the most damning evidence against the judge, and on the first day of the January 1892 court session, Mary Van den Heuvel released a statement absolving Aikens of the purported assault against her. "I have never met Judge Aikens and would not know him if he were standing before me," she said.

But Mary would soon be standing before the judge as a witness. Maggie's case had been set for trial.

◦⧏◈⧐◦

THERE WAS A time when Maggie had thought she could buy freedom for herself and her daughter. After she fled her husband's attempts to institutionalize her in Paris in 1890, she believed that what he wanted more than anything was her money. She was willing to pay in exchange for his acquiescence in court; after all, she had already left behind a house filled with the fine furniture, fashionable frocks, and priceless mementos she had acquired over her lifetime. Such collusion between spouses in pursuit of a divorce was illegal under South Dakota law, and indeed under the laws of most states, but it was also common. It was the reason Charles Andrews was so confident in his ability to end his own marriage.

Charles was another of the Cataract's long-term guests and a frequent companion of William Elliot and Edward Pollock. The trio lived a louche life in the frontier city, spending their days prowling the city's illegal saloons, its billiard tables, and its impromptu gambling dens. On his new horse, a white umbrella attached to the saddle, William led the men on excursions into the countryside in fair weather, but now that snow blanketed Sioux Falls, they were most likely to be found with a clutch of other colonists sledding down Sixth Street.

Charles was known as the "dude of the colony"—an eastern dandy with no place on the western frontier—but his antics were mostly a source of amusement. The husbands who came to Sioux Falls for a divorce did not attract the same derision as the wives who did the same and were not held to the same impossible standards. A man who expected his freedom was not as outlandish as a woman who demanded hers.

Charles had traveled to Sioux Falls in August 1891 in the uncertain weeks after Benjamin Mann was refused a divorce decree, but he never doubted the successful completion of his own errand. He had convinced his wife, Kate, to consent to a separation a year earlier. By agreement, the couple split their assets; Kate received the title to the brownstone in Boston's exclusive Back Bay neighborhood where they had lived during their three years of marriage. Charles had been surprised when Kate hired a lawyer to contest his Sioux Falls case, but a generous payment to his soon-to-be ex-wife solved the problem.

Maggie now knew her wealth would not spare her a protracted court battle. When her husband had filed his response to her case in early November, he had likened her efforts at negotiation to bribery. The Baron claimed he "absolutely and peremptorily refused to listen." The months since had been a parade of delays and of depositions taken in London and Paris. Among those sworn to tell the truth about Maggie's marriage were her brothers, Arthur and Harry. Maggie did not expect them to be kind to her. They had not been shy in expressing their disapproval of her decision to divorce.

It all worried her sick. Maggie had spent much of December in Chicago recovering from a nervous attack and returned to Sioux Falls in the last days of 1891 to find herself enmeshed in the Aikens affair. Around her the city rang in the new year with grand receptions and much dancing, but Maggie had little reason to celebrate. She was still married, and the words of her husband's lawyer echoed in her mind. "This case will be fought to the bitter end," J. L. Glover had declared. "The baron is determined that no divorce shall be secured by his wife."

It was big news, then, when word arrived from Paris in the first week of January that the Baron would not be coming to Sioux Falls for the trial; his lawyers blamed his professional commitments. But any sense of relief was illusory. Maggie would not have to face her husband in the courtroom, but she would have to confront his words. His deposition was on its way from France, giving Maggie several weeks to worry about what her husband would tell the court. On Wednesday, January 27, just after 2 p.m., Maggie—and all of Sioux Falls—learned the answer. Standing before Judge Aikens, J. L. Glover announced that his client, the Baron, wished to charge Maggie with adultery.

"For the sake of the good name borne by me and my children, and to avoid that there should be a stain upon the reputation of the plaintiff, I was inclined to give the plaintiff the benefit of the doubt," Glover read, giving a voice to the Baron's grievances. In the seventy-five-page deposition, the Baron chose his words carefully, explaining with legalistic precision and little emotion that he had heard rumors of Maggie's infidelity, but he had not found proof until his lawyers had deposed several witnesses in London. Maggie had been seen there in the company of a man. The Baron described it as "an open state of adulterous intercourse."

In court, Glover sketched the outlines of the affair. The Baron's tale filled in much of the missing months between the time when Maggie left their home and her arrival in Sioux Falls. From England, he claimed, she and her lover had departed on a steamship for the Indian Ocean, visiting Ceylon and India before returning together to London. The Baron had found evidence of their liaison in the register of the Caledonian, a hotel on the Strand overlooking the Adelphi Gardens and the Thames. The entry, dated February 10, 1891, read "Mr. and Mrs. William Elliot."

⌜❈⌝

THE NEWS THAT William Elliot was more than Maggie's private secretary shocked sensibilities. Despite the sordid tales the newspapers told of her marriage, Maggie had appeared to Sioux Falls society to be one of the less offensive divorce colonists. She did not expect to be accepted in the city and was rarely seen by the public, apart from the regular visits she and William made to St. Augusta Cathedral. But those same Sioux Falls gossips had to admit that the discovery was not a complete surprise. As Maggie's private secretary, William arranged all her affairs and served as a buffer between the baroness and those who sought something from her.

He had done that job well, perhaps too well. William had on occasion been too bold in his advocacy for Maggie—too loyal, too intimate, and too attentive to be a mere employee.

The man had the bearing of one born to wealth. William stood six feet tall, every inch of his lean frame clothed in the slim-cut three-piece suits that were the latest in European fashion. His dark brown hair was slicked back, highlighting his sharp profile: a heavy brow, a prominent nose, and a pointed chin. The thirty-five-year-old was charming when he wanted to be but also exclusive in the company he kept and voluble in his displeasures. He had a fondness for the pursuits of high society—fox hunting, horse racing, polo—and an insouciance that bordered on recklessness. Unlike Maggie, he welcomed the attention this attitude attracted. William was "so queer in his actions," wrote one newspaperman, "that he causes the average Western hustler to smile." Yet no one had ever heard of William Elliot before he boarded the steamship for Ceylon.

The Baron's accusation that Maggie had sailed with William, posing as husband and wife, was true. About a year earlier, she had been standing on the deck of a west-bound steamer, gazing out into the Indian Ocean, smoking a cigarette plucked from a gold case encrusted with diamonds, a habit her husband deemed "unladylike." The others on board were as suspicious of Maggie and William as the people of Sioux Falls, but at least on the ship Maggie was an anonymous, if slightly odd, woman. She seemed to be American, but she also had "the air of a woman accustomed to Continental life," one fellow passenger recalled for a newspaper reporter. She caused a great fuss when she demanded to be let ashore to explore when the steamer paused for coal in the British colony of Aden at the tip of the Arabian Peninsula. The ship's purser claimed the couple was an English duke and duchess by the name of Elliot, traveling incognito from Bombay, where they had purchased a cache of silver— they'd "taken up pretty much half the ship"—and several horses. But the English on board knew there was no duke in the peerage by that name.

The handsome man remained a mystery to most until that January day in Judge Aikens's court when Maggie's husband tore off his rival's mask. "I had heard from various sources," the Baron's lawyer read aloud from the deposition, "that the baroness was living on intimate terms with one Elliott Zborowski, alias William Elliott [*sic*]." The man who had been Maggie's constant companion since the summer of 1890 was not the unknown William Elliot but rather William Elliott Zborowski, well known to the Four Hundred as a New York theater landlord and the hero of the polo fields of Newport and the hunting grounds of Melton Mowbray.

The man who was known to his friends by his middle name, Elliott, had kept up the charade convincingly for a year and a half; he had some practice at reinventing himself. Elliott was the son of Martin Zborowski, a prosperous landowner, who had, until sometime in the mid-1860s, called himself Martin Zabriskie. In his later years Martin reclaimed the ancestral Polish name of Zborowski, and he cultivated a foreign mien. Though the Zabriskie family had been in New Jersey for generations, Martin did little to counter stories of himself as an immigrant and claimed close ties to a seventeenth-century Polish king. Elliott also affected an air of the exotic, and after Martin's death in 1878, he left for Europe, returning as Count Elliott Zborowski. His sister Anna had married her title when she wed a French nobleman; the origins of Elliott's new moniker were unclear. Many suspected he had bestowed the title on himself, but even so, it stuck.

No one was exactly sure, either, when and where Maggie and the count had first begun their romance, an inconvenient truth that did not for a moment stop the Baron, newspaper reporters, and Maggie's acquaintances back in New York from speculating on the matter. The Baron believed the affair dated back to the fall of 1888, when Maggie stayed at the Chateau de Fontenay at the invitation of the Comtesse de Montsaulnin. The De Stuers knew the comtesse from Parisian society, but she was also Elliott's sister, Anna. The *New York World* now claimed that Maggie and Elliott's relationship had been an open secret for much longer than that. Elliott had been enamored of Maggie since their childhood, and she reciprocated his feelings, the newspaper wrote, retroactively expressing surprise that Maggie had ever wed the Baron at all. Certainly, Maggie's family and Elliott's had known of one another. The Zborowskis were not among the Four Hundred who were entertained at the Astor home, but both families were active in New York real estate, both traveled through Europe's capitals when Elliott and Maggie were children, and both vacationed in Newport.

Despite the impropriety of their relationship, whenever it began, it was generally agreed that Elliott, three years her junior, was a better match for Maggie than the much older Baron. Maggie and Elliott shared a passion for sports and the outdoors, while the Baron was disdainful of all forms of exertion and was happiest surrounded by his books and his art collection. When she was in high spirits, Maggie's temperament complemented Elliott's playfulness; her moodiness was always at odds with the Baron's perpetual reserve and sarcasm. Formal and polished, with a reverence for proper manners, the Baron was at home with the strictures that governed good society. Maggie and Elliott had each been raised with the same rules but rebelled against them.

Still, the most generous of society gossips were determined to write a romance for the pair that was nearly respectable. In this telling, Maggie and Elliott had fallen in love two years earlier at the Metropolitan Opera House late on the evening of January 2, 1890, amid the pomp of the most magnificent ball New York had ever seen. Arriving at the front entrance of the impressive building, Elliott would have been directed to the Fortieth Street side, where gentlemen could leave behind the elegant coats that protected them from the night's rain. Maggie paraded down the grand staircase and into the auditorium, where her aunt Lina Astor, in a diamond and pearl tiara, greeted guests.

The concert hall had been transformed into a bucolic spring landscape. The opera boxes were filled with hyacinths and tulips, and garlands of roses were strung between them. The ceiling was a canopy of greenery sparkling with Edison lights. More than twelve hundred people—all invited by the notable families who financed the event—swirled on the dance floor, but Maggie stood out. She "was among the most admired women in the room," one reporter noted. Her intention to divorce the Baron after she completed her residency in Rhode Island was known by then, but it would not have been a proper topic of conversation at such an event. Somewhere between the first waltz and the final cotillion, the largest ever organized in the United States, Elliott and Maggie crossed paths. Perhaps they danced; the choreography of the cotillion made for unexpected couplings. By the time the guests streamed out just before dawn, so the story went, Maggie and Elliott were love struck.

Maggie herself had no comment on the various tales—disgraceful or charming—spun about her life, and Judge Aikens had no interest in them. He listened to Glover's late motion to amend the Baron's response and then to Cap Stoddard's rebuttal. Maggie's lawyer argued that the motion was nothing but an effort to delay the trial and smear his client. Aikens then delivered his ruling: proper court procedure would be followed; the motion would not be amended, and the court would hear no more testimony about the alleged adultery.

New York society passed its own judgment on the Baron's accusations. Maggie might become a pariah for pursuing a divorce, but she was not to be shunned as an adulteress. "The strongest count on the lady's side," opined *Town Topics*, "is that while charging her with long-continued unfaithfulness, still, the Baron does not want a divorce. This is truly an extraordinary state of things."

Chapter Five

A SAVAGE AMERICAN

J UST BEFORE 9 a.m. on the clear and cold morning of Monday, February 8, 1892, Maggie entered the Minnehaha County Courthouse. It had been 252 days since she first glimpsed the building from the Illinois Central depot. With Elliott at her side, Maggie climbed the wide oak staircase to the second-floor courtroom and walked with her lawyers—Cap Stoddard and Herbert Shipman, in from New York—to the plaintiff's table. The defense table was unoccupied. Elliott and Mary Van den Heuvel seated themselves in the first row of opera chairs reserved for the public; Charles Andrews joined them, as did several newspaper reporters. A handful of ladies, including Anna Nevins, who was in Sioux Falls with her soon-to-be-divorced sister, Mary Nevins Blaine, settled into the theater-style seats in the gallery overlooking the bench. Otherwise, the two-story room was empty.

Long minutes ticked by before the defense team, J. L. Glover and his partner, Alpha Orr, arrived. Finally, at 9:15, the usually punctual Judge Aikens brought the court to order. A few minutes later, Cap Stoddard called Maggie to testify. Her skirt swished as she ascended the two stairs to the round witness dock. She knew she would spend most of the day on the stand in the front of the courtroom, protected from bad memories and harsh questioning only by the dock's waist-high wooden lattice.

Three weeks earlier, it had been Edward Pollock's wife, Ellen, sitting on the same witness dock for hours, fielding accusations of subterfuge and adultery. The courtroom had been full for the first contested case to arise in the divorce colony. Ellen arrived in the city from New York just one day before the start of her trial; unlike Maggie, she had come not to end her marriage but to save it. Her husband, Edward, had been in Sioux Falls since his unhappy parents had sent him west in April 1891.

The Pollocks' case lent itself to headlines as readily as Maggie's did, providing the baroness both a brief respite and a preview of the scrutiny that was sure to come. Edward and Ellen had been joined in marriage secretly in 1887. When Edward's family learned of his union with their household maid, they threatened to disown him. The primary question before the court was whether Ellen had abandoned her husband when she realized he would be poor. Edward had filed his divorce suit on the grounds of desertion and needed to prove that claim to get his decree. If, instead, the evidence showed that Edward had abandoned his wife to keep his income, he would not be entitled to a divorce. The court was also tasked with deciding if Edward was the father of little Mary Ellen, barely one year old. The accusations flew. Ellen accused Edward of arranging the kidnapping of Anna Amelia, their three-year-old daughter. Edward accused Ellen of threatening to poison him and pointing a revolver at him.

Ellen had been a pitiable defendant. Dressed plainly in clothes that were not warm enough for the Dakota winter, she sat with her lawyers, clutching her two children, and addressed the court in a high-pitched, quavering voice. At the plaintiff's table, Edward ignored his wife and daughters, seemingly oblivious to the proceedings. He was focused instead on the diamond ring on his finger. For those who opposed divorce, there was no clearer portrait of its evils. This poor wife needed to be protected from the husband who would cast her off. In his closing statement, Edward's attorney, C. S. Palmer, addressed the narrow legal questions before the court. Ellen's attorneys, in turn, lambasted him for talking of the "dollars and cents in a case where the dearest and most sacred rights of society are at stake." "It would take the pencil of a master to depict the villainy of this man and the suffering of this woman," one lawyer lamented of Edward and Ellen.

Edward's divorce petition was still pending as Maggie stepped up to the witness dock. Her testimony was unlikely to engender the same tender emotions Ellen's had elicited. Even in the most trying moments, the baroness exuded elegance and authority. To ward off the chill of that February day, she was dressed in a three-quarter-length Persian lamb cloak. A brown soft-felt hat with a broad feather hid much of her dark golden hair. Her fair skin may have been paler than usual, but she spoke in a clear and musical voice as she answered her lawyer's questions.

Cap Stoddard led Maggie through a litany of the Baron's cruelty toward her over the sixteen years of their marriage.

"What was your husband's treatment of you in London?" he asked.

"He was very unkind to me," Maggie testified. "He would scold me before people. He said I was 'a savage American' and a 'baby,' and that I didn't know how to behave myself."

"What was his conduct in Paris?"

"It was about the same. He was rude to my friends, especially my American friends, and humiliated me in their presence," Maggie told the court.

"Was he cruel to you at Madrid?"

Maggie remembered a commercial treaty the Baron was negotiating in Spain. He needed the cooperation of the minister of commerce and had tried to enlist Maggie's help. "Make him fall in love with you," the Baron demanded. "You know how." "I told him I was not doing such work," Maggie said. "I refused flatly to thus place my womanhood at the services of the state."

Maggie continued her stories, the gallery of the courtroom slowly filling as word spread through the city of the drama unfolding there. She needed little prompting from her attorney. She recalled how her husband had accused her of adultery years before. When she denied the charge, he demanded she go to a church and swear to her faithfulness. She did, but he still refused to believe her. She also recounted his controlling nature: "My husband objected to my reading anything but history. One day I was reading a harmless English novel when he entered the room, snatched the book from me, and went out, slamming the door." And she related his threats of physical violence. One morning, as Maggie prepared to venture out from their Paris home, her husband demanded to know why she was taking a cab instead of their carriage. "He came up close to me, screamed in my face, grabbed my parasol from me, and swung it ten or twelve times over my head," Maggie said. Her husband had later told her that he did it to frighten her. "I told him, 'You might frighten your Dutch women that way, but you can't thus scare an American.'"

It had been like this for almost as long as Maggie could remember. A decade earlier, shortly after her parents died, Maggie had hosted a small dinner. "We had present some eight or ten guests," she told the court. "I made some remark which he didn't like. He jumped right up from the table, screamed at me, spit in my face, and said, 'I wish to God I had not married you.'"

⚛︎

MAGGIE HAD BEEN seated in the witness dock for almost four hours when the Baron's attorneys rose for the cross-examination. Alpha Orr began with deceptively simple questions: "When did you come to Sioux Falls? Who came with you? For what purpose?"

"To establish myself and to get as far away from my husband as possible," Maggie said in answer to this last query.

In his deposition, the Baron described a very different woman than the poised one who stood before the court. In his version Maggie was a depressive and abusive wife. She did not take proper care of the household or support him in his career, the Baron claimed. She drank and smoked and behaved erratically. In his deposition, the Baron told of a marriage as difficult as the one Maggie detailed, but in his telling, Maggie was the one with a temper, and she became cross "at everything and nothing."

The Baron's words were damning on paper, but they were hard for those who had witnessed Maggie's testimony to believe. She had remained calm in recollecting the worst moments of her marriage and broke down in tears only as she recounted her final morning in her husband's home, the same story of attempted institutionalization she had told the *Chicago Daily Tribune*. After the doctors departed that day, the Baron had locked his wife in her boudoir. From the window, she watched her husband and children ride away in a carriage. Maggie threw open the window and shouted for the coachman to stop.

"That was the last glimpse I had of my children," she told the court in a tremulous voice. "I have not seen them since."

The Baron, in his quest for custody of his brood, claimed that Maggie had "never shown much tenderness for any of her children, nor paid much attention to them." But that issue was not central to the case his lawyers wanted to make. Instead they tried to recast the incidents Maggie had described, suggesting that it was Maggie who treated her husband poorly. It was her insults that caused the Baron to react in anger. "She at first loved me dearly and now has taken a dislike to me," the Baron charged in his deposition. "Since 1885, Mrs. De Stuers' manner toward me has gradually become worse and worse."

In front of a standing-room-only crowd, the lawyers for the plaintiff and for the defendant argued over the questions that would be posed to Maggie; she responded to those that met Judge Aikens's approval with polished and even witty answers. But no one—not the Baron's counsel and not her own—asked why her attitude toward her husband had changed in 1885. Had the court inquired, Maggie would have likely explained that she had been mourning; indeed, she still was. Though the court was concerned with the fate of three De Stuers children—John, Margot, and Bertie—Maggie had borne another child, Mary Alida, in April 1876. She was John's twin and shared a name with Maggie's mother and sister. Maggie bestowed the nickname May on her daughter; it was a tribute to Maggie's beloved little sister who had died in an Alpine spa town at the age of nine. As a child John resembled the Baron, with wide-set eyes, a long nose, and a sharp chin, but May De Stuers took after Maggie, with her oval face, almond-shaped eyes, and full lips. May was just eight years old when, on July 7, 1884, she died in Paris; her cause of death went unrecorded.

That day, Maggie lost both her daughter and, it seemed, all her hopes for happiness. In March 1886, the Baron recounted, he had chided his wife for her lack of interest in John, Margot, and Bertie. "It is well that I should not care much for anybody, because people die as soon as I love them," Maggie told her husband. "I have no more heart. I cannot give what I don't possess." Maggie remembered watching her mother fall apart after her own daughter's death. That was not how she wanted to live. The sorrow overwhelmed her, but she would have given all her inheritance for another chance at happiness. "If I could buy a heart on the road, I would buy a big one," she said.

The Baron's attorneys were interested not in the events of 1885 but rather those of 1890 and 1891. Maggie and her maid had left Paris on the night of June 13, 1890, for Wiesbaden, a German spa town, and then they disappeared. The Baron wrote to Maggie's family, but they did not know where she was either. In the courtroom, J. L. Glover took over the questioning and pressed Maggie: Where had she been between her June 1890 trip to Germany and her July 1891 arrival in Sioux Falls? And whom had she been with? He wanted her to tell of her travels with Elliott. He wanted her to confess to the adultery of which the Baron accused her.

Maggie's attorneys objected, and Judge Aikens agreed. The judge rebuked Glover. "This case closes on June 13, 1890." But Glover raised the issue again. "Isn't it true," the lawyer asked Maggie, "that in case you get a divorce, you intend to marry Mr. Elliott [*sic*]?"

On the witness stand, Maggie just laughed.

⚭

MAGGIE'S TRIAL TOOK one day, but almost a month passed before Judge Aikens ruled on her petition. At the conclusion of the trial, the judge claimed the planned delay was typical bureaucracy. "My stenographer is three weeks behind with his work," Aikens said. "I am behind that much more. Of course, I must take these cases in their order."

But that backlog was not the true cause of the holdup. Aikens had heard from only two witnesses in court: Maggie and her maid, Mary. The French woman had told the judge, in stumbling English, that "the baron's conduct was often wild and foolish—screaming loud." The rest of the story would be found in hundreds of pages of depositions, from doctors, diplomats, and servants on two continents, and Aikens had made the somewhat unusual decision to keep the court record open for at least three weeks as the defense waited for more testimony to arrive. Arthur Carey, Maggie's brother, was among those whose sworn statements had not yet been submitted. He had never had much sympathy for Maggie's nervous condition. As far back as 1889, he and the Baron had met with Dr. Eugene Cheurlot to discuss Maggie. The men reached the conclusion then that she was an unfit mother. Arthur was also inclined to believe "that a false and ignorant point of view is at the root of many forms of nervous suffering." "As to the baron's treatment of my sister," Arthur said, when asked under oath, "I should say that he never treated his wife in a cruel or inhuman way. He was intentionally kind and considerate. My impression is that he was patient and forbearing."

The ordeal was too much for Maggie. Shortly after her day in court, she was again felled by her nerves. Her health was so worrisome by late February that two doctors were summoned from Chicago to her bedside at the Cataract House, where Maggie still lived; she had backed out of buying a home in Sioux Falls. After examining the patient, Dr. James Stowell delivered his diagnosis to the press as pointedly as if he had been a plaintiff's witness. "There were positively no traces of insanity. The Baroness is suffering from a nervous trouble," he concluded. He had no doubt about what was causing the affliction either. "For some time past, her condition has been serious, the anxiety and distress caused by the divorce suit, the brutal accusations made by her husband, which have never been substantiated, and the enforced separation from her children."

It wasn't until Saturday, March 5, 1892, that the *Sioux Falls Gazette* noted that Maggie was recovering from her illness. That same day, the newspaper reported that Judge Aikens had returned to town from Flandreau, where he had been holding court. He registered at the Cataract; rumors of his banishment from the establishment had been overblown. Late that afternoon, Aikens signed the final paperwork in the case of *De Stuers v. De Stuers*. After the courthouse closed for the day, Albion Thorne was summoned back to his office, and shortly after 6 p.m., thwarting both the newspapermen who would report on the verdict and the lawyers who would certainly appeal it, the clerk filed the judge's decision: an absolute divorce.

Aikens found the Baron guilty of "acts of extreme cruelty" toward his wife, "which have inflicted grievous mental suffering upon her." He concluded that the Baron had, as Maggie had charged, schemed to institutionalize her and abscond with her children. Dr. Charcot's "pretended examination" of Maggie was dismissed as insufficient to form an opinion on her well-being and her fitness as a parent, and the judge awarded Maggie custody of her still-missing daughter, Margot.

A few weeks shy of her seventeenth wedding anniversary and nine months after her arrival in Sioux Falls, Maggie was free.

FOR WEEKS, MAGGIE's illness had kept her confined to her rooms at the Cataract House. But on the Monday morning after her divorce decree was issued, she ventured out. Maggie had one more piece of business to attend to in Sioux Falls. At about 11 a.m., accompanied as always by Elliott, Maggie again climbed the quartzite steps of the courthouse. She needed to see Albion Thorne, who would once more issue judgment on her life. In the clerk's office on the second floor, Thorne considered the applicant before him and, finding her acceptable, handed over the form she requested. Maggie signed the name Margaret L. De Stuers one final time, on a document attesting that she was "single and unmarried" and that she was "of sound mind, not deprived of civil rights, and could lawfully contract and be joined in marriage." Elliott affixed his signature beside Maggie's on an application for a marriage license.

A half an hour later, Maggie and Elliott were married in a small ceremony in her suite at the Cataract House. It was a far cry from her first wedding. Maggie had hoped that Reverend George Wallace, who preached at St. Augusta Cathedral when Bishop Hare was on mission trips, would bless the union. The reverend had a fondness for the couple— they had been consistent and generous parishioners—but the rules of the Episcopal Church clearly forbade Maggie's remarriage. The state of South Dakota might recognize extreme cruelty as just cause for ending a marriage, but the church did not. Instead, Reverend John A. Cruzan of the First Congregationalist Church blessed Maggie and Elliott's union. The state's Congregational ministers were united in opposition to the permissiveness of the South Dakota divorce law, and Cruzan had himself spoken against the colony, but the $500 fee might have changed his mind.

Maggie and Elliott took their vows in front of Herbert Shipman, the couple's New York attorney, and John Lewis, the treasurer at St. Augusta. Lewis was considered one of the kindliest gentlemen in the city, so perhaps it was no surprise that he befriended Elliott when most Sioux Falls residents shunned him, but Lewis's association with the newlyweds came with a price: there were whispers that he had taken to drink and fallen into "bad ways." Over an elaborate luncheon, the small group, all well versed in how quickly rumors spread throughout the city, vowed to stay mum about the marriage. Despite that precaution, the dishes were hardly cleared before reporters learned that the baroness was now the "Countess" Zborowski. Marriages—like divorces—were public record.

"One of the Astor family, after cultivating our church in Sioux Falls and playing the role of an injured woman, has turned a disgusting somersault," Bishop Hare wrote to his daughter-in-law Rebecca of the shocking news. "She was accompanied by her adviser, so called, William Elliot by name, whom she *married at once upon her divorce*, and it turns out that he is one Elliott Zborowski, or some name of that kind!"

The bishop's disgust was rooted in his sincere religious convictions and his chivalric duty toward wives who could be unfairly cast aside by their husbands. But Maggie was not a victim of divorce; she was its perpetrator. And her presence had made the issue personal. The bishop's reputation was inexorably linked to that of the Astors, who had been his benefactors. Maggie herself donated $1,000 to St. Augusta for memorial glass windows to be installed above the altar. Reverend Wallace had cultivated the gift, and Bishop Hare had written a cordial note of thanks. He commissioned an artist in New York to create stained glass images of crucifixion, resurrection, and benediction. Below the depiction of Christ cradling a girl with an oval face, his hand outstretched in blessing, the artist painted a dedication to May, the daughter Maggie mourned. "I won't have them," Hare insisted in the weeks after Maggie's divorce and her rushed remarriage. "I'd as lief"—gladly—"paste up the flaming placards of a low circus."

The bishop had not witnessed Maggie's divorce trial firsthand. For the first several months of 1892, he had been on another mission trip, this one to China and Japan. But the distance did not temper his revulsion at Sioux Falls' sullied reputation. Maggie and her fellow divorce colonists threatened what Hare had built in the city. The bishop now found himself ashamed to ask parents to send their young daughters to his All Saints School. What kind of education would they get in a place that allowed such immorality to thrive? "The rain, the deaths, and worse than all, the scandalous divorce mill which is running at Sioux Falls, with revelations of the silliness and wickedness of men and women, have made my return home a very gloomy one," he wrote to Rebecca. "I despise people who trifle with marriage relations so intensely that the *moral* nausea produces nausea of the *stomach*. I have a continual bad taste in my mouth."

That Bishop Hare would no longer see Maggie among the worshippers in the pews at St. Augusta did not soothe him. Maggie and Elliott left Sioux Falls shortly after their wedding. Though they claimed they would return in a month, it was strategic bit of fiction designed to provide some legal cover. Ninety days' residency was required to file for a divorce in South Dakota, but no one was yet sure if continued residency was required to keep the hard-won decree.

Embarrassed by the church's embrace—however brief—of Maggie and Elliott, Hare took to the pages of St. Augusta's *Church News* to express the discomfort he and his parishioners felt at being forced to intermingle with the colonists. He asked that the divorce seekers "abstain, therefore, from seeking any more intimate connection with a congregation than attendance on the public service." Even that tepid invitation was strained. Hare did not commit to celebrating communion with the divorce seekers. Instead, he quoted the canons of the Episcopal Church, which assigned to a bishop's own "godly judgement" the right to refuse the sacraments to those who disobeyed the marital edicts of the church, except in cases of "imminent danger of death."

The lines Hare recited had been enacted twenty-five years earlier at the Episcopal Church's 1877 general convention, and the church's stance against divorce stretched nearly back to its founding in the late eighteenth century. Maggie surely knew the doctrines she was flouting. The threat of church disapproval had held no more sway over her decisions than the near certainty of social alienation. Hare had watched his fellow religious leaders in Sioux Falls and beyond rail against the divorce colony for nearly a year, to no avail. The petitioners kept coming.

Perhaps there was another remedy to quell his moral nausea. The bishop had an abiding faith in God's laws, but he recognized the power of man's laws too. If the men of the cloth could not protect the institution of marriage from those, like Maggie, who trifled with marriage relations, the responsibility would fall to the men of the country's legislatures. As Hare had said at the annual convocation in 1885, "It is by no means safe therefore to say, 'What the law allows must be right.' In the matter of marriage and divorce the law allows much that is not right."

···· **PART TWO** ····

MARY

Chapter Six

ARDOR AND INEXPERIENCE

M ARY NEVINS BLAINE and her husband had been happy. Even in February 1892, as she counted down the final days until her divorce trial, Mary wanted people to know that. She wanted them to believe she had not married for social status or for a bank account, though she had gotten both, for a while. Her marriage had been a love match, the affection so strong that it had propelled Mary and her suitor, Jamie Blaine, from their meeting in Augusta, Maine, in the late summer of 1886 to the Church of St. Leo in New York City in just eighteen days. Indeed, it would have gotten them there faster but for the Catholic Church's reluctance to marry a woman of its flock to a man baptized Protestant. It took the young lovers two days to win a dispensation from Archbishop Michael Corrigan.

They had been happy on the afternoon of Monday, September 6, 1886, in the vestry of the church on East Twenty-Eighth Street, just a few blocks from the mansion where Maggie De Stuers had been married for the first time eleven years earlier. There, in the room that Father Thomas Ducey typically used to don his vestments—and not in front of the white marble altar beneath St. Leo's elaborate frescos—the priest pronounced Jamie and Mary husband and wife. The only witnesses to their union were two of the church's employees. The newlyweds departed immediately on their honeymoon. Their boat steamed through the night from Long Island Sound to Boston.

They had been happy until, that is, Mary and Jamie realized they had to tell their parents what they'd done.

From Boston, Jamie went north, back to his family home in Augusta. Mary went south, returning to Manhattan, where her mother and father were in residence at the New-York Hotel. Neither expected a warm reception.

On the surface, the match appeared to be a respectable, if hasty, one. Jamie was more properly known as James Gillespie Blaine Jr., the youngest son of the influential former senator from Maine of the same name, who was the de facto leader of the Republican Party and a perpetual presidential contender. The Nevins family did not have such name recognition, but Mary's mother, Flora, was the daughter of Samuel Medary, who served as the territorial governor of both Minnesota and Kansas (he had also been the head of the Dakota Land Company in the 1850s when it first staked a claim on Sioux Falls), and Mary's father, Dick, had established himself as a businessman and politico in their hometown of Columbus, Ohio.

But Jamie had not yet shown any of the ambition promised by his family name. He was only seventeen years old and had already been expelled from at least three preparatory schools for drunkenness, theft, and some dalliances best left unmentioned. His parents had declared he would attend Harvard in the fall of 1886, but they also thought Jamie was studying with a tutor when he was instead romancing Mary. Jamie had no profession and seemed to have no desire for one. The Nevins were shocked by their daughter's choice. They scolded her severely.

James Sr. was in the midst of a barnstorming tour through Maine when Jamie reappeared at the Augusta house. That day, the elder man attracted a crowd of five thousand to Farmington, an industrial central Maine town of just three thousand. He railed against tariffs and endorsed the Republican candidate for governor, then returned home to the news of his son's marriage. To James and his wife, Harriet, it did not matter that Mary was tall and slender, with a tumble of ash blonde hair, pale skin, and gray-blue eyes. It did not matter that she had been well educated by the nuns of the Visitation Order or that she was an accomplished singer, the rare woman who could voice the lowest notes of a tenor.

All they saw was an older woman whose once well-to-do family was now in reduced circumstances. Nineteen-year-old Mary, they were certain, had set out to corrupt their underage son and cajole him into a secret marriage. Jamie was an impressionable young man, and his parents would not countenance such a bride for him, a schemer who was not only Catholic but also an aspiring actress and a Democrat.

Several days after parting ways with Jamie, Mary finally received a letter from her husband. He could not yet return to her; his parents forbade it. "We may be separated for a long time, my darling," Jamie wrote from Augusta, "but do not doubt my love." Mary had closed herself in her room and cried.

Finally, a week after he had said good-bye to his new bride in Boston, Jamie arrived in Manhattan on the early train. Just before 7:30 a.m., the young man rushed into the New-York Hotel, his tall, loose-limbed frame clothed in a dark suit. He wore a short-brimmed derby, a style that emphasized his Roman nose and strong, square chin and disguised his protruding ears, and he carried nothing but a light overcoat and a small gripsack. Mary had passed the first days as his wife in her parents' suite at the hotel, but with the stroke of a pen, Jamie secured their first, if temporary, marital home. "Mr. and Mrs. James G. Blaine, Jr., Maine," he had written in a firm, bold hand in the hotel's register.

Not even five years later, though, Mary's name appeared without her husband's on the register of the Cataract House in Sioux Falls.

THE BLAINE NAME was already in the headlines when Mary first arrived in Sioux Falls in late April 1891. Most expected that James G. Blaine Sr. would run for the highest office in the land again the next year, and much ink had been spilled on the fraught politics of such a challenge. The sitting president, Benjamin Harrison, was a member of Blaine's Republican Party, and James currently served in his cabinet as secretary of state.

James's past campaigns had been brutal. In 1876, he was the front runner for the Republican nomination until accusations arose that the Union Pacific Railroad had bribed the then Speaker of the House of Representatives, paying him $64,000 for some worthless bonds. In the subsequent investigation, a man named James Mulligan came forward with a cache of incriminating letters James had written. One ended with the demand "Burn this letter." James made a valiant attempt to salvage the situation, going to Mulligan's hotel room and leaving with the fifteen damning letters in hand. James reported he simply demanded the papers; Mulligan, however, claimed that James had tried to buy them and, failing that, had sobbed and threatened suicide. James then read from the letters on the House floor, choosing only the excerpts that bolstered his claim of innocence. The performance almost saved his candidacy. At the convention in Cincinnati that year, Robert Green Ingersoll placed James's name into contention. His rousing speech gave James his enduring nickname, "the plumed knight," and would have earned him the nomination, James believed, had the forces allied against him not adjourned for the night immediately after the speech. Ohio governor Rutherford B. Hayes became the Republican nominee and nineteenth American president.

After another failed bid for the Republican nomination in 1880, James was tapped by his party in 1884 to challenge New York governor Grover Cleveland for the White House. James was still plagued by the Mulligan letters. "James G. Blaine, continental liar from the state of Maine," chanted Democratic crowds. But Cleveland had personal baggage. In the summer of 1884, it was revealed that he had fathered an illegitimate child. "Ma, Ma, where's my Pa?" chanted Republican crowds in response. Voters appeared to face a choice between a candidate dogged by a private scandal and a candidate dogged by a political one, until James's marriage ended up in the headlines. "James G. Blaine betrayed"—seduced—"the girl whom he married, and then only married her at the muzzle of a shotgun," charged the *Indiana State Sentinel*.

The claim was intentionally sensational, but upon closer examination, there were some unanswered questions. James's own campaign biography noted that he wed Harriet Stanwood in Pittsburgh on March 29, 1851. Their first child, Stanwood, was born ten weeks later on June 18 of that year. (He died at the age of three.) After a month of increasingly wild public speculation in the fall of 1884, James attempted to defend his wife's reputation in a passionate "private" letter written to a friend who promptly released the missive to the media.

"You can imagine how inexpressibly painful it must be to discuss one's domestic life in the press," James wrote, before recounting his courtship with Harriet. They had met in Georgetown, Kentucky, in 1848, when James was only eighteen and Harriet was twenty. Six months later, they had committed themselves to one another in a private engagement. Two years after that, on June 30, 1850, James explained, he and Harriet had quietly married. They married again nine months later in Pittsburgh because James had come to fear their first wedding, undertaken without a marriage license, was not legally valid. "At the mature age of fifty-four, I do not defend the wisdom or prudence of a secret marriage suggested by the ardor and inexperience of youth, but its honor and its purity were inviolate, as I believe, in the sight of God, and cannot be made to appear otherwise by the wicked devices of men." That secret wedding had been the start of a successful marriage. "It brought to me a companionship which has been my chief happiness from boyhood's years to this hour," James attested.

There were, however, some odd details in the story James told during the 1884 campaign. He had misstated the marriage laws of Pennsylvania and Kentucky. June 30, 1850, was a Sunday, a day on which Protestants rarely married. Not one of the witnesses to the first union was still alive. And James, like his wayward son Jamie thirty-six years later, had not yet reached the legal age for marriage on his professed wedding day. The tale was deemed true enough by the voters in 1884—James's narrow loss was unrelated to the charge of private immorality—but the personal experience of all-consuming young love and a secret wedding that flouted society's expectations did nothing to soften James and Harriet's hearts when Jamie confessed to the same in 1886. The companionable marriage that had grown from inauspicious beginnings for James and Harriet did not give Jamie's parents hope for their son and his new bride.

Upon hearing the news of Jamie's wedding, James had immediately dispatched his eldest son, Walker, from Augusta to New York in hopes of finding a way to invalidate Jamie's vows, but the groom soon confessed to consummating his marriage on the northbound steamer. Unable to insist on an annulment, Walker advised that the newlyweds must follow in his parents' footsteps. The union would be kept a secret until Jamie graduated from college, and then they would be married again in a proper ceremony, with no mention of this youthful indiscretion. This plan, too, was thwarted when news of the pairing leaked to the New York newspapers. "The young people are very young and their marriage has surprised everyone," a representative for the Nevinses said, attempting to downplay the family drama. "Whatever feeling there is, is of surprise, mingled, perhaps, with a little temporary disgust at their disregard or, perhaps, evasion of the advice their elders would have given them. There is no anger in either family against them."

The public was fascinated by the young couple, and as the 1886 election approached, James's speeches on behalf of Republican candidates competed with Mary and Jamie's romance for the country's front pages. Archbishop Corrigan had warned the young lovers about that very thing. When Mary and Jamie had appealed for a dispensation to be married, the archbishop spent an hour trying to talk them out of their rush to the altar. The archbishop told Jamie directly that he should be careful not to do anything that would interfere with his father's political plans.

Mary now knew the consequences of—and saw the opportunities in—failing to heed that warning. She had seen her personal life entangled in the national elections of 1886 and 1888, and her divorce seemed destined to be an issue in the 1892 presidential campaign too.

⚬◈⚬

TRY AS THEY might, the reporters in Sioux Falls could not get Mary to say a cross word about her estranged husband or about her famous father-in-law, the man who attempted to end her marriage in its first week. She did not avoid the newspapers, as Maggie tried to do. Mary had understood the power of publicity since the days when she had imagined her future as a star of the stage; she knew exactly what she was doing when she invited Fannie Tinker to her "quaint little" Sioux Falls cottage, appointed with "artistic taste and refinement," for Fannie's otherwise shocking feature in the *New York World*. But Mary did not refrain from scolding the correspondents who hounded her. "It is too bad that you are out here to stir up all these people who are trying to get out of trouble," she chastised one from the *Pittsburgh Daily Post*. "Are they not unhappy enough? You ought to be more merciful." If the reporter thought that enduring Mary's scorn would earn him an answer to his question, he was mistaken. "I have no feeling in my case against the Blaine family," she said. "I have nothing to tell you."

Mary believed her father-in-law to be a good man, one of unwavering loyalty to his family, which included her son, his grandson and name-sake, a darling three-year-old who, like his father, bore a strong resemblance to the elder statesman. Mary and James had met for the first time about six weeks after her wedding. James was in Pittsburgh for a rally in support of the state's Republican gubernatorial candidate. Jamie and Mary, without resources to set up housekeeping, were living there with her brother, Richard.

Jamie was nervous about introducing his wife to his father. He went first to James's room at the Monongahela House, emerging fifteen minutes later with an anxious expression. He beckoned to Mary, who kissed him as she strode into James's room alone, leaving Jamie to pace the white marble floors and black walnut stairways of Pittsburgh's most elegant hotel. He walked and smoked cigarettes for nearly an hour before Mary reappeared, smiling. Jamie's brother Emmons wrote to his mother about the meeting. "Father saw Jamie's wife. I could not prevent that, though I tried," he reported. James had made peace with the newest addition to the family, but not all of the Blaines were ready to embrace Mary. "She made such an impression on him that I think that if I had not been there he would have had them in Augusta this fall," Emmons wrote. "That, I hope, I stopped."

The couple did not go to Augusta, but James agreed to provide Jamie with a small allowance to support himself and his wife. They moved to a house in Pittsburgh's East End, and Jamie took a job as a reporter for the *Pittsburgh Times* at $15 a week. His tenure there was not distinguished; he was later remembered primarily for his "lordly and patronizing air and manner" and the dramatic yellow ulster coat he wore through town. Mary also contributed to the newspaper's literary coverage on occasion. It was her handwriting that left a lasting impression. One compositor called it the "worst he had ever seen."

Mary didn't meet Jamie's mother, Harriet, until more than eight months into her marriage. By May 1887, Mary and Jamie were settled into a flat on East Nineteenth Street in Manhattan. Jamie had taken a job at a brokerage firm that paid three times what he had made at the newspaper in Pittsburgh, and Mary was delighted to be near the Lyceum Theatre. She became a frequent visitor to the lofts above, where Franklin Haven Sargent had established the country's first acting school. Harriet was in New York for two days early that May, and Mary visited with her twice in that time. She next saw the Blaine family—James, Harriet, Jamie's brothers, and his two younger sisters; only Alice was missing— at the Fifth Avenue Hotel for dinner at 6 p.m. on July 6, 1887, and then accompanied them to the Hoboken pier the following day to wave good- bye to her in-laws. James and Harriet, along with their young daughters, were headed to Europe. They would be gone more than a year.

The next twelve months were an adventure for Mary and Jamie too. They vacationed in the beach resort of Sea Bright, New Jersey, that sum- mer, and come fall, they moved uptown into a larger apartment on East Fifty-Fifth Street. They filled it with beautiful furniture. The bed was carved of ash and the bureau of oak, its grain reflected in a large, beveled plate glass mirror. Elegantly corkscrewed red cedar legs supported a white pine table. Mary and Jamie inked their names over and over on its pristine surface: "M. N. Blaine," "J. G. B." The mahogany rocking chair they chose would be perfect for when the baby came. Mary was pregnant with Jamie III. She gave birth to the blue-eyed boy at their home in January 1888. A few weeks later, Mary and Jamie were spotted walking on Broadway. "They swung along as joyously as children," the *Brooklyn Times*'s infor- mant reported. Jamie was "making money and friends." He'd also been taking boxing lessons. Mary was "a happy mother" and a theater patron.

No one would have known it from watching the couple vacationing in Sea Bright again in the summer of 1888—Jamie playing lawn tennis and Mary, often dressed all in red, riding in a horse-drawn cart along the ocean—but the clouds were rolling in. That spring, Jamie had lost his job at the brokerage house. He had stopped going to the office regularly, and he was drinking again. Another firm sued him for several hundred dollars in fees sustained when Jamie lost big in a speculation scheme. The neighborhood grocer had extended the couple a line of credit, but he was growing impatient. The butcher and the dressmaker hadn't been paid either. "Wait until my father gets back from Europe," Jamie told the creditors. "He will settle everything."

Jamie's father returned to New York in August 1888 to great fanfare. There was hardly a hotel room available in Manhattan, and the guests were all decked out in white hats with white plumes and gold badges emblazoned with "Blaine." The transatlantic ship was delayed, and James's admirers spent two days waiting by the bay, Mary and Jamie among them. Finally, at 7:10 a.m. on August 10, a steamboat chartered by the Republican Club of New York chugged away from Pier 18 to meet the arriving ship, which had been spotted during the night. There were some eight hundred people on board, including the members of the Seventh Regiment Band. They played the national anthem and, when James boarded the steamboat, "Hail to the Chief." James was not running in the 1888 election—Harrison had been nominated the month before—but many continued to dream of a Blaine administration.

Mary was among the first to greet her in-laws, and she was seated with the family on the upper deck of the steamboat as those gathered below hollered in approval. "Three cheers for Mrs. James G. Blaine!" someone shouted, and the crowd yelled in response. "Three cheers for Mrs. James G. Blaine, Jr.!" The crowd roared louder. On the upper deck, Harriet turned her back to her daughter-in-law.

When the case captioned *Blaine v. Blaine* was filed—not in Sioux Falls but in Deadwood, in the far southwestern corner of South Dakota—it listed two causes for the divorce action: "James G. Blaine, Jr. disregarding the solemnity of his marriage vow, willfully, wrongfully, unlawfully and without any cause and against the plaintiff's consent, desire and wish deserted and abandoned the plaintiff," and he had "willfully and wrongfully neglected to provide for the plaintiff." In private conversations, however, the plaintiff was quick to describe the true source of her marital troubles in far fewer words and with a bluntness she denied to reporters. "The fault is with his mother," Mary said.

Chapter Seven

THE CAMPAIGNS

S ENATOR JAMES H. KYLE had been a regular visitor to Sioux Falls
through the summer of 1891. The newest member of the US congressional delegation from South Dakota, Kyle spent those months meeting with his constituents, in his words, "looking up the needs of the state
in the way of national legislation." Now, on February 3, 1892, he stood
on the floor of the US Senate preparing to speak, for the first time in his
tenure, on a proposal he had carried with him from Sioux Falls to Washington, DC.

The Senate chamber in the north wing of the Capitol Building,
where James G. Blaine Sr. had spent five years of his political career,
was an impressive space, befitting high-minded aspirations. Eighty-eight
mahogany writing desks were arrayed in concentric arcs facing the dais.
The carpet was the rich purple of royalty, and the ceiling was embel-
lished with intricate ironwork. Sunshine streamed in through twenty-
one skylights.

The experience of speaking in the chamber, however, held little of
the same grandeur. Senators frequently complained about the acoustics,

especially when rain drummed on the roof, and they bemoaned the dimness of the room on cloudy days and during late nights of debate. Those same senators buzzed in and out of the chamber conducting business at their desks and in the cloakrooms, paying little heed to the member who held the floor. The speeches would be published in the *Congressional Record*, where members could peruse them quickly, if at all.

And who could blame them for their inattention? The events of this particular day—like most of the previous two months—were dull. Kyle was growing tired of the minutia. He took to the floor. "It is my belief," he said, "that we can well afford to turn from questions, such as claims and public buildings, to a subject which is eminently fitting to command the attention of our country's wisest and best minds. This is a proposition for an amendment to our national Constitution."

The din in the chamber lessened a bit. Senator Kyle, tall and broad shouldered with a mustache almost as formidable, still had the commanding presence of the Congregational preacher he had been just eighteen months earlier, and his proposed amendment, though not novel, was provocative, especially coming from a man of South Dakota. If Kyle got his way, the sixteenth amendment to the United States Constitution would read, "The Congress shall have exclusive power to regulate marriage and divorce in the several States, Territories, and the District of Columbia."

Kyle had penned the amendment after seeing the growing divorce colony firsthand in Sioux Falls. He claimed that in his time there he had counted some two hundred colonists who had traveled from elsewhere to obtain their decrees. This phenomenon made his amendment "of vital interest to the life of our Republic."

For Kyle, national control over marriage and divorce was even more important than the Thirteenth, Fourteenth, and Fifteenth Amendments, which had stitched back together a nation riven by the Civil War. "They refer to slavery, citizenship, and the electoral right and are therefore of great moment," he read aloud from his speech. "But the first institution given to mankind is greater than all questions touching subsequent rights between man and man. If the sacredness which has attached to marriage in the past is to be eliminated, the family is in peril and the associate institutions of society rest upon insecure foundations."

Kyle was not alone in his concerns about the state of the American family. Similar proposals for a constitutional amendment giving the federal government jurisdiction over marriage and divorce had been introduced in 1884, 1887, and 1889, though their impetus was widespread fear of the Mormon practice of polygamy, which the Church of Jesus Christ of Latter-day Saints officially ended in 1890.

On the Senate floor that February day, Kyle claimed the support of South Dakota for his amendment and defended the state. "Our laws upon divorce are not more lax than those of numerous other states," Kyle said. "The privilege of instituting divorce proceedings, however, upon a ninety days' residence has brought us applicants from many States, and in consequence of fraud and perjury as to bona fide residence divorce proceedings are often corrupt and farcical." He could have been describing Mary Nevins Blaine in that moment, though it is unlikely he ever encountered her outside the newspaper headlines. In the nine months since she had arrived in Sioux Falls to establish her residency, Mary had spent less than half her time there. As Kyle made his plea to the Senate, Mary was again residing at the Cataract, but she had spent most of the previous two months in New York.

When Kyle finished his speech, several senators offered their congratulations. In the days and weeks afterward, religious newspapers also rose up in support for the former minister's secular solution to divorce. The language of the proposed amendment was neutral—"regulate"—and provided no guarantees as to what the government would do with the newfound power, but the country's clergy heard in Kyle's speech a call for stricter divorce laws. Others remained more skeptical of the little-known senator, who had formally declared himself an independent.

South Carolina, which had no provisions for divorce, could not imagine trusting a legislative body that included representatives from South Dakota to craft a better law. In South Dakota, the idea divided the populace. The *Sioux Falls Press* wondered why the "apostle of divorce reform" was focused on an issue with as much practical value "as a constitutional amendment to prescribe the sort of clothes the people of this country should wear in different kinds of weather." Meanwhile the newspaper in Mitchell, seventy miles west of Sioux Falls, suggested that the main flaw in Kyle's plan was that it could not be enacted fast enough. "Senator Kyle ought to put an emergency clause in his divorce amendment," the *Mitchell Capital* wrote, "so as to shut off the filth which is just now inundating the state of South Dakota from the social sewers of the East."

MARY HAD RETURNED to Sioux Falls from New York just a few days before Maggie De Stuers's divorce trial. If she joined her sister Anna in the gallery as the case began, her presence was not noted, but when the court reconvened that Monday afternoon in early February, Mary was among the hundreds jostling for space in the crowded courtroom. As she listened to Maggie detail the Baron's cruelties, small and large, Mary likely saw little familiar in Maggie's marriage. Jamie had never scolded her, never threatened her. He was careless with money, but it was Blaine money he risked. He did like to drink—a weakness Maggie did not level at the Baron—but in the first year of their marriage, it hadn't been so bad. Mary was willing to indulge Jamie's occasional carousing, caring for her tipsy husband like a child. Jamie could be imperious, a trait he shared with the Baron; Mary had to overlook his off-putting habit of asking, "Do you know who you are talking to?" But Mary's husband's fatal flaw was a mirror image of the one Maggie found in the first man she married. Whereas the Baron was domineering, Jamie was docile and easily led. His father thought him "the most helpless, least responsible" of his children, "erratic, but controllable through his strong affections," and a "source of constant anxiety, but not of despair, because he is as readily influenced to the right as the wrong."

Harriet believed Mary had influenced her son to the wrong. The awkwardness between the two women had begun with the circumstance of Mary and Jamie's wedding, and they had spent little time together in the four and a half years of Mary's marriage. Mary had not been able to win over her mother-in-law as she so quickly had her father-in-law. Harriet was everything that flirtatious and charming Mary was not: straitlaced and sharp-tongued, with no patience for silliness. She indulged only her husband and her children, perhaps Jamie—her dear "J'aime," French for "I love"—most of all. Harriet was used to being the most important woman in her teenage son's life, and her word had always been inviolable in the Blaine household, so it must have been a shock when, at Mary's urging, Jamie refused Harriet's invitation to Augusta after the family returned to the United States in August 1888.

Mary's victory was short-lived. By the middle of that month, Harriet prevailed, and the couple traveled to Augusta with Jamie III and his nurse, Honor Fuller. They planned to stay with the Blaines until Mary discovered that Harriet's other grandchildren, who were also visiting, had the whooping cough. She sent her seven-month-old and his nurse to the Augusta Hotel, over Harriet's objections. Mary and Jamie remained at the Blaine house, a large white mansion in the Italianate style of the 1870s with a picket fence; James had bought it as a birthday gift for Harriet years earlier. But Mary was often seen out alone in the family's phaeton, not even Jamie by her side, as horses pulled the carriage through the streets of Augusta.

The elder Blaines had discovered what James called "the dismal failure of their New York life." Jamie was broke, made poor by an extravagant lifestyle, ill-advised investments, and a slipshod work ethic. He had been too confident in his parents' willingness to cover his debts. His father, certainly, could understand some of Jamie's excesses; he too was prone to lavish expenditures and speculation and on occasion even misplaced his paychecks. But for his mother, such inattention to finances was unimaginable. The family was well-off, with elegant homes in Augusta, Bar Harbor, and Washington, DC, but Harriet still worried about every dollar. After a "family council," James and Harriet agreed they would support their son and his wife financially, but only if the couple agreed to certain conditions.

Jamie was sitting with his father on the front lawn of the Blaine house, a green expanse dotted with apple trees, when James made his proposal. Mary and Jamie were to leave New York. They would live here in Augusta. James and Harriet planned to spend the winters in Washington, DC, and the summers in Bar Harbor. This house would be vacant. James would pay for the upkeep of the property, as well as the wages of a manservant and the cost of a horse and carriage. He would also provide Jamie with $2,500 a year—far more than he was making in his new job as an exchange reader, scouring the newspapers for tidbits useful to the Republican National Committee—until, James added optimistically, such a time that Jamie was earning that much on his own.

The money must have been attractive to Mary. She had lived well as a child in Columbus, while her father was the state printer, but his business faltered, and there were accusations of fraud. The years after that, as the family moved to Washington, DC, and then New York, had been lean ones. It would be difficult to forsake the luxury Mary had rediscovered with Jamie in their New York life. But Mary felt unwelcome in Augusta, and she must have at least suspected another big change was coming. She was pregnant again.

Shortly after James made his proposal, he left for a speaking tour through Maine, and a few days after that, on the stormy, final Friday in August, Jamie followed. Jamie, it had been announced, would join his father on the stump that fall, rallying Republican voters. For now, James just needed some documents delivered. Mary expected her husband to be gone a day, but he did not return on Saturday or on Sunday. He did not even send a telegram, but word got to Mary anyway. Jamie was in Bar Harbor, flirting his way through the hotel piazzas.

Perhaps Mary thought of this moment when she sat in the Minnehaha County Courthouse listening to Maggie recount the final days of her own marriage. Surrounded by the oppressive darkness of her mother-in-law's house in the hours before dawn on Monday, September 3, 1888—two years to the day since she had departed Augusta bound for the Church of St. Leo—Mary made a decision: she was going to leave.

Later that morning, Mary told Harriet that Jamie III was dangerously ill. Augusta was no good for him, the doctor advised; he needed to be in Sea Bright. Mary still remembered Harriet's response: "If you go, I never want to see you again. I will make you rue it the longest day you live." Mary took her son, her dog, and her trunks, leaving behind only a note for Jamie. "You shall live to regret all this," she wrote.

⟨∞⟩

IN HIS SIOUX Falls courtroom, Judge Aikens had ruled that the law's interest in Maggie's story ended the moment she left her husband's home; he did not hear testimony about the events after that date. In Mary's trial, what happened after she left the Blaine household would make all the difference. In Deadwood, a judge would be asked to determine if Mary had abandoned her husband on that September day or if Jamie's subsequent actions were the true cause of the separation. Mary needed to prove that Jamie was at fault to have legal grounds for a divorce. She had been preparing just such an argument since the moment she left Augusta without her husband in 1888.

That day, as Mary's train headed south toward Boston, where she would transfer to another bound for New York, she spotted Martin McMahon passing through the train car. She hurried after the lawyer. McMahon was a close friend of the Nevinses and was godfather to Jamie III. He was also well acquainted with the strain between the Nevins and

Blaine families. He had served as a go-between two years earlier when the fate of Mary's marriage had first been in doubt. Now Mary recounted the story of her visit to—and sudden departure from—Augusta. McMahon offered what reassurance he could, becoming the first of many attorneys consulting on Mary's marital problems, even as she denied her split with Jamie. "We are as happy a couple as there is in the country," she insisted publicly.

The legal team Mary assembled was an unlikely crew: McMahon was a Democratic politician, a prominent New York Catholic, and a former lieutenant colonel in the United States' Army of the Potomac. Roger A. Pryor was a Confederate carpetbagger, a Southern Democrat, and a vocal secessionist who had served in the Confederate Army and the Confederate States Congress. And Robert Green Ingersoll, a staunch Republican nicknamed "the great agnostic," was the very same man who had crowned James G. Blaine "the plumed knight" at the 1876 convention. Ingersoll's relationship with the elder Blaine had cooled several years earlier for reasons neither man would divulge, though one version circulating pinned the blame on Harriet's bluntness. James wrote to him to dispute Mary's charges, but that did not sway Ingersoll's determination to help her. He might have made the same decision if James had still been a friend. A progressive thinker on the issue of women's rights, Ingersoll was firm in his belief that divorce was not the evil so many condemned it to be. He thought marriage should be governed by contract law, not the laws of the church. "Is it possible to conceive of anything more immoral than for a husband to insist on living with a wife who has no love for him?" Ingersoll asked. "Is the wife to lose her personality? Has she no right of choice? Is her modesty the property of another? Is the man she hates the lord of her desire? Has she no right to guard the jewels of her soul?"

These three men and numerous other advisors offered Mary conflicting guidance, but there was one constant refrain: as a resident of New York, Mary could not file for divorce on grounds of abandonment; if she did not have evidence of adultery on Jamie's part, she would have to find a different solution to her marital woes. Pryor's advice was blunt and far more practical than Ingersoll's abstract musings: Mary should reconcile with her husband. "In all cases of trouble between man and wife, I always try to have them make up," he said. "Even if a suit is brought and decided in favor of the woman, she is in the end the real sufferer."

Mary had tried to heed Pryor's counsel. "Indeed I am so wretched without you that I can bear it no longer," she wrote to her husband. "For the sake of our child and the one to come I will go to whatever home you may provide, even under your parent's roof." She wrote to him again and again. When she received no response, she sent a registered letter: "As your true and faithful wife, I will go with you wherever you say and make my home with you as a wife should." The return receipt was signed by Walker Blaine. Finally, Mary traveled to Augusta. In the parlor of the Blaines' home, Mary pleaded to see Jamie. Harriet refused her entreaties. Mary rushed up the stairs to her husband's room, but Harriet had locked the door. In tears, Mary departed. "I am going to leave Augusta, but not you, Jamie," she shouted.

The image was a pitiful and painful one of a woman in a delicate condition, ill-treated and abandoned by both her husband and his influential family. Mary's misery played out in great detail in the newspapers. She was suffering, as Pryor had predicted, but could it be a strategy? Mary's actions had given her a distinct advantage, both in the courts and in the public eye. This intense scrutiny of her family's affairs was exactly what Harriet, exhausted by the spotlight on her marriage in the 1884 election, had hoped to avoid when she advised James not to run for president in 1888. It was clear now that she had miscalculated. The Blaines would face a fierce campaign that fall without any hope of ending up in the White House.

The newspapers were willing accomplices, chronicling Mary's every move. With equal credulity, the tabloids detailed Mary's race to Newspaper Row at midnight to suppress an article about her unhappy marriage— "I knew it would hurt my husband's family," she explained—and printed long interviews in which she told of her abuse at the hands of her mother-in-law. When Mary's lawyers announced that they were preparing a $100,000 civil suit against James and Harriet for alienation of affection on behalf of their client, who was so distressed by the situation she was confined to bed, reporters gleefully counted down the days until James's next campaign trip to New York, hoping he would be served. No court papers were ever filed, but the night that James arrived for a raucous speech in front of eleven thousand in Madison Square Garden, Mary took a turn for the worse. The headlines the next day announced that she had been stricken with nervous prostration and hysteria brought on by James's rally.

Mary's life was "hanging by a thread," her physician told newspapermen on the evening of October 27, 1888. But he did not reveal the true cause of her distress. Mary, three or four months pregnant, had miscarried. Jamie, in Augusta, read about Mary's illness in the paper. The real cause of this personal suffering would not be used in her public battle with the Blaines, but her husband must have known the truth. He was "visibly affected" by the news, one observer noted, speculating that the man would soon be at his wife's bedside.

As the days passed, however, Jamie did not arrive at the New-York Hotel to comfort his wife, and the war between Mary and the Blaines began anew. Mary's recovery—from nerves, as far as public would ever know—was a daily source of tittle-tattle, and her relapse conveniently coincided with Harriet's next visit to New York. The whole country was focused on the feverish young woman lying in a dark and quiet room on Broadway. When tens of thousands of supporters of Democratic presidential candidate Grover Cleveland paraded through Manhattan, the bands fell silent in front of the New-York Hotel in deference to the woman who had proven herself a campaigner as adept as their rival, James G. Blaine. A few days later, supporters of Republican candidate Benjamin Harrison paid the same respect to James's estranged daughter-in-law. Forty thousand marched passed the hotel in a hush.

Mary had won the battle of public opinion. By the summer of 1889, newspapers depicted her as a refined young woman, "the picture of trim simplicity," lounging on the oceanfront piazza of the Brighton Hotel in Point Lookout, Long Island. She wore gray-green silk with a flounce of green and white embroidery, old-fashioned white silk gloves, and a buttercup-yellow cashmere shawl. She was cool and coy about her failed relationship: "When the proper time comes I will talk about my unfortunate marriage episode." Jamie spent that summer covered in ash, doing penance in his latest job as a fireman on the Central Maine Railroad. His family forbid him from taking the season off to relax at the Bar Harbor house. Instead, Jamie was assigned to stoke the boiler on the express train between Bangor and the seaside city and even carried his father and his touring party one July day.

But Mary's apparent victory was an empty one. She had not reconciled with Jamie; nor had the embarrassment the Blaines endured brokered an extralegal separation and the settlement she needed. Mary and Jamie remained married, but the remnants of their short life together were disappearing. Even the white pine table on which the young lovers had tattooed their names was gone. Along with all the furniture that once adorned the Fifty-Fifth Street flat, the table was carted off to James P. Silo's auction house on Liberty Street downtown. The sale was advertised as "the entire household furniture of a young couple who have deemed it wise to discontinue housekeeping," and each piece bore a yellow tag with the name "Blaine" scrawled in pencil. But unlike the rest of the country, the auctioneer had nothing more to say about Mary or Jamie. "People send their things here and we sell them," he said. "It isn't our business to know anything about their misfortunes."

❦

SPECULATING ABOUT MARY's misfortunes had become a national pastime. It was not just the particulars of her marriage, which would be aired in court, that interested the public. People also wondered what kind of life a well-known divorcee would be allowed to lead. She had garnered sympathy as an estranged wife, but once she went to Sioux Falls, the sentiment began to shift. After her divorce, could Mary pursue her long-held dream of appearing on stage? Would she marry again and erase the name Blaine from her signature?

If she had a choice at all, it was a binary one. If Mary did not go on the stage, she would likely need to marry. She had no other obvious source of income. And if she married well, she was unlikely to go on the stage. She had been contracted to perform in 1886 when she eloped with Jamie. One explanation Mary offered for their hurry was Jamie's insistence that he could not wed an actress. The stigma once associated with women in the profession was fading, but there were still social barriers between the bohemians of the playhouses and the moneyed elite. Once he was Mary's husband, Jamie had the authority to void the legal agreement she had previously signed with an acting troupe, and he did so, much to the disappointment of the patrons who had financed her arts education.

Mary had stood center stage only once, in 1885, playing Paul in the opera *Paul et Virginie*. Though it had been an amateur performance, with most roles undertaken by notable Washingtonians, all two thousand seats of the new Albaugh's Grand Opera House, within sight of the White House, had been filled. President Chester A. Arthur was in one of the boxes overlooking the stage; James and Harriet, still strangers to the teenage actress dressed in a loosely knotted tie and men's top boots singing about lost love, sat in another. The reviews of Mary's performance had been largely positive. She was an "exquisitely pretty girl with a phenomenal voice," the *Chicago Daily Tribune* critic opined.

After she left Jamie in 1888, Mary had decided to capitalize on that long-ago moment of fame, but she wasn't confident about her prospects. "When I stop to think I am nearly frightened at what I have undertaken," she said in December of that year. "When I first contemplated going on the stage I was a young girl and only saw the rosy side of such a career.

To-day I am a woman with a child to support and my success or failure means everything to me." She needn't have worried. Theater owners didn't want her talents; they wanted her name and notoriety. Those would sell tickets. For her star turn, Mary—who had been billed by her childhood nickname "Marie" in her debut—rechristened herself "Mary Nevins Blaine."

But that name never appeared on marquees. A handsome costar had been cast, a new play commissioned, and a tour of eastern cities announced when Mary fell ill in late August 1889. The show's director blamed her condition on a sudden summer rainstorm Mary had been caught in. For nearly a year afterward, she suffered from what her doctors diagnosed as rheumatism. The disease stiffened her joints, twisted her limbs, and threatened to cripple her.

During the long, painful months of 1890, Dr. William Tillinghast Bull, the attending surgeon at New York Hospital, had begun treating Mary. Under his care, she emerged from her morphine haze, and the distinguished forty-one-year-old surgeon successfully operated on her right arm and leg, a procedure that involved breaking and resetting the extremities. William was constantly at Mary's bedside, so, of course, rumors began to spread that Mrs. Blaine Jr. would soon be Mrs. Bull. Confronted with the story when Mary first traveled to South Dakota, William said only, "It seems to me if such a thing were true that I would naturally know something of it." Nevertheless, the whispers followed Mary as she limped through the streets of Sioux Falls.

Chapter Eight

UNDESIRABLE CATTLE

D EADWOOD WAS a long way from Sioux Falls. The smaller city—
population twenty-three hundred—lay 350 miles almost due west.
If a traveler followed the crow's path, she would cross the fertile plains,
ford the Missouri River, skirt the arid badlands, and climb into the pon-
derosa pine forests of the Black Hills. Much of the land between the two
points had been Sioux territory until 1889, when Congress opened the
center of the new state to homesteading; all of it had belonged to the
tribes just two generations earlier.

No train running from the east yet crossed the Missouri into the
Sioux lands. In the 1870s, prospectors determined to mine their fortune
in the hills had ridden the rails as far as Pierre and braved a thirty-six-
hour stagecoach trip, numbingly cold in the winter, stiflingly dusty in
the summer, and sure to be robbed in any season. By 1891, though, one
could board a train south from Sioux Falls to Sioux City. From there two
railroads raced across Nebraska, tracing the boundary of the American
Indian reservations before heading into the hills. The first had arrived
in Deadwood in December 1890; the second, a month later. In February

1892, Mary, accompanied by her son, his nurse, and yet another attorney, C. S. Palmer, made the journey in about forty-eight hours. It was a hard trip for her. On the second night, as the engine turned north toward Deadwood, she fell ill. Palmer called it a hemorrhage of the lung and demanded silence aboard the train to allow Mary to rest. From the depot, where many locals had hoped to glimpse the woman in the headlines, she was rushed to the Keystone Hotel to recuperate.

The Keystone was as close as it got to first-class accommodations in Deadwood. It didn't look like much from the outside. The wooden structure on Main Street had been built piecemeal over the last twelve years, growing larger in fits and starts with the boomtown. It could now accommodate forty or fifty guests in some style; those larger rooms had been repapered just a year back. The other one hundred or so were quite small but more than enough for the traveling men who called the Keystone home when passing through Deadwood. Like the Cataract House, the hotel was the city's town square. Its twenty-four-hour dining room and its billiard tables were always busy, and it served as headquarters for, at various points, visiting doctors and dentists, safe salesmen, and cigar stockists. It was also a de facto mining exchange, and when a particularly impressive chunk of ore was unearthed in the nearby hills, it was displayed, to much speculation as to its worth, in the Keystone office.

It had been fifteen years since Deadwood's most famous residents, "Wild" Bill Hickok and Martha "Calamity" Jane Burke, walked the muddy streets, but the city maintained its outlaw image. Once an illegal settlement, Deadwood had been incorporated in 1881, and the city's leaders had the authority "to restrain, prohibit and suppress tippling shops, billiard tables, ten-pin alleys, ball alleys, houses of prostitution, and other disorderly houses and practices, games and gambling houses, desecration of the Sabbath, commonly called Sunday, and all kinds of indecencies"—but there was little evidence they tried. Vice coexisted with proper Victorian society relatively peacefully in Deadwood. Its residents had come from all over the country and the world, and they prided themselves on a particular kind of tolerance, one based primarily on commerce.

But in this town where money outweighed most societal considerations, there was no cadre of hotel owners, restauranteurs, and lawyers eager to make their living from the unhappily married. Deadwood still cultivated its aura of anarchy, but when it came to divorce petitions, the city wanted no part of the lawlessness. "The parties to them are undesirable cattle," the *Deadwood Daily Pioneer* opined, "and the details of the cruelty and crime brought out in the suits are extremely shocking to the sensitive morals of Deadwood people."

Deadwood could afford to put on airs. It didn't need a divorce mill to draw people and money from the East; it had the mines. But countless other towns in South Dakota—and in North Dakota, which adopted the same old territorial laws—desired the colony. Once Sioux Falls had laughed at the envy of its neighbors. "We notice that some jealous contemporaries are throwing rocks at Sioux Falls' flourishing divorce industry," the *Argus-Leader* had written. "They covet Sioux Falls' success." That was before Mary and Maggie arrived along with the country's disapprobation. Deadwood did not want the notoriety, but Sioux Falls now wondered, with equal parts hopefulness and fear, if another town would lure its most famous industry away.

One courtroom was just as good as another to C. S. Palmer. The forty-seven-year-old lawyer and politician—bow tied, with a stubborn cowlick—had seen many of them while traveling across Dakota as an associate justice of the territorial supreme court in the 1880s. When the Vermont native resigned from the bench in 1888, he stayed in the West, hanging out his shingle in Sioux Falls and partnering for a time with Judge Aikens. The competition for clients was fierce, and Palmer was a practical man. He was a Congregationalist who had opened each court session over which he presided with a prayer, and he was a Republican who pledged his support to James G. Blaine, but he had shown no reluctance to take divorce cases, including Mary's. The only drawback was the Dakota newspapermen who scoured the appearance books and filled the courtroom gallery in Sioux Falls. Palmer had a contentious relationship with the "penny-a-liners," as he called them derisively, which could explain why he'd filed Mary's lawsuit in Deadwood. It was becoming a common tactic for a divorce colonist to plead her case in one of the smaller eastern South Dakota towns, hoping the distance would discourage the press, but Mary had gone clear to the western edge of the state's jurisdiction—and so had the correspondents.

Would the penny-a-liners notice that Palmer was selling the same story in the Blaine case in Deadwood that he had in the Pollock case in Sioux Falls a few weeks earlier? A wealthy boy meets a girl below his station. They marry secretly to the dismay of his parents. An heir is born and a spouse abandoned. In the Pollock trial, though, Palmer stood with Edward and argued that his wife's despair and destitution were of no matter to the court; Edward deserved a divorce nonetheless. Here, Palmer would argue the opposite. Mary's ill health and financial straits made her desire for a divorce all the more urgent. In both cases, he believed, he had the law on his side, but this time he hoped to reclaim the public's sympathy too.

⟨∞⟩

JAMIE HAD NOT come to Deadwood; nor had his lawyers. There was little suspense for Mary in the outcome of the proceedings about to take place. She would get her divorce. Though she could not admit it to the court—that would be evidence of illegal collusion—the arrangements had all been made months earlier in New York, where depositions were taken for the convenience of the witnesses who lived on the East Coast. For more than a week in December 1891, lawyers for the Nevinses and the Blaines haggled in a conference room in the Equitable Life Assurance Building on Broadway. In the offices of Lord Day & Lord, Mary had faced Jamie for the first time since he left Augusta for Bar Harbor in the summer of 1888. Mary believed that her husband had tried to return to her once. It had been that October when she visited Augusta and argued with his mother. She later heard that Jamie had attempted to follow her, boarding a train to Portland only to be intercepted at the next stop by his sister. But if Jamie's commitment to their marriage lingered beyond the day court papers said he abandoned her, there was no sign of it in front of the referee. Husband and wife did not acknowledge one another.

The settlement had not come easily. "We are going to fight the matter clear through," Jamie's attorney said. Mary would not be guaranteed her freedom unless the parties reached an agreement. They had tried once before, as Mary was preparing to leave for Sioux Falls in March 1891. Through intermediaries, she offered to file on grounds of nonsupport and forgo alimony in exchange for custody of Jamie III and an uncontested divorce. But things had changed in the intervening months, and everything was open to negotiation again: money, which Mary needed; custody of Jamie III, which she dearly wanted; and Mary's silence, which had become her most valuable bargaining chip as the elder Blaine again eyed the presidency.

The court had already ordered Jamie to pay temporary alimony and a portion of Mary's attorneys' fees, a total of $1,000. Jamie, also in court that month for failing to pay a doctor's bill for his wife and child years earlier, pleaded poverty. His job prospects had not improved considerably in recent years. He had, for a time, been a clerk for the House of Representatives Committee on Foreign Affairs and was dispatched to Spain on a diplomatic mission, but now he was a clerk in the Pennsylvania Railroad ticket department. He claimed to make just $60 a month. At the same time, though, he argued that he could better provide for his son who had not, he said, been living in a "wholesome atmosphere" while with Mary in Sioux Falls. Jamie III remained in the West with his nurse as his parents argued over his future. Jamie wanted his parents to raise the boy. Mary had planned to bring him east for Christmas, until she began to worry he could be kidnapped.

While in Manhattan, Mary had grown nervous. She was certain that she was being spied on. There was a suspicious woman who had taken a room near Mary's at the New-York Hotel and a man in the lobby who seemed familiar from Sioux Falls. She'd led another man on a horse-drawn cab chase through Manhattan before leaping from her carriage to confront him: "I know you are a detective and are following me," she shouted. The man had laughed. The Sioux Falls divorce colonists suspected every stranger to be a spy, but their paranoia was not necessarily misplaced. Pinkerton's National Detective Agency, the best known of the investigative firms and the colonists' favorite bogeyman, had decreed from its earliest days that it would not take divorce cases—a business it characterized as "disreputable in its character"—but plenty of other snoops were happy for the work. Mary herself employed one in early 1891 in hopes of finding evidence that Jamie was committing adultery, evidence that would have allowed her to get a divorce at home in New York. James, too, had investigated Mary's life after she filed her suit against his son. He wrote to his lawyers about a tantalizing "new clue" he had discovered but ultimately decided that nothing should be done with the closely held information unless absolutely necessary to protect the family's interests.

In New York, there were days of depositions detailing Mary's time in Augusta and the circumstances of her miscarriage, and passions ran high. Estelle Doremus was among those who spoke on Mary's behalf, describing a proud mother and proper lady. Estelle also listened to the testimony of other witnesses. She was incensed by what she heard and turned to the person next to her. "The man in this case is a scoundrel and poltroon!" she said.

"Do you know who you are talking to?" the man snapped. It was Jamie Blaine.

Estelle, a friend to Mary and so many of the city's actors and musicians, flushed but was not finished speaking her mind. "I did not know that you were Mr. Blaine when I spoke. But I repeat it now. A man who would abandon not only his wife, but his innocent child, at the dictates of his father and—"

"Don't mention my mother's name," Jamie warned her.

In the end, that seemed to be the agreement. Mary would get her divorce, her child, and whatever alimony the court ordered—provided poor Jamie could pay—in exchange for sparing the Blaine family further embarrassing headlines in an election year.

⚬❦⚬

THE MINNEHAHA COUNTY Courthouse towered over Sioux Falls, an always visible symbol of the city's lofty ambitions—one that had become for many a reminder of its moral failing. In Deadwood, that space in the skyline and the city's psyche was filled by the hills and the detritus of those ever hopeful of digging, panning, milling, and smelting their way to a fortune. Its courthouse was a two-story structure at the corner of Pine and Sherman Streets downtown. It was a modern brick building, a vast improvement over the original wood-framed one that had burned in the great fire of 1879 and far more comfortable than the makeshift courtrooms constructed in rented spaces through the city for a decade after the blaze, but it had not been built to inspire. With large windows spanning the length of the first floor, it looked—like much of Deadwood—as if it had been built for commerce. A peek through the glass seemed more likely to reveal the latest in women's finery than the comings and goings of judge and jury.

The Lawrence County Courthouse was the domain of Judge Charles M. Thomas, a forty-four-year-old Kentuckian, who retained the speech patterns of his native Bowling Green and its politics; Thomas had joined the Confederate Army at the age of fifteen. Appointed as an associate justice in the Dakota Territory by President Grover Cleveland in 1886, Thomas had found himself a Democrat in a predominantly Republican town, but he was earnest and eloquent and talked his way to election as a circuit judge after statehood, the only Democrat among their number. Surely C. S. Palmer, who had been a colleague of Thomas's on the supreme court bench, took his politics into consideration when he filed Mary's case.

On the morning of Friday, February 19, 1892, all of Deadwood seemed to be crowded into Thomas's courtroom. Some 250 people were in attendance, by one count, among them many of the city's best-known women and a stranger, whom locals eyed suspiciously as he jotted notes about proceedings. They suspected him to be a spy for the Blaine family. The trial lasted just a few hours. Palmer entered the depositions taken in New York into evidence, reading some portions aloud, and then he ushered Mary to the stand and asked her about her ill-fated trips to Augusta. Mary recounted the harsh words the newspapers had already put in Harriet Blaine's mouth, but she refrained from lodging new complaints against the Blaine family. The only drama came when Palmer handed Mary a photo of her son. She broke down in tears, and a correspondent for the *Sioux City Journal* noted, "Not a few of the men in the room made suspicious gestures by which handkerchiefs passed across the eyes."

In the absence of defense counsel, Judge Thomas posed a few questions to Mary. In her response, Mary suggested that part of the trouble between the families had arisen because the Blaines did not consider the Nevinses to be their social equals. Thomas could not let that comment pass without reassuring Mary. He had known Mary's grandfather and her father, and the Nevinses were the equal of any family in the country, he told her. Finally, Thomas asked the witness the most important legal question in any South Dakota divorce trial.

"Mrs. Blaine, I want to ask you a question concerning your residence in Dakota," the judge said. "I suppose you came to Dakota to avail yourself of the liberal laws of the state?"

Like Maggie before her, Mary was well prepared. "Your Honor, I came to Dakota to establish a bona-fide residence here. Since my husband's separation from me my constant aim in life has been to secure the legal control of my boy. To this end I have struggled for him through sickness and ill-health. For his sake I have invoked the laws of my country, and but for him I would never have troubled this or any other court for a decree."

The very next morning Judge Thomas resumed his place on the bench. Mary hadn't expected to be summoned so soon, but the judge had spent the night mulling the young woman's predicament. He didn't want Mary to wait any longer for the decree he felt she was entitled to.

The finding of fact the judge produced was straightforward: that Mary and Jamie had married in September 1886; that they had had a child, now in the care of his mother; and that they had lived together as husband and wife until the seventeenth day of October 1888, when Jamie abandoned Mary and stopped providing for her. The court further found that Mary was a resident, "in good faith," of Sioux Falls, and that she had, throughout her marriage, "conducted herself in an exemplary manner and in every respect as a wife do should towards her husband." Judge Thomas awarded Mary everything she asked for: a divorce, custody of Jamie III "without any interference on the part of the defendant," and $100 per month in permanent alimony, plus the $1,000 in court-ordered alimony and legal fees Jamie had never gotten around to paying. Mary was overjoyed by the judge's decision, but he wasn't done yet.

Judge Thomas had something else to say. He'd given careful thought to the statement. His words wouldn't carry the force of law, but they were certain to echo across the country's front pages. He was inclined to invective but had, over the course of the previous evening, reined himself in. He now thought his sentiments moderate and conservative, befitting a member of the judiciary.

With a court stenographer at the ready, Judge Thomas began his own version of Mary and Jamie's love story, from "their ill-considered, ill-advised, and in many respects unfortunate" wedding to their first years of an "affectionate, happy, and contented" marriage. What had gone wrong? Judge Thomas was not satisfied with the explanation of abandonment and neglect the law provided. "The cause of the estrangement and separation, so far as the court is able to judge from the testimony, was the unfriendliness on the part of the family of the defendant, especially his mother," he told those gathered in the courtroom.

"Mrs. Blaine the elder did all within her power to make the life of the plaintiff unhappy. That she was evidently opposed to the marriage and had concluded that the best thing for her son's welfare was to have them separated, and laid a shrewd plan, and surrounded them by circumstances which would result in an apparent desertion on the part of the plaintiff."

Jamie's conduct was "reprehensible," the judge concluded. The boy had a "hardness of heart" and a "reprobacy of mind," but Harriet was culpable as well, as the devious, angry, demanding woman who raised him.

Chapter Nine

A PERSONAL STATEMENT

J AMES G. BLAINE SR. was a master orator. On the stump, he commanded attention like a leading man standing in the spotlight. He spoke rapidly and forcefully, his whole body animated. And then he would quiet, as if he were addressing a confidant in his parlor, his sincerity drawing the audience in. James understood the power of a well-crafted performance. Faced with the Mulligan letters in 1876, he had stood on the floor of the US House of Representatives and raised the offending documents above his head, slamming them back down on the desk. "I am not afraid to show the letters," he declared. "I invite the confidence of forty-four million of my fellow countrymen while I read those letters from this desk." It was, one of his Democratic adversaries said, "one of the most consummate pieces of acting that ever occurred upon any stage on earth."

But before he was a politician with a national platform and the ability to draw thousands to a rally, James had been a journalist, and he still often turned to the pen to make his case. In office, James had pioneered the art of the Sunday night news release. Knowing from personal experience the difficulty of filling the Monday morning edition after a quiet

Sunday, James picked that moment to send statements or share his correspondence with friendly papers sure to print them as news. In this way his voice reached not thousands but millions. Over the years, he used this platform to inform the public about his travel plans, his health, and his candidacy for high office. Most recently, on a Monday less than two weeks before Mary's trial, the country awoke to another missive from James. It was addressed to the chairman of the National Republican Committee. "My dear sir," he wrote, "I am not a candidate for the presidency, and my name will not go before the Republican National Convention for the nomination." As was typical—and perhaps intended—James's announcement did not end the conversation but instead inflamed it. Both his supporters and his detractors carefully dissected each word of the two-paragraph letter to divine the man's true intentions. The campaign was far from over.

In the days after Mary received her decree, James sat down again to write. The recent years had been difficult ones for the Blaine family. In early 1890, James's eldest son, Walker, his confidant and political heir, had died suddenly of pneumonia. Two weeks later, his eldest daughter, Alice, died after a brief illness. Now James's youngest son's ordeal weighed heavily on him. Jamie, for his part, seemed unperturbed. On the night Judge Charles Thomas dissolved his marriage and denied him his child, Jamie had been spotted enjoying the various entertainments Washington, DC, had to offer. James was surely sorry he would not get to know his grandson, but he too saw cause to celebrate the severance of familial ties with Mary. He had once been fond of his daughter-in-law but had since come to believe that "disaster is the only legitimate conclusion" of a marriage as impulsive as his son's.

And what a disaster it had been. For three and a half years, James had stayed mum while his family's private matters played out in the papers, and the reward for his discretion had been an assault on his wife's character from the judicial bench. The whole affair had plagued his political ambitions too. C. S. Palmer had put it bluntly in an interview a few months earlier. "You know that Blaine suffered more when he ran for the presidency over the slanderous accounts of his marriage than over anything else which was brought up in that memorable campaign," he said of the 1884 election. "The Blaines are anxious to make a family name for themselves, which will be carried down through the history of our country, and I believe that they would suffer more from the outcome of another campaign than they would care to endure." It sounded a lot like a threat coming from Mary's lawyer, but Palmer was also an astute political observer. "Every act young Blaine has figured in, and they are numerous enough, would be exaggerated and made a thousand fold worse," he said. It would be enough to "turn the feelings of every moral man in the country." Palmer's comments caused such a furor that he had been forced to deny ever making them, but the firestorm only served to prove his point, which numerous other Republicans echoed: Jamie's divorce had given the Democrats ample ammunition against a candidate Blaine.

Silence had not proven to be a winning strategy for the man known for his conversational excesses. It was time for a new approach. Members of the press gallery liked to joke that James G. Blaine Sr. could usually be relied upon to report "what the weather was yesterday in Dakota; what the Emperor's policy will be touching Mexico; or what day the 16th of December, proximo, will fall; who is the chairman of the school committee in Kennebunk; what is the best way of managing the national debt; together with all the other interests of today." Today, the topic of interest was his wife, and as when his marriage was assailed in the 1884 campaign, James was overwhelmed by the need to defend Harriet. "To remain silent would be to accept and perpetuate a great wrong to my wife," he decided, and "a greater wrong to my grandson than even a publication of the truth can inflict on him." And so, on Sunday, February 28, James released "a personal statement" to the press. The next morning it filled two full columns on the front pages of the country's newspapers.

James's diatribe read as if it were the closing statement he had paid his lawyers not to deliver in Deadwood. It was less a defense of Harriet than a direct attack on Mary. James had at hand letters she had written to Jamie through their courtship and marriage, and he marshaled them as evidence that Mary had manipulated his son. He quoted excerpts from the love notes she had penned in the first weeks of her romance.

"Write nothing until I see you. Let me know at once about the law," she had scrawled to Jamie while she waited to learn where they would be permitted to marry. "I can't wait to hear. It makes me ill."

A few days later: "Don't ask any questions that may lead people to suspect anything. Remember that we are in the mouths of every man, woman and child in Augusta. Every word you speak is repeated and misconstrued, every flush of your face is talked of."

Mary was impatient in love. "All else can wait," she wrote.

In James's telling, Mary had penned her own indictment, but he added some rhetorical flourishes. "It was thus," James wrote, "that a boy of seventeen years and ten months, in some respects inexperienced even for his age, was tempted from his school books and led to the altar by a woman of full twenty-one years"—Mary was only nineteen on her wedding day—"with entire secrecy contrived by herself and with all the instrumentalities of her device complete and exact."

The statement was not an argument against divorce, per se, but implicit in his condemnation of Mary was a threat against any woman who would avail herself of the courts to find freedom from her husband. He had harsh words, too, for those he felt had aided and abetted Mary. Her mother, Flora, who had accompanied her daughter on her ill-fated return to Augusta, was "insulting" and "violent" toward his wife, James wrote. And with his statement James released a letter he had sent to Father Thomas Ducey after discovering the man had blessed Mary and Jamie's union. "Of whatever evils resulting from this deplorable marriage my son may be the author or the victim," James had written to the priest in September 1886, "the guilt be on your head."

As for Jamie, James shrugged: "When his youth, his uncompleted education, his separation from the influences of home, the exchange of a life full of hopes and anticipations for premature cares and uncongenial companionship, are considered, I hold him more sinned against than sinning."

✧❈✧

MARY TREATED HER divorce decree with the care and reverence typically reserved for a holy book. It was nothing more than a few typewritten sheets, the text x-ed out where the clerk had struggled with spelling, but Mary tied the pages together with a blue ribbon and stored the precious document in a case she had chosen just for that purpose. Already, though, the potency of the decree's words was fading. With his statement, James had appealed the South Dakota court's decision to the court of public opinion, and Mary found herself again preparing for a showdown as eagerly anticipated as a prizefight: the diplomat versus the divorcee.

Mary had left Deadwood for Sioux Falls the morning after her trial concluded. Since then she had shuttered herself in her rooms at the Cataract, claiming illness when reporters sent up their cards seeking comment on James's accusations. C. S. Palmer advised her "to make no hasty answer." Her response needed to be as deliberate and damning as James's had been. But Palmer could not control the actions of those around Mary who felt their reputations impugned.

Mary's mother, Flora, leapt to her own defense, offering paragraph after paragraph of colorful quotes to any reporter who inquired at the New-York Hotel. She had her own version of the October 1888 trip to Augusta. In it, Flora "sat by quietly and patiently," allowing her daughter to "fight her own battle with the elder Mrs. Blaine," who "instantly flew into a fury. She almost foamed at the mouth." Flora lashed out at James too. "Mr. Blaine speaks of his dear little grandson," she spat. "Why do you know he never offered to pay so much as that poor child's milk bills? He's worse than his wife."

Finding himself again embroiled in the Blaines' affairs, Father Ducey charged that Jamie had lied to obtain his blessing, saying the groom claimed to be twenty-one, when he was really a few weeks shy of eighteen. The priest deflected any blame onto Archbishop Michael Corrigan, who had granted Mary and Jamie the necessary dispensation to marry. Through a spokesman, the archbishop fired back at the clergyman. "It was the duty of the priest who performed the ceremony to ascertain if there were any obstacles to the marriage." The spokesman was also careful to remind the Blaines that the archbishop had been willing to assist in the family's efforts to invalidate the marriage. In Deadwood, Judge Thomas, too, sought to make amends. "The statements of the distinguished Secretary of State not being before me on the trial of the case, I could not consider them in arriving at my judgement, however true or weighty they may be," he now said.

The clamor of voices opining on the circumstances of her marriage and divorce threatened to drown Mary out. She waited a day and then two before entering the fray with a carefully crafted open letter addressed to James that was published as widely as James's missive had been. "I acknowledge your well-rendered, richly deserved fame as a diplomat, and appreciate fully the weight which your utterances possess— as fully as do I appreciate my own weakness and my total inability to cope with you in a personal encounter—but I shall expect from you that considerate and honorable treatment which I am sure your keen sense of equity and fairness will dictate," she wrote. "The powerful man of a great nation will surely accord to a weak and defenseless woman her full meed of justice."

The public's eagerness to re-embrace the image of Mary as a helpless woman had served her well, blunting the criticism of her divorce. Now she played the role to her advantage again, issuing an ultimatum that was both polite and pointed. "Have the kindness to publish in connection with your statement the full text of the letters you have quoted from. Do not, like a shrewd and unprincipled person, select only such pages as may be needed to make your case," she wrote. "I will give you sufficient time in which to conform to my reasonable demand—say ten days. If, at the end of that time, you fail to respond, I shall deem it my duty to give in substance their content and corroborate my statement by publishing letters from your son."

It was a risky game of brinkmanship with the country's top negotiator, and Mary still had a lot to lose. She had no source of income except the alimony Jamie was unlikely to pay, and any prospect of a future on the stage—or of finding a respectable new husband—hinged on rehabilitating the reputation James was further destroying. But with her legal obligations to the Blaine family dissolved, Mary was no longer powerless, and she was not a good enough actress to fully obscure that truth. "I wish it distinctly understood by you," she wrote to James, "that I am not asking sympathy. I respectfully demand justice."

⚮

MARY AND JAMES seemed determined to stay in the headlines. This unceasing attention to the issue of divorce should have been helpful to South Dakota senator James Kyle and the constitutional amendment on the subject he had introduced two months earlier. But in the capital, the freshman senator, not yet adept at the politicking necessary to move his proposal through the Senate, instead watched his effort wither in committee.

In the House, however, a similar proposal, authored by Republican representative George Ray, became the subject of much debate. Ray had several advantages over Kyle in pushing his agenda: he had previously served in the House, he had a seat on the Committee of the Judiciary, which would consider the amendment, and he hailed from New York. That fact gave Ray credibility among divorce opponents who mistrusted the South Dakotan's intentions.

In committee, Ray argued that the nation's founders did not foresee the multitude of conflicting statutes that governed marriage and divorce at a state level. They had not envisioned a future in which a woman might be a wife in Maine but find herself a mistress in California, should that state choose not to recognize her marriage, Ray said. Nor did they imagine a country in which a man could be divorced and remarried in South Dakota, but guilty of bigamy in New York if his decree was not honored there. If they had, the founders would have given the federal government the power to preserve marriage and limit divorce, he said.

But only a minority of the committee was persuaded to join Ray in his conviction that "the most sacred relation of our citizenship can be best preserved and protected by lodging a power in the hands of the general government." The majority took a much dimmer view of the role of the federal government in legislating that which had long been the domain of the states. "If Congress were given power to legislate upon the subjects of marriage and divorce, it would soon extend that power by construction to all the domestic relations," read the statement the committee submitted in opposition to the proposed amendment. The committee members who signed on to the adverse report had found something they feared more than divorce: interracial marriage. If such an amendment passed, the report warned, "who can doubt that there soon would be a law enacted securing the right of marriage between any man and woman of lawful age, without regard to race, color, or previous condition, and thus to encourage the mixing of races."

With no hope of action by Congress, those who opposed divorce shifted their attention to other ways to align the diverse laws of the forty-four states. Some small measure of progress had been made on that front. In 1890, New York became the first state to formally embrace the effort when the legislature authorized the governor to appoint three people as "Commissioners for the Promotion of Uniformity of Legislation in the United States." The disparity in divorce laws had been the impetus for the action, but the commissioners would also address less controversial concerns such as standardizing legal forms. Now, seven other states had appointed commissioners with the same mandate, and the group—dubbed the Uniform Law Commission—was planning to meet in the summer to begin drafting model legislation.

In Deadwood, where the disgrace of the Blaine divorce still smarted, the *Daily Pioneer* bemoaned both the ease with which Congress dismissed the proposed constitutional amendment and the slow, incremental promise of the Uniform Law Commission. "Some good in this direction may be accomplished in time," the newspaper wrote, "but not the radical change needed."

MARY'S VERY PUBLIC spring deadline had passed without a word from either the Nevinses or the Blaines. The letters Mary had demanded James publish in full remained hidden, as did those she had threatened to release. They had seemingly fought to a draw. Each had inflicted serious wounds on the other's reputation and prospects; it remained to be seen if those blows would prove fatal. It had all sent Mary to her sick bed again. Doctors diagnosed heart failure, and then decided she was simply suffering another attack of nervous prostration. James was felled by the grippe and sweated through dangerously high fevers for several days.

Both had suffered self-inflicted harm too. James, friends reported, was "extremely sorry that he ever attempted to wash his family linen in public." He had released his tirade on Mary without consulting these friends, and they believed he had made "one of the greatest mistakes of his life." Political observers were surprised by the tactical error the consummate campaigner had committed. In attacking Father Ducey, James had attacked the country's Catholics, a valuable voting bloc already wary of the might-be candidate. Even those who understood James's need to defend his wife opined, "Nevertheless, it is true in such cases that 'silence is best and noblest to the end.'"

Mary's New York lawyers certainly agreed. Her retort to James had been published the day Mary left Sioux Falls for the East. On her arrival, her legal counsel advised that she not follow through on the ultimatum she had foolishly issued. "You have taken your case into court; you have produced your evidence; on it you have been sustained by the court, and you certainly ought to be satisfied with the opinion expressed by the judge," one chastised her. "For your own sake, it would be far better to let the matter drop where it is."

When Mary set sail on a months-long European tour with one of her cousins in the spring of 1892, it appeared the spectacular feud had finally fizzled out. There were other tales from Sioux Falls to sate the public's appetite. Edward Pollock had finally received his divorce from Ellen. Judge Aikens ruled that it was Ellen who had abandoned the marriage, but he also found that both children were Edward's heirs and awarded Ellen custody and $50 a month in child support. Ellen announced that she would continue to fight for her marriage in the South Dakota Supreme Court; Edward made it known he would soon wed Florence Cuthbertson, the two-time divorcee he had met in Sioux Falls. Charles Andrews had gotten his decree, too, and promptly returned home to Boston where he had begun courting the sister of his brother's wife. And, of course, Jamie never strayed far from gossip columns. It was said he was engaged to one of the Miss Pattens, a quintet of sisters so ubiquitous in Washington, DC, society that they were rarely distinguished from each other. Whichever one of them Jamie was wooing had two clear advantages over his first wife: she was extremely rich and an orphan.

James G. Blaine Sr. turned his attention to Minneapolis, where the Republican Party would gather in early June to select its nominee for the 1892 presidential election. On June 4, James resigned from President Benjamin Harrison's cabinet in preparation for his campaign. He would be a candidate for the nomination. He had carefully orchestrated the convention, filling the leadership positions and the hall seats with boisterous supporters. When his name was put forward, a roar of support went up. For sixty seconds, the proceedings came to a halt as feet stomped and hats and handkerchiefs waved to the chant of "Blaine! Blaine! Blaine!" Later in the proceedings, when another supporter rose to extoll James's candidacy, the room echoed with the Blaine name for a full thirty minutes.

But the pageantry wasn't enough. The party decisively renominated Harrison.

James would not be president—and he would not escape the shadow of his son's divorce. At the height of the convention, with thousands cheering his name, James was forced to deny a very detailed accusation about the letters Mary had sworn to publish. It was said that months of negotiations between Father Ducey and Secretary of War Stephen Elkins, a longtime Blaine confidant, had produced a settlement. Multiple sources insisted that $65,000—raised by Richard C. Kerens, a Republican politician from Missouri, and five other dedicated Blaine men—had purchased the potentially damaging letters. James challenged the story. On June 8, a Wednesday night, he released a letter addressed to the editors of the *New York World*: "Will you please state in your columns that it is utterly false that I, or any one for me, or in my name, ever paid or offered to pay, Mary Nevins Blaine, or any one for her, 1 cent, or any other sum for any alleged letters she holds." The truth of the situation never came out. Neither did the letters.

Chapter Ten

LET NOT MAN PUT ASUNDER

O N NEW YEAR'S DAY 1893, Bishop Hare stood in the chancel of
St. Augusta Cathedral and looked out at the congregation he had
built. He had been preaching in South Dakota for two decades and had
made his home in Sioux Falls for some ten years. He was a young man when
he had first come west, but now he was in his mid-fifties, and his brown curls
had faded to white. As his hairline receded, his sideburns grew into long,
bushy muttonchops, a style that seemed old-fashioned by the 1890s. His
otherwise clean-shaven face was remarkably unlined and his eyes bright,
though the tall, slender man appeared thinner than ever in his robes.

Hare's mission work over the previous two years had taken him far
from his brethren. At first, he was reluctant to accept the House of Bish-
ops' call to carry their message to Japan, but on further consideration, he
decided the community of the faithful across South Dakota was strong
enough to endure his absence. In an open letter to the clergy and laity of
the state in early 1891, Bishop Hare asked each of them to "stand fast in
his place, so that I may find you on my return in unbroken rank, the work
of the Lord prospering in your hands." Instead, he had returned to find

the divorce colony flourishing, and nothing Hare had said in opposition to this outrage seemed to have had the slightest effect.

On that fair first Sunday of the new year, worshippers streamed in through the massive red doors of the cathedral. They filed into the pale wood pews, any hushed conversations echoing off the nave's vaulted ceiling. Nearly every seat was filled, at least fourteen of them by members of the divorce colony. The names had changed. The pioneers of the colony—Edward Pollock, Florence Cuthbertson, Charles Andrews, Mary Nevins Blaine, and Maggie De Stuers among them—had all left Sioux Falls. But Maggie still haunted the bishop. Her aunt's name was carved in stone on the wall of the cathedral; the stained glass tribute to her daughter remained hidden in the church basement. And there seemed to be an endless supply of unhappy spouses streaming into Sioux Falls. The divorce mill continued to grind.

Bishop Hare had seen enough. He stepped to the pulpit to deliver his prepared sermon. He always drafted his remarks carefully but rarely consulted his notes as he spoke. On this day, the topic was one that had preoccupied him for months. "Any institution or practice carried on in a community, which is sapping the moral life of that community, should be exposed and suppressed," he began. "The time has come in the history of our fair state when the divorce industry carried on here should receive such treatment.

"Some say that it is a good thing for South Dakota to have divorces and divorce suits," he said, nodding to the city's lawyers and hoteliers. "I say that it is alarming, and our lax divorce laws have become a national scandal." Bishop Hare continued in his clear, ringing voice. "It is not so much the securing of a divorce which is so shocking, it is the consecutive polygamy which is practiced in marrying again so soon to a man or woman who has been courted while the suit for divorce to the former husband or wife was pending. It is the perjury committed by the applicants, who swear that they intend to make their home here, and no sooner get their decree than they leave town."

"Do we wish to be famous?" he exclaimed. "This makes us infamous. Do we want credit? This is discredit . . . A shadow is being cast on the city's prosperity."

Hare's words had the familiar cadence of his sermons. "What then are we to do with the divorce industry? Dread it! Dread it! It is the disruption and destruction of the family." But his solutions were those of a politician. Any hope that the constitutional amendments Senator James Kyle and others had proposed would rein in divorce across the country had faded, and the uniform divorce law movement was only in its infancy. South Dakota would have to do this for itself. The bishop now advocated for changes in the state's law: a longer residency requirement, revamped notification procedures, and a provision for a temporary separation. Hare had not expected to lead the charge in the state legislature. "Imagine me in the lobby, 'the third house,' as they call it!" he wrote to his sister Mary with amazement and no little discomfort.

The bishop was going to Pierre. "We must ventilate, agitate and educate," Hare exhorted his flock. "What better object can the church of Christ have in view, the beginning of this new year than to work for a new law?"

⸎

EMMA CRANMER WAS going to the state capital too. "Women should have a voice in the making of the law equal to that of men," she believed. The thirty-four-year-old from Aberdeen, a town some two hundred miles northwest of Sioux Falls, was an ardent suffragist, an outspoken temperance advocate, and the founder, with her husband Simeon, of a school for working women who had not received an education. A rising star in the national women's rights movement, Cranmer chafed at "all unjust laws of South Dakota pertaining to women," and she included the state's divorce statute among those she held up for derision. She believed it was far too easy to get a divorce in South Dakota.

Months before Bishop Hare declared his intention to lobby for a longer residency requirement, the Woman's Christian Temperance Union of South Dakota—Emma Cranmer, president—had resolved to strengthen the law. The women of the South Dakota WCTU pronounced the divorce industry "a disgrace to the state" and "a menace to public morals." Cranmer—whose allegiance to the standards of social morality espoused by the WCTU was so strong that she named her daughter in honor of the national organization's president—wanted to empower women; in the view of the many in the WCTU, divorce was a threat to that goal and to Christian ideals of family. But even within the evangelical group, there were those who saw the importance of allowing women to end their marriages. The WCTU's newspaper, *The Union Signal*, had argued in 1886 that limiting the grounds for divorce to adultery—as the Bible and New York State did—was insufficient. For as long as the saloons remained open in the country, the editorial board wrote, drunkenness must be recognized as permissible grounds for divorce as well.

The question of divorce had vexed the women's rights movement for decades. Though there was near-universal agreement among activists that the statutes governing the relations between husband and wife should not be shaped by men alone, there was little consensus on what those laws should say. Some within the movement feared the harm "easy" divorces could do to women left by their husbands. Others thought the current laws sufficient in most states and rued the attention the divorce colony had drawn to the question. And there were a few radicals who advocated for "free love"—a world in which the government had no authority over marriage or divorce. The divide led to deep concern that focusing on the controversial issue would splinter the movement and derail progress toward suffrage.

But for some, the ability to divorce was more important than the right to vote. Elizabeth Cady Stanton was among those who had been outspoken on the issue. She had first seen the difficulties faced by a woman trapped in wedlock when a childhood friend married an abusive man.

"I impulsively urged her to fly such a monster and villain, as she would before the hot breath of a ferocious beast of the wilderness," she later recalled. It was bold advice in the first half of the nineteenth century, but "she did fly, and it was well with her."

Cady Stanton could not now condemn those who skirted the laws of their home states in search of freedom. "The States which have liberal divorce laws are to women what Canada was to the slaves before Emancipation," she believed. She opposed constitutional amendments like James Kyle's and efforts like those underway in South Dakota to further restrict divorce access. Indeed, she wondered what right society had to exercise such control over the intimate relationship between two people. In an article published in 1890 she wrote, "The question of Divorce, like Marriage, should be settled as to its most sacred relations, by the parties themselves, neither the State nor the Church having any right to intermeddle therein."

Cranmer understood the power of a provocative argument delivered by an impassioned advocate. She was herself a celebrated lecturer who toured the state, delivering her messages of suffrage and temperance. But while she surely appreciated the attention that Bishop Hare's New Year's Day sermon had brought to the cause they shared, Cranmer knew it would take more than words to woo the South Dakota legislature. Instituting divorce restrictions—as well as gaining suffrage for women in municipal elections and repelling an attempt to repeal prohibition, issues she felt even more strongly about—would require adept political maneuvering. That was a task Cranmer was well suited for. She was widely admired and often underestimated. A dainty woman, with delicate waves framing her face, a blue ribbon tied at her neck, and a black bolero jacket decorated with beads that had been replaced countless times, she did not look like a lobbyist. But while the bishop and his fellow clergy served as the face of the effort, Cranmer spent her days in whispered conversations in the corridors of the South Dakota House and Senate, making deals and making threats.

Outside observers were certain that the divorce colony would soon be eradicated. "Sioux Falls is doomed as the Mecca of the grass widows"— abandoned women—"of the East," the *New York Sun* predicted. Within the state, however, many were ambivalent about the current law. When a senator from rural Spink County proposed a one-year residency requirement for all seeking divorces and a two-year residency requirement for any divorce seeker whose stated cause had arisen out of state, the *Argus-Leader* called the bill "radical." "Overdoing the matter," the paper opined, "is likely to prevent any action at all. General apathy prevails on this subject among the members."

The ensuing debate was anything but apathetic. Three dueling bills proposing a one-year residency requirement—two in the House and one in the Senate—were introduced, but the representatives ultimately rallied around a fourth bill with a six-month wait. The vote in the House was unanimous. In the Senate, however, some thought the bill was too lenient. To remedy this, they added an amendment to require one-year residency in any case where the defendant could not be personally served. Just before the final vote was called, a small number of senators, including Charles L. Brockway, a Sioux Falls attorney, made a final, long-shot argument for maintaining the three-month rule in most cases. According to the *Argus-Leader*, Brockway and his allies "spoke against the change on the ground that we should not try to fit our actions to suit the criticisms of outsiders." Brockway was adamant that the current divorce law "did not injure in any way the state or its people, but did bring relief to hundreds of the worthy and despondent."

Senator Brockway's pleas on behalf of unhappy spouses went unheeded. The South Dakota Senate passed the bill, and in March the governor signed into law a residency requirement of at least six months— still a shorter wait than in most other states. In the first weeks after the bill became law, there was a brief surge in the number of divorce seekers in the city. The change would not go into effect until July 1, 1893, leaving the smallest window of opportunity to gain residency and initiate divorce proceedings under the three-month rule. But the rush did not last. New arrivals dwindled as the deadline approached.

⌒∞⌒

THE CROWD BEGAN to gather outside the South Reformed Dutch Church in Manhattan mid-morning on Tuesday, May 30, 1893, but the doors to the Protestant parish remained stubbornly closed. Those gathered on the sidewalk were hoping to see a wedding—a second wedding.

For perhaps the first time in her life, Mary had done her best to avoid this attention. Just the night before she had denied that she and the surgeon William Bull would be married in the morning, as she had done many times since her divorce. But here she stood, in the vestry, wearing a pearl-gray silk dress with a fitted lace bodice and a diamond brooch. A short train fanned behind her, and she clutched a spray of pink roses as she awaited her groom, the man who had nursed her back to health and had done the same for five-year-old Jamie III when the boy had fallen dangerously ill with scarlet fever a few months earlier.

As the clock ticked closer to noon, the mass of spectators on the street swelled. The Decoration Day parade had just ended nearby, and the throng of fashionably dressed women in front of the church gate attracted more curious onlookers to their number. Some were likely drawn in by the very name Mary was relinquishing. James G. Blaine Sr. had died several months earlier, but for his political devotees, the family still possessed an irresistible aura of power. Others were probably there for the celebrity. Mary had never become a star, but perhaps the guest list might include some notable names from the stage whom Mary counted as friends. Most, though, seemed eager for the brush with notoriety.

A forbidding sexton kept the gawkers outside the church. Inside, young Jamie III, in a bright white sailor suit with blue trim, was seated in the front row of the church. The other pews were occupied with Mary's family and William's, as well as a small number of their close friends.

William, with just enough silver in his hair to look the part of the accomplished surgeon he was, stood at the altar, as Mary, accompanied by her father, processed up the aisle with little evidence of the limp that still sometimes slowed her. Theirs was a love match, friends attested, but there was no denying that the well-established forty-four-year-old was also a smart, stable choice for the once impetuous twenty-six-year-old mother.

As a divorcee, Mary could not be wed in the Catholic Church, but at least one part of the Reformed Church ceremony was familiar to her. After she swore her fidelity to William, Reverend Frederick Roderick Terry quoted from Matthew 19:6: "What therefore God has joined together, let not man put asunder." This was a celebration of a marriage, but the verse continued, "And I say to you, whoever shall put away his wife, except it be for fornication and shall marry another, committeth adultery; and whoso marrieth her which is put away doth commit adultery." They were the same words that Bishop Hare had quoted in his argument to the South Dakota legislature railing against divorce.

Mary had sympathy for those driven to Sioux Falls by the same pressing necessity she had felt, but it is unlikely that the politics of the state she once claimed she would make her home weighed on her on her wedding day. Mary wanted nothing more than to put that all behind her. She had her decree, she had her son, and she had William. It mattered little now that Mary had been one of the first Sioux Falls divorce colonists—or that, it seemed, she would be one of the last.

PART THREE

BLANCHE

Chapter Eleven

A MORAL SUPERSTITION

T HE WOMAN who strode across the Cataract House lobby on the
morning of Sunday, November 16, 1902, cut a memorable figure.
She wanted anonymity, but she had not dressed for it. She was wrapped
in luxe furs, and when she unbuttoned her black silk traveling gloves,
she revealed long, slender fingers heavy with diamonds. Her burnished
chestnut hair was piled atop her head in the intricate pompadour of a Gibson Girl, adding several inches to her five-foot, ten-inch stature. Stop-
ping in front of the clerk's desk, she fixed her eyes on the man, but she did
not reach for the pen to sign the hotel register. The clerk paused too. The
woman's stare could be disconcerting. Few held her gaze long enough to
realize why; one of her wide brown eyes was made of glass, the lifelong
consequence of a childhood injury.

"Just take my name, please," the woman instructed the clerk. Her
voice was low and musical and had, inexplicably, a hint of a British
accent. It was said she had a laugh that sounded like "bubbles of champagne breaking against the rim of a glass," but there had not been much
merriment in her life for several years. "Mrs. L. C. Johnson," she said,

without offering any more information for the register. "May I have your best room?" The clerk led Mrs. Johnson to a suite on the fourth floor of the hotel, with solid oak furniture, leather upholstery, and two large, lace-fringed windows looking out onto Phillips Avenue, and then he left the woman alone without further interrogation.

Could remaking one's identity really be so easy? The hotel's newest guest was not named Mrs. L. C. Johnson, but the clerk had not questioned her. And he had not glared at her with the dismay and suspicion she had grown accustomed to in New York. In Sioux Falls, it seemed, the twenty-eight-year-old woman could be anyone she wanted to be; it was, after all, the same desire that had drawn so many of the earliest white settlers west.

If Mrs. L. C. Johnson could reinvent herself, she would fashion herself as a "New Woman," a term popularized in 1894 to describe those who threw off Victorian strictures. There were many forms of rebellion. Mrs. L. C. Johnson would give little thought to the issue of suffrage or the politics of feminism. She would be a bohemian, an independent spirit, and a sexual being. She would not have children; she would instead pursue a career on the stage and a life of travel.

If she had the same power to mold the perfect husband, "Mr. L. C. Johnson" would be a passionate, forceful man; the woman admired what she called the "masculine element." He would be confident in his own endeavors and unintimidated by his wife's interests. He would be playful, genial, and quick with a joke, but he would also be cultured, at home in a fashionable restaurant or an exclusive salon.

Or maybe, sequestered in her rooms at the Cataract after several days of train travel, the woman imagined Mr. L. C. Johnson to be no one at all. She had never wanted to marry.

Yet she had wed. Back in New York, Mrs. L. C. Johnson was known as Blanche Molineux. It was a name she had come to despise, because it yoked her to her husband of four years. He was Roland B. Molineux, but Blanche referred to him only as "that man." When she married him, with some reluctance and much pragmatism, on a snowy day just after

Thanksgiving 1898, that man seemed to possess at least some of the qualities that Blanche desired. But just a few days after their honeymoon in the bridal suite at the Waldorf-Astoria—a month Blanche had spent largely alone and with little physical affection from her groom—the man she had married began to reveal his true self.

Blanche had come to Sioux Falls for the same escape Maggie Zborowski, Mary Bull, and scores of others had pursued a decade earlier, but her reason for seeking a divorce was more dramatic than any the city had heard before: Blanche believed her husband was a murderer.

THE CITY BLANCHE had decided to make her home—at least temporarily—was changed from the one Maggie and Mary had known a decade earlier. As Bishop Hare had hoped, the unhappy spouses who might have sought relief in South Dakota were discouraged by the longer six-month residency requirement enacted in 1893. The truly desperate continued onward to North Dakota. Fargo, 240 miles north, became the destination of choice for those few. It did not have much to recommend it besides the three-month wait. In 1893, a great fire had ripped through the town, leveling thirty-one blocks of wooden homes and businesses. To the south of the destruction, though, the castle-like courthouse remained standing. The people of Fargo were as conflicted about the divorce seekers as Sioux Falls' residents had been in the earliest days of the colony, but the town was struggling to rebuild. Free-spending visitors from the East could bring a needed boost to its economy.

For the lawyers, hoteliers, restaurant owners, and shopkeepers of Sioux Falls, the loss of the divorce industry could not have come at a worse time. Elsewhere in the country, there had been signs of looming economic hardship, and South Dakota was also suffering the effects of a years-long drought. Sioux Falls had still felt flush in the early 1890s, buoyed by legal fees and dinner tabs, but by May 1893, as the first wave of colonists departed, the coming calamity could no longer be ignored.

Every day brought news of another bank closure as the country tumbled into a depression that would last nearly five years. The Dakota boom was over. Immigration to the state slowed and then nearly stopped. Meanwhile, export of Sioux Falls' second most famous product—quartzite stone—plummeted too.

For many who had ventured west in the 1880s to make their name in the young city—"a second Chicago," boosters said—it seemed time to move on. Among the departures were many divorce lawyers: Cap Stoddard left Sioux Falls for Buffalo to open a new firm with his law partner, William H. Wilson. C. S. Palmer departed for New York City when his wife fell ill with cancer; Mary's new husband, William Bull, tended to the ailing woman. And J. L. Glover also relocated to Manhattan, not long after his fellow lawyers tried to disbar him for fraud in a divorce case.

In 1902 the courthouse still stood tall over Sioux Falls. At a glance, the only change was the clock that had been installed in its tower; a bell tolled each passing hour in the city. But Albion Thorne could no longer be found in the clerk of courts office. He had been driven from the post by accusations of embezzlement that had turned out to be minor accounting errors. And Judge Aikens no longer presided over the massive courtroom. After the tumultuous final years of his term, Aikens had decided not to run for reelection in 1893. He issued his last divorce decree in December of that year and set up his law office in Sioux Falls. Judge Joseph W. Jones, ten years older than Aikens, with a full head of graying hair, replaced him on the bench and remained there almost a decade later.

One could no longer find Harry and Henry Corson holding court at the Cataract House either. Starting in 1894, the pair leased out the hotel they had owned and operated for nearly a quarter century. Under new proprietors, the Cataract managed to survive the loss of the divorce colony and the downturn that followed, and it remained central to life in Sioux Falls. Senator Richard Pettigrew used it as his de facto headquarters, as did the amateur theater company and visiting fortune tellers. It was heartbreak for the city when, on the evening of Saturday, June 30, 1900, smoke was seen billowing from the Cataract's windows. The hotel had been dressed up for the Fourth of July, with tissue paper streamers and fireworks in the front windows. When a clerk lit a gas lamp, the decorations exploded. Within hours, the building, and much of the block, had burned to the ground. Only a few sections of exterior wall, a chimney, and a vault were spared. Tens of thousands of dollars' worth of property was destroyed, but fortunately no one had died. For months, the Corson brothers debated rebuilding, and eventually a new, bigger, better Cataract rose—five stories, 1.5 million bricks, two and a half miles of carpet, and a legal saloon. By a vote of the populace, South Dakota had repealed prohibition in 1896. By the time Blanche arrived, the city had more than twenty licensed liquor dealers.

A divorcee who had bided her time in Sioux Falls in 1892 would recognize little in the city a decade later—except for the man who had banished the colony. Bishop Hare remained on the pulpit at St. Augusta. He had thought of leaving his cathedral church and his beloved All Saints School. "If the legislature had not wiped out the divorce scandal, I should have accepted a call elsewhere," he said in 1893, "but now that we have eradicated this evil, I feel that I can hardly leave this state."

While many of the clergymen he had rallied in opposition to divorce had abandoned Sioux Falls for more prosperous parishes, the bishop considered the city his home. "I now expect that I will pass the remainder of my life in South Dakota, following up the work now underway." His doctor—the same Silas Weir Mitchell who had ordered Maggie to rest, lest she be overtaken by neurasthenia—had tried to persuade the bishop to leave Sioux Falls in 1895 when he fell ill. The shortness of breath and fatigue he felt were signs that the weak heart Mitchell had diagnosed in 1875 was worsening. "It's probably not too late," the Philadelphia doctor wrote. "It is none too soon." But as he had two decades earlier, the bishop consented to only a brief respite in the East, away from the South Dakota climate and his sermons and speeches. Even as the symptoms grew more pronounced, Hare traveled for weeks at a time through the region by train car and wagon, welcoming the converted and proselytizing to the unconvinced. When he was in Sioux Falls, the bishop ministered to his students at All Saints. Divorce no longer occupied his mind, but he had not forgotten about the unfortunate events of the early 1890s.

A constant reminder awaited the bishop in the chancel at St. Augusta. A new stained glass window had been installed above the altar after the death of Reverend Charles Smith Cook in 1892. Cook had been a protégé of the bishop's, a man of Sioux heritage who had been ordained by the Episcopal Church and preached on South Dakota's reservations. "The eternal God is thy refuge and underneath are the everlasting arms," read the inscription below the dedication. Above was a depiction of the crucifixion with three women mourning at Christ's feet. It was one of the three windows Maggie had donated to the church; the memorial pane honoring her family had been replaced.

Bishop Hare had not forgotten about the divorce colony. But he had not expected it to return.

⚮

THE STAFF AT the Cataract House expressed no surprise at Blanche's arrival—not at her mystery or her extravagance or her obvious alias—because they were accustomed to it. Billy Cornell, the cheerful day clerk, had been working the hotel desk for almost two decades. He'd seen it all. The stunning sums lost and won in games of chance, the elaborate garb donned for a stroll on Phillips Avenue, and the over-the-top divorce dinners staged to celebrate a decree. One had been catered by the New York steakhouse Delmonico's; the divorcee dressed in her wedding gown. There was even the memorable case of mistaken identity that had, late one night in 1892, led a colonist with a revolver at her bedside to fire several shots at a fellow hotel guest. (She missed.)

If he was in a chatting mood, Cornell could also tell tales of the handful of divorce seekers who had traveled to Sioux Falls after the residency requirement was changed. They came because a vote of the legislature was not enough to erase the indelible mark divorce had made on the city's reputation. They came because, for some, the amenities of Sioux Falls outweighed the lure of a shorter stay in Fargo. And they came because they still needed their divorces. For those in the city who had thrived on the divorce industry, those few arrivals were not enough. For those who had sought to abolish the colony, even one was too many. The fight over South Dakota's law did not end in 1893.

When the state legislature had convened for its biennial session in early 1895, divorce supporters were on the offensive. Several bills were introduced to reduce the amount of time it would take to get a divorce in the state. As one lawyer explained in support of such measures, "The change of the law two years ago as the result of Bishop Hare's personal efforts has been of no benefit to the morals of the state and has sent elsewhere hundreds of thousands of dollars which might as well have come to South Dakota." After weeks of debate, it looked like the state would relax its laws. Under a bill passed by the Senate, residency would no longer dictate when one could file for a divorce. Instead, applicants could file as soon as they arrived in the state; they would only need to live in South Dakota for six months before a divorce could be granted. A year's wait would be required if the defendant was not personally served, but for most the divorce mill would grind as quickly and effectively as it had back in 1891.

Bishop Hare, who had been traveling in the East, was unprepared for this attack on the divorce laws. Returning to the city, he quickly mustered a coalition in opposition to this "unsavory subject." On a Sunday morning in February, he again held forth on the issue from the pulpit at St. Augusta. With his characteristic drama, he likened a divorce to a revolver, too dangerous to hand to someone in a passion. "We consider the offering a non-resident the right the moment he steps into South

Dakota to take advantage of our divorce law the putting into his hand a deadly weapon," Hare thundered.

But that same day, Joseph Andrew, the new reverend at the All Souls Unitarian Church, gave voice to a group heard little during the debates of 1893: those who truly supported divorce, not because it was good business but because it was good social policy.

Reverend Andrew had given the sermon first in front of his sixty-five-person congregation; he reprised the speech in the city's largest venue, the eight-hundred-seat opera house. He told the crowd he considered divorce "a tragedy in human existence" but believed that tragedy should not be prolonged. "The reason why people came to South Dakota to get divorces is not because our laws are bad but because their own states have not become civilized enough to enact proper divorce laws," he said. The thirty-five-year-old Englishman, who had clashed with some among the city's clergy since his arrival two years earlier, did not mince words, writing in the *Argus-Leader* the next day, "For any man in this age and country to claim that divorce is morally wrong for any but one reason—that neither cruelty, desertion, crime, indignity, or any other grievous cause is sufficient to justify it—has abandoned his conscience to the tyranny of a moral superstition." Two days later, he delivered the same message in the state capital.

That year, the legislature fought to a draw. In 1897, when those who opposed divorce were on the offensive, the debate again ended in a stalemate. During the 1899 legislative session, Bishop Hare floated a proposal to reduce the causes of divorce in South Dakota to just two: "biblical causes"—that is, adultery—and "great personal abuse." For a third time, the status quo prevailed in the South Dakota legislature—but things were about to change anyway. Ever since it first earned attention for granting the country's easiest divorces, North Dakota had been trying to extend its own residency requirement. Finally, in the winter of 1899, it succeeded. As of July 1, North Dakota would require one year of residency before a divorce claim could be filed.

The colony was headed back to Sioux Falls.

"Many of the lawyers of Sioux Falls now have clients on hand and they are receiving daily inquiries," one newspaper reported in May of that year. But the new arrivals had learned from the trials of those who had preceded them to Sioux Falls. Their lawyers filed their cases in smaller South Dakota towns and then quickly removed the paperwork from the court record to thwart nosy reporters. Oftentimes, news of the proceedings did not break until the decree was issued and the applicant, newly single, was packing for the trip home. It was willful ignorance on the part of the Sioux Falls establishment to pretend that these well-dressed visitors from the East were so entranced by the city that they stayed for months at a time without any legal inducement, but it was a flattering fiction that South Dakota, emerging from its economic doldrums, was eager to believe. For a time, there seemed to be an unspoken agreement: if the divorce seekers did not flaunt their immorality and draw the country's attention back to Sioux Falls' unorthodox industry, the city would tolerate the colony.

Chapter Twelve

FREE AS AIR

BLANCHE PLAYED the role of Mrs. L. C. Johnson for just twenty-four hours. She remained in her rooms throughout the day Sunday, taking her meals in private, and arose late on Monday morning, about the time the Western Union messenger brought a telegram to the Cataract House. The yellow envelope was addressed to Mrs. Molineux. This name should have sounded familiar to the clerk, but it was not listed in the ledger, so he set aside the telegram with the other messages already collecting in the letter holder on his desk. An hour later, Blanche appeared in the Cataract's two-story central rotunda dressed for an excursion in a fashionable brown afternoon frock and a black hat. Before she departed, she stopped in the hotel office and asked to see the envelopes. She riffled through the stack and withdrew the yellow one from the pile. Now the clerk knew the truth. Mrs. Johnson was in fact Mrs. Molineux, a woman whose love affairs—and their fatal consequence—had dominated headlines for nearly four years.

Blanche was oblivious to her slip. She asked the clerk to recommend a music store nearby and headed out to rent a piano for her room. But as she undertook her errand, the telegraph lines to New York began to buzz with the news of her arrival in Sioux Falls, and typewriters in both cities clacked with a rehashing of her romances.

Blanche Chesebrough first met her husband in Maine in August 1897. It had been a stunning summer day in Portland harbor. "Bluest of skies were above," Blanche remembered, "bluest of waters below." Blanche and her eldest sister, Izcennia Stearns—whom Blanche called Isia—were aboard a friend's yacht. Blanche, who was making $10 a week singing at Hill Church in Brooklyn, was wowed by the wealth Isia had married into. She thought the boats bobbing in the Atlantic to be "luxurious toys," and she and Isia had been invited to lunch on the most extravagant of these playthings, the *Viator*, skippered by Albert J. Morgan, heir to the Sapolio soap fortune.

Blanche was so overwhelmed by the well-appointed ship and the spread of Russian caviar and iced Moët & Chandon delivered by the steward that she took little notice of her new companions at first. Only later that afternoon, giddy from sunshine and champagne, did she turn her attention to one of Al's guests, a man reclining in a deck chair, his feet balanced on the boat rail. He was reading and smoking a cigarette. Seeing Blanche, he rose to greet her. The dark-haired man was not as tall as she was, Blanche noticed, but he had the body of a gymnast, "slender, muscular and beautifully proportioned." Blanche admired his nonchalance, poise, and fine manners, which she recognized immediately as evidence of good "breeding." When he offered her a "quiet, infectious smile," she later said, "something flashed between us."

Al had called the man Mollie. He was Roland B. Molineux, the middle son of Harriet and Edward Leslie Molineux. His father—known to most as "the General"—had been the Civil War commander of the 159th Regiment of the New York National Guard. During the fighting, he proved himself a tireless and committed leader. Back in Brooklyn after the war, the left side of his face permanently scarred by a rifle ball, the General brought the same energy to business, politics, and civil society, earning the family a place among the city's commercial aristocracy. In many ways, Roland's upbringing in the Molineux house had been as proper as Blanche imagined. The general had endeavored to raise devout Episcopalians steeped in the American ideals of patriotism and capitalism. Roland, however, had not always walked this narrow, respectable path. He had a loftier image of himself as an upper-crust gentleman, and he had far lower appetites. But Roland had flourished in the industry that had made his family rich, first as a chemist in his father's paint company and then as the superintendent of another firm, a position that brought him the money and prestige necessary to take a room at the popular Knickerbocker Athletic Club on Central Park.

Blanche had lived a very different sort of life. Her father, James, had been a largely luckless inventor whose pursuits had taken her mother, Harriet, and the six Chesebrough children from the Northeast to the Midwest to the South and back again. Sometimes there was money; sometimes there was not. The family had grown smaller as they traveled, the older siblings marrying and scattering across the country. Blanche, the fifth of the six children, was almost two decades younger than Isia, the oldest of them. When Blanche was a teenager, Isia had been more like a mother to her than a sister, bringing Blanche into the Boston home she shared with her husband, Waldo Stearns, and paying for her musical education.

After a year, though, Blanche moved in with her parents again, first in Boston, then in New York, where she remained when her parents relocated to Rhode Island. "That great center of metropolitan life" awed Blanche. She was astonished by what she described as "the splendid shops, the hotels, the restaurants and theaters," and she imagined life in the "magnificent abodes" of Fifth Avenue "that gave the impression of royal palaces—the owners royal not because of birth but because of wealth!" This was Roland Molineux's New York; it did not belong to Blanche, who scraped by in the city.

The circumstances in which Blanche met Roland seemed like a dream to her, and the months afterward were some of the happiest she could remember. She did not hesitate to show her interest in the man, contacting Roland the day after she returned to New York in early September. Roland responded with near-daily gifts. Fruits, flowers, and sweets filled Blanche's rooms—first at Mystic Flats, just off Broadway, and then at a smaller boarding house on the Upper West Side, a move necessitated by Blanche's meager income. Roland's invitations were almost as frequent. Most evenings found the pair at the Casino Theater or the Metropolitan Opera, to which Roland had season tickets. After the shows, they would dine at the Waldorf or Delmonico's. For Blanche, it was an entrée into the magical world she had only seen from afar. It was the life Blanche wanted to live, and she did her best to fit in. She may not have been able to afford the newest frocks, but she had a talent for dressing up her old gowns with a colorful sash or a well-placed piece of jewelry.

Roland's gifts helped. Through the fall, they grew more and more expensive: an opal broach, a butterfly pin encrusted with one hundred diamonds, and, most precious of all, a custom-designed ring from Tiffany & Co., that palace of jewels on Union Square that was shorthand for wealth in Manhattan. The ring sparkled with diamonds that spelled out the word *mizpah*, Hebrew for "watchtower," and the gleaming metal was engraved with a reference to a biblical verse from Genesis: "The Lord watch between me and thee when we are absent from one another." In earlier decades, such a gift was a declaration of the deep bond between two people, and Roland surely meant it that way, but Blanche accepted the ring as blithely as she had received the other baubles he had presented to her. She enjoyed his company, but he was not the perfect man for her. She was most disappointed by his reserve. Though they often spent the night together in her small room, Roland had not tried to ravish her.

Blanche had been raised with the mores of an earlier generation. Her mother had frequently warned her daughters to be "ever on their guard" against men, and she never so much as mentioned the word "sex" in their presence. But that omission only made Blanche more fascinated by the intimacies between a man and a woman. Roland possessed, she feared, none of the "brute masculine force" she craved. He seemed uninterested, even incapable, of consummating their relationship. "I wanted passion and love in my life," she later said.

She did not, however, want a husband. At age twenty-three, she felt on the verge of the life she had always desired. Though Roland had introduced her to this new existence, she did not believe she owed him a lifetime commitment in return. When the topic of marriage came up, she joked it away. She did not love Roland, and to be a wife, she had come to believe, was "a narrowing of horizons" and "a curtailment of freedom." Blanche rejoiced in her singlehood. Her pleasure was so evident that when she visited friends in a Rhode Island town where her family once lived, one newspaper reported that "half the young married women were beginning to wish they had waited awhile before they settled down." Blanche thought herself "free as air" and believed she "owed no allegiance to anyone."

And so on Thanksgiving Day 1897, when Roland knelt before Blanche and asked for her hand in marriage, Blanche said no.

⟨◇⟩

HOW HOPELESSLY NAIVE that young Blanche Chesebrough must have seemed to the woman who now used the alias Mrs. Johnson. At the moment Blanche turned down Roland's proposal, she had not fretted for her future. She saw only opportunity in her independence. She did not intend her refusal to be the end of her flirtation with Roland. There was no need to give up the frequent theater outings or the fancy meals or the fashionable company he kept. Blanche continued to wear his *mizpah* ring. But after her declaration, she also felt free to pursue another man: Henry Barnet. Barney, as Blanche knew him, was a friend of Roland's from the Knickerbocker. Roland had himself introduced the pair at the opera. From the start, Barney had been far more interested in his new acquaintance than in the arts. He was an incorrigible charmer, and Blanche delighted in the attention.

That was then. Now Blanche strolled through Sioux Falls alone, hoping not to attract any notice at all. She had but a few hours before the next edition of the *Argus-Leader* came off the presses. Already the typesetters were placing the headline that would unmask Blanche to all of Sioux Falls. The South Dakota newspaper had followed Blanche's tribulations as closely as any in the country. Blanche was new to Sioux Falls, but the city already knew her secrets.

It had been a blustery evening in late January 1898 when Blanche began her affair with Barney. She had arrived at a late-night party near Washington Square with Roland, but she had not donned her black tulle dress and satin slippers studded with sparkling jewels for him. The diamond-encrusted butterfly pin on her décolletage was meant to attract another man's gaze. Barney arrived at the soiree with someone else too, but he quickly found Blanche in the crowded room and suggested they slip away to an apartment uptown. Its owner was in Europe, and Barney had the key. He had set the scene for a seduction—a roaring fire, a carefully placed chaise piled with damask pillows, and two crystal glasses filled with scotch and soda. He raised his to Blanche and kissed her roughly, pulling her down onto the chaise. This was exactly what Blanche imagined. "It was an ecstasy!" she still remembered. The couple returned to the party hours later, clothing askew, lips bruised. Barney's hand bore a long scratch from the butterfly on Blanche's breast. Roland didn't seem to notice anything amiss.

Within a few weeks, however, Roland discovered the illicit relationship. He confronted Barney first, and when Blanche heard about the men's encounter, she demanded to see Roland. She did not wish to apologize. She was angry about the way he had handled the matter. Facing him in her parlor, she threw the *mizpah* ring across the room. Roland scrambled to retrieve it and stormed out. "Tell Barnet the coast is clear," he shouted. "He wins."

For a few months, Blanche felt like the victor. Henry Barnet was so different from Roland. They both belonged to the Knickerbocker, but while Roland was there for the prestige and the gymnasium, Barney was there for the camaraderie and the dining room. Barney's appearance reflected his lifestyle. At thirty-two, he was round and fleshy, but his blue eyes were bright with laughter, and his broad face always creased with a smile. Whereas Roland had been reserved and aloof, Barney's jovial manner made him a favorite with women, including Blanche's landlady and the housekeeper.

As the summer approached, though, reality intruded. The freedom Blanche relished was not free. Barney's job at the Jersey City Packing Company did not earn him the salary Roland's job brought, and Barney did not have the Molineux family accounts at his disposal. Still, he was so stingy, Blanche wondered if he was seeing another woman. She wrote to friends with increasing desperation, hoping someone would invite her to the seashore for the season. She needed to save on rent and get some distance from the suitor she had begun to doubt. Blanche escaped to Isia's summer home on the Rhode Island coast in June, but her sister's marriage was falling apart, and Isia closed the house and returned to Boston that same month. Determined not to return to New York at the height of the summer—which would have revealed her precarious financial situation—Blanche instead imposed on the kindness of one friend and then the next.

When it was the proper time to go back to New York in September 1898, Blanche found a letter from Roland waiting for her; there was no message from Barney. Blanche had seen Roland only once since their argument, a seemingly chance encounter in front of her boarding house as she and Barney had departed for an evening on the town. Roland's note, on eggshell blue paper, was friendly but not intimate. He spoke of his time abroad and hoped that Blanche's getaway was as pleasant. Then he invited her to lunch at the Waldorf-Astoria on any Thursday that suited. She agreed to meet him on the very next Thursday.

At a prime table with a view of Fifth Avenue, Blanche and Roland dined on filet of sole and quaffed white wine. It seemed, for better or worse, as though no time had passed. Blanche had not changed her mind about Roland. She still did not love him. And she had not changed her opinion of the dark side of marriage. But her relative poverty had brought to the surface a practical streak. To finance her musical education, luncheons at the Waldorf-Astoria, and European adventures like the one Roland had recently returned from, she would need to become someone's wife. When Roland reached across the table and slipped the glittering *mizpah* ring back on her finger, Blanche made her choice. She engaged herself to Roland and the life he promised her.

But a terrible plan had already been set in motion. In the late summer, two unsolicited packages had arrived in the mail for Barney. One contained a sample tin marked with the logo of Kutnow's Improved Effervescent Powder. The gourmand was familiar with the remedy, said to be made with salt from the Carlsbad mineral springs; he often used it to treat hangovers. The other, to Barney's amusement, was labeled Calthos. The powder-filled pills were for anyone suffering from "lost manhood or weakness of any nature in the sexual organs." Barney tossed both aside until the morning of Friday, October 28. He had overindulged the night before, and when he couldn't stomach breakfast, he had taken a dose of Kutnow's powder. Within moments, he was racing for the bathroom.

The vomiting and diarrhea lasted a day, then came the inflamed throat and tongue and the loss of appetite. A doctor diagnosed Barney with a mild case of diphtheria, a bacterial infection for which an antitoxin had recently been discovered. But Barney's condition continued to deteriorate. When Blanche heard about his illness, she sent a bouquet of chrysanthemums and a desperate note to her former suitor's bedside. She had not seen him in weeks, not since he had learned of her engagement and refused Blanche's offer of friendship. "I want so much to see you," she wrote in the note. "Do not be cross anymore and accept, I pray you, my very best wishes." She signed it, "Yours, Blanche." Three days later, Barney was dead.

Blanche married Roland in a small ceremony at the Church of the Heavenly Rest on Fifth Avenue and Forty-Fifth Street in Manhattan later that same month. As she stood at the altar beneath a dramatic painting of Christ the Consoler and committed herself to a lifetime with Roland, Blanche believed her former lover's death to be an inexplicable tragedy. And when a sixty-two-year-old widow named Kate Adams died on December 28 after taking a dose of Emerson's Bromo-Seltzer, Blanche didn't pay any mind to the news stories about the stranger. She and her new husband had just returned home from their honeymoon at the Waldorf-Astoria. She was already bored of marriage—"somehow, all glamour seemed gone," she thought—but she had done her best to enjoy her first holidays with the Molineuxes.

It wasn't until the knock on the front door at 6 a.m. on the morning of January 2, 1899, that Blanche learned that Kate Adams and her Barney had both likely been murdered.

Roland's father had rushed to their house with a copy of that morning's *New York Journal*. Her husband stood in their bedroom, clutching the tabloid. By the light of the bedside lamp, Blanche, still in her nightclothes, saw the headline: "Police Want Roland Burnham Molineaux [*sic*] in the Poisoning Case."

⚭

KITTREDGE, WINANS & SCOTT was tucked between a bookstore and a carpenter's office on the west side of Phillips Avenue in a building full of attorneys. The first name on the sign set the law firm apart from the others. Alfred B. Kittredge was the state's junior senator, a Republican selected to fill James Kyle's spot after his death in 1901. Kit, as he was known, agreed with his predecessor on many issues but not on divorce. Kyle had introduced a constitutional amendment designed to end the colony; Kit, forty-one, had spent the last decade representing Sioux Falls' colonists. But when Blanche arrived that Monday afternoon after acquiring a piano, it was the second named partner, Edwin R. Winans, twenty-seven years old and fresh out of school, who ushered the new client in.

Blanche was cagey in her first meeting with the attorney. She refused to reveal the grounds on which she hoped to sue for divorce. To the outside observer, she seemed to have a strong case for the separation she desired, but if Winans knew even the barest outlines of Blanche's saga, he would have realized that the case was more complicated than it appeared.

Just three months after Blanche's wedding, Roland had been arrested for the death of Kate Adams and marched across the "bridge of sighs," a prisoner catwalk suspended above Franklin Street in Manhattan, to a small, squalid cell on the second floor of the Tombs—Murderer's Row.

A weeks-long coroner's inquest had preceded Roland's detention. The jury in the inquest had been charged with determining not guilt or innocence but the existence of a crime. The case was a complex one, in large part because Kate's murder seemed to be a mistake. The prosecutor argued that her cousin, Harry Cornish, who received mercuric cyanide disguised in an Emerson's Bromo-Seltzer bottle in the mail, had been the poison's intended target. Harry was the athletic director at the Knicker-bocker, and Roland had clashed with the man over petty management issues. Roland had tried to get Harry fired, but in the end, it was Roland who had been forced out of the club. "You win," Roland had said at their final parting in December 1897.

Barney's death had not been the subject of the inquest, but it had been eerily similar, down to Roland's pique that Barney had "won" something that Roland had wanted. What doctors thought to be diphtheria turned out to be symptoms of mercuric cyanide poisoning, the deadly dose hidden in a Kutnow's tin. Prosecutors pursued charges only in Kate's case because the evidence of that crime was far stronger. They presented the jury with letters on the eggshell blue stationery Roland used, written in his stilted, upright penmanship. Each requested that a sample of medicine be sent to a postbox, and each was forged with the signature "H. Cornish." But a love triangle was a more believable motive than a tiff over gymnasium equipment, and so Blanche was forced to take the stand and defend the affectionate note she had sent to Barney. She felt that she was on trial.

While Roland spent months in the Tombs, Blanche was confined to the Molineux family home in Brooklyn, unable to venture out without attracting a crowd. Challenges by the Molineux family lawyers led to three separate grand jury hearings, and Roland's case didn't come to trial until November 1899. The prosecution made its opening statements on Blanche's first wedding anniversary. She visited Roland regularly in the Tombs, and when she appeared in court, she kissed her husband with a loving smile, but Blanche had already decided that she could not remain Roland's wife.

Just what kind of man Blanche had married became clear over the course of the murder investigation, which revealed debauchery that dated back decades. In 1883, at the age of fifteen, Roland had been named in a divorce suit as the adulterous companion of a married neighbor; Roland's father sent the boy away from New York until the incident was forgotten. Six years later, twenty-one-year-old Roland started a sexual relationship with Mamie Melando, a thirteen-year-old girl employed at his father's company. The relationship lasted years, and Mamie moved with Roland to his new company, where they frequently met in the apartment he kept above the factory. Roland promised he would marry Mamie, but after meeting Blanche, he instead ended the relationship and fired her. In recompense, he had bought her a new dress. Cornish and other members of the Knickerbocker Athletic Club were quick to reveal Roland's collection of "immoral books" and pornographic images. He was a habitué of the dives of Chinatown, and Roland himself had admitted on the stand that he smoked opium.

Was he also a murderer? Like the inquest, the almost three-month-long trial focused more on Henry Barnet than Kate Adams, though Roland stood accused only of her murder. The prosecution's case was damning, and the defense rested without presenting any evidence. In his closing remarks, Assistant District Attorney James Osborne addressed the jury. "Gentlemen, it is not often that a motive assumes a real, concrete personality. This one is endowed with flesh and blood. It has the form of a human being. And there"—Osborne swung around and pointed at Blanche—"there the motive sits." After a day of deliberation, the jury found Roland guilty of murder in the first degree. He was sentenced to death and scheduled to be executed six weeks hence, in March 1900. Blanche saw her escape: she would soon be a widow.

But Roland was not executed. The family appealed the verdict. With Blanche, they moved upstate to be closer to Sing Sing, where Roland sat on death row. Blanche still visited her husband, at the urging of her father-in-law. She wanted to leave, but she had given the General her word. She would not abandon the family while Roland's life hung in the balance. In October 1901, the court of appeals overturned Roland's conviction and ordered a new trial, in large part because of the emphasis placed on Barney's murder and the disparagement of Blanche's character in the first case.

Cracks began to show in the family's united front. Roland was transferred back to the Tombs to await another day in court, and his family moved back to Brooklyn. By then, though, Blanche had stopped visiting her husband. She stopped writing. She moved out of the family home and into the Murray Hill Hotel in Manhattan. She did not attend the new trial, which commenced on October 13, 1902. It lasted a little less than a month, and the jury deliberated for just thirteen minutes: not guilty. Roland was free; Blanche was trapped. She left for Sioux Falls the next day.

She recounted little of this to Winans during their first meeting, which lasted for less than a half hour. The firm's third attorney, Wallace D. Scott, spotted Blanche as she left his partner's office. Scott's first thought was not about the woman's purpose in engaging Kittredge, Winans & Scott. Nor was it about the fee such a well-dressed client might be able to afford. "By George there's a handsome woman," he marveled as Blanche departed. He quizzed Winans: Who was that? When he heard her name, though, Scott's interested shifted. Blanche Molineux was striking, yes, but it was her legal predicament that intrigued him now.

Scott had followed Roland Molineux's court proceedings in the press. He knew that for all the charges leveled against Roland, few were actionable causes for divorce, even in South Dakota. Roland's lechery predated his marriage to Blanche. With no evidence that the sexual affairs continued after their wedding, Blanche would be unlikely to triumph in a suit that claimed her husband had committed adultery. South Dakota did allow for divorce when one spouse was convicted of a felony, as Roland had been, but with his subsequent acquittal, that path to freedom too seemed closed to Blanche. She was left with a claim of desertion. She had not lived with her husband for years, not since February 27, 1899. But even that argument was legally fraught. Roland had not willingly left Blanche; he had been imprisoned by the state. Scott asked Winans to let him handle the fascinating case, which he had already been pondering for months.

As Roland's second trial had begun in the fall of 1902, the Sioux Falls lawyer wondered aloud about the final outcome. Scott was concerned not about Roland's fate or, really, Blanche's but about the prosperity of his city. "What if she should come to Sioux Falls?" he had proposed to friends gathered in the clubroom of the new Elks lodge, within sight of the Cataract House. "It would be a big advertisement for the town," he said. Then he delivered the punchline. "It would be a bigger one though if she should fall in love with and marry some local man," Scott joked. "He would probably get more advertisement out of it than would please him."

Chapter Thirteen

THE SENTENCE

"THANK GOD my time is up soon," one colonist moaned to her companion in the days after Blanche's appearance in Sioux Falls. "Only six weeks more."

The *St. Louis Post-Dispatch* reporter eavesdropping on the conversation did not name the women, but only a few divorce seekers were staying at the Cataract in early December 1902. Many had retreated to smaller boarding houses, and despite the stylishly upholstered davenports and easy chairs in the hotel's parlors, those who remained were wary of venturing into the common areas since the newspaper correspondents had taken up residence. Perhaps the reporter had been lucky enough to spot Baroness Louise Wolfbauer, in her silks, chatting with Millie DeWint—who had not mustered enough evidence to earn a divorce from her husband in New York—or Baltimore author Margaret Pennington.

"How fortunate you are!" her friend responded. "I have eight weeks and three days yet. I do hope that Mrs. Molineux won't get us all into trouble."

A third woman chimed in. "Yes, it's a shame," she said. "To think, after serving here four months and two weeks, that now I might be exposed at the very end, just because of that woman from New York."

"That woman from New York" had rarely left her room since her identity was revealed. Blanche had tried, once, to take a stroll, only to find herself besieged by passersby. Since then she had limited herself to checking for mail and posting the numerous letters she penned each day. During her first week in Sioux Falls, other Cataract guests had heard her playing the piano in her room, but after a few days, the music stopped. Blanche's only visitors had been John Emmke, the hotel manager, who worried about his guest's health, and Senator Alfred Kittredge, one of her lawyers, who fretted over her case.

Blanche had not overheard the divorce colonists lamenting her presence, but she knew what people were saying. As she had so often in her life, Blanche had run afoul of rules of behavior that she had not even known existed. She had thought that a woman in this new century could lead an independent life, only to be reminded by her dwindling bank account that such freedom was only available to those with money. She had thought the sexual inhibitions of the Victorian era were long discarded, but following her passions landed her in the midst of a murder trial. Roland had been acquitted, but Blanche would be forever guilty of indulging her desires. And she had thought she would be accepted in Sioux Falls.

Blanche had tried to do what she was supposed to. She'd left New York without a word and with just a few belongings. The Molineuxes thought their daughter-in-law was going shopping; the family lawyer who handed over some pin money believed it was for dresses, not train tickets. She had traveled the same railroad lines, stayed in the same hotels, and hired the same lawyers as so many before her. And she had refused to see the reporters who came knocking. That last was no hardship. Blanche often struggled to hold her tongue, but she had an intense dislike of cameras. In the rare instances that she consented to be photographed, she ducked her head to the left, a coquettish pose designed to hide her glass eye. The reporters tried all kinds of ruses. One offered her services as a maid, another as a manicurist, a third as a hat saleswoman. "As I do not go out I have really no use for a new hat," Blanche wrote in response to a note about the fine Parisian bonnets on offer. There was said to be a bounty on Blanche's head: $50 for a surreptitious snapshot, $500 for a portrait.

Blanche wondered if she'd made a mistake coming to Sioux Falls. She requested her trunks be sent from New York, then countermanded the order, telling the hotel staff she didn't plan to stay long enough to require them. She had hoped to live in Sioux Falls without the scrutiny she endured back in New York. She wanted to go to the theater—a comedy entitled *Divorce* was opening at the Academy—play a round of golf, take a drive; she missed those things. Hers had been a dull and lonely life with her in-laws for most of the last four years. It would be too much to expect the residents of Sioux Falls to embrace her—they merely put up with the divorce seekers—but perhaps she would make some friends among her fellow colonists. At last she was among kindred spirits. These women had shown themselves, by their very presence in Sioux Falls, to be "free as air," as Blanche had once imagined herself.

The other divorce colonists would have paled at that comparison. They considered themselves to be nothing like Blanche, who departed for Sioux Falls too hastily and arrived in the western city alone. Couldn't she have exercised some discretion and waited a week or two before making her escape? Why hadn't she traveled with a companion? Most women arrived with a sister, a friend, or at least a maid. Even a husband-to-be disguised as a private secretary would have been a nod to propriety. But Blanche was estranged from her sisters. She had few friends, no household help, and no marriage prospects. "I thought that out here in this Dakota town I could once more breathe freely and forget that I had ever known sorrow and despair," Blanche said. "But no, the dread terror seems to pursue me even here."

Blanche's exile was so complete that one acquaintance felt moved to write a letter to the editor of the *Sioux Falls Press*. From her home in upstate New York, Dr. Mary Walker made a simple request: "Will you say to the women of Sioux Falls that all humane women will appreciate them if those outside of Blanche Molineux's hotel will share a little of sisterly kindness by calling on her?"

Everybody knew Mary Walker. She was that woman who wore trousers. A prominent advocate of dress reform, Mary was also a surgeon, a Civil War veteran, a Medal of Honor recipient, and a suffragist. But she had a better understanding of the situation Blanche found herself in than one might have expected. In 1860, at the age of twenty-seven, Mary abandoned her medical practice in Rome, New York, and moved to the tiny town of Delhi, Iowa, in hopes of obtaining a quick and quiet divorce from her adulterous husband, Albert; the process had been neither quick nor quiet.

Mary had also played a small role in the events that led Blanche to Sioux Falls. Mary was an outspoken opponent of the death penalty, and she saw Roland's case as an opportunity to make her argument against it. She thought Blanche's husband to be innocent, and she told anyone who would listen: the press; the New York legislature, which was debating the state's capital punishment statute during Roland's first trial; and the New York governor, whom she petitioned for his pardon. She still believed Roland had been "wronged" by the judicial system, but that view did not quell her conviction that Blanche should be allowed to leave her husband. Mary had once written that "to be deprived of a divorce is like being shut up in a prison because someone attempted to kill you. The wicked one takes his ease and continues his course, and you take the slanders, without the power to defend yourself." Now she took it upon herself to defend Blanche: "Why she desires a divorce is her own secret and no polite person will inquire. Throw a little sunshine into her life. The sun will not miss the same."

But Blanche's missteps in Sioux Falls had been more than mere social faux pas. On the second evening of her stay, she received a note at the Cataract House from the offices of the *Sioux Falls Press*. The reporter requested an interview, but if Blanche could not oblige, she was kindly asked to state her intentions in writing. On the same piece of stationery, Blanche scrawled her response: "There is really nothing to say save that it is true that I am in Sioux Falls for the purpose of instituting divorce proceedings. My plans? I only know I shall, of course, be a resident here the coming six months."

How Wallace Scott must have cringed when his new client's statement appeared in print the next day. Those twelve words—"I am in Sioux Falls for the purpose of instituting divorce proceedings"—uttered before she had served her sentence in Sioux Falls were a legal minefield, both for Blanche and for her fellow colonists.

⌒∞⌒

BACK IN NEW YORK, Roland Molineux appeared to be preparing for another long legal battle. Four years of trials had given him an unexpected ease in the courtroom. Confronted with news of his wife's trip to Sioux Falls, he had rushed to the Centre Street Courthouse. This time Roland sat not at the defendant's table but in the gallery, reading a newspaper as the magistrate ruled on the fate of the vagrants and drunks rounded up the night before. Some were released, others ordered held for trial in the Tombs next door, a place Roland still thought of as "more like home than anywhere else." His presence caused a stir among the newspaper reporters covering the court, but Roland refused to even acknowledge their questions. He was slightly less reticent when the Tombs barber, a man known to most only as Joe, entered the courtroom to greet his former client. "I see you're in trouble again," Joe said with a smile and a handshake.

"Oh, I guess I'll take care of this all right," Roland responded, reassuring Joe that he had not been arrested. He'd come to the court to meet his lawyers on a personal and "urgent" matter. Bartow S. Weeks and George Gordon Battle were scheduled to appear before the judge that morning to defend two high-profile clients accused of blackmail. Weeks and Battle had won Roland his freedom; now he wanted them to prevent Blanche from gaining hers. With a barber's eye, Joe likely noted that Roland was well put together for court, clean shaven and dressed formally in a cutaway coat, but despite his nonchalant words, Roland's face was ashen and drawn, and he appeared more agitated than he had when he stood accused of murder.

Roland met with his lawyers for hours that morning. He had brought evidence with him, documents he spread out before them. He pressed his case so loudly that the meeting was relocated from a Broadway restaurant to law offices nearby, where his father joined them. Roland looked haggard as he left the building, but General Molineux was more collected. Of Blanche the General said, "She has had the first word in this matter. Perhaps she will have the last, and perhaps she will not."

Roland's circuitous trip through the judicial system had taught the Molineuxes a lesson that most divorce colonists remained ignorant of until after they received their decrees: few court decisions were ever final. Even if Blanche filed for and was awarded a divorce, her jilted husband could pursue numerous legal avenues, at great cost to Blanche's bank account and her reputation. A contested South Dakota divorce could be tied up in the courts for years.

Just ask Edward Pollock. His "easy" divorce had not been easy at all. First, there had been the dramatic and well-attended trial in Sioux Falls in the winter of 1892, where he faced accusations of abandonment and kidnapping leveled by his destitute wife, Ellen. Then came a months-long wait as Judge Aikens weighed the evidence. The judge awarded Edward his decree in April 1892—but another four years passed before the case's final adjudication. By that time Edward and Florence, his new wife, were about to celebrate their third wedding anniversary; their daughter was almost two years old.

Ellen was behind the delay. She had appealed the divorce twice to the South Dakota Supreme Court, putting Edward, the *Argus-Leader* wrote, in "an embarrassing position, for there was a chance for the divorce being dissolved, which would have annulled his second marriage." The first trip to the state's highest court had been a procedural one. In early 1893, Judge Aikens had refused to sign the bill of exception necessary for an appeal to proceed. The judge said the paperwork had not been filed in a timely fashion; Ellen's supporters said he had accepted a large bribe from the Pollock family to ensure the divorce stood. In December 1893, the supreme court laid the blame instead on clerk of courts Albion Thorne for not passing along the filing to the judge promptly. The decision cleared the way for Ellen to again ask the court for reconsideration. In his final days on the bench, Judge Aikens had refused her request for a new trial, and when Judge Joseph Jones donned his judicial robes as Aikens's replacement, he did the same, putting the case on the path to the South Dakota Supreme Court once again.

While awaiting South Dakota's decisions, Ellen had also filed a lawsuit in New York. This one named her former father-in-law, millionaire merchant Alexander Pollock, as defendant. She was seeking $50,000 in damages for alienation of affection. It was Alexander's meddling that had brought an end to her marriage, she claimed. Alienation-of-affection claims were not an unusual accompaniment to a divorce suit; years earlier, Mary Nevins Blaine had considered mounting one against her in-laws before going to Sioux Falls.

The new lawsuit guaranteed another sensational trial. All the New York tabloids covered the case in vivid detail; the staid *New York Times* was only slightly less dramatic in its retelling. On the first day of the trial in June 1893, Ellen—"the picture of poverty," wrote the *Times*, "a poor young woman, without education and even without good looks"—tearfully testified that, on learning of her marriage to Edward, Alexander had offered her money to commit adultery, which would have given his son cause for divorce in New York. When she refused, Ellen claimed, Alexander told his son to seek a divorce elsewhere. On cross-examination, a defense lawyer charged that Ellen, three years older than Edward and then a member of the Pollock's household staff, was running a long con, "a plan," he said, "that began when this boy, her husband, was a schoolboy coming home during vacation." The judge himself objected to the questioning, and the jury, the *Times* wrote, "burst into applause. The spectators quickly took the cue from the jury box and in a second the big room was ringing with shouts of approval, hand clapping, and other demonstrations of satisfaction."

This court had no power to reunite Ellen with her ex-husband, but it could declare that Ellen was not to blame for the divorce. Stumbling through his testimony, Edward admitted to lying to the South Dakota court. Ellen's attorney conducted a rapid-fire cross-examination, covering all manner of ills. Then, he asked the key question: "You abandoned her then, didn't you?"

"I did," Edward acknowledged.

The testimony had lasted more than a week, but the jury deliberated for just ninety minutes before awarding Ellen $37,500. It was a fortune for the occasional seamstress—and it was vindication. But this case, too, would be appealed. A year later, a three-judge panel overturned the jury's judgment, finding there was insufficient evidence for the award. In South Dakota, the supreme court upheld the original divorce decree and denied the $1,500 in attorney's fees Ellen had asked for. In the process, at the request of Edward's counsel, the court revisited the question of support, revising his bill downward from a permanent $50 a month to $25 a month for each child until they reached the age of twenty-one—or about half the $20,000 Alexander was said to have offered his daughter-in-law to drop her objection to the original Sioux Falls divorce suit in 1892.

It seemed impossible that the divorce colonists of the 1900s could be unaware of such legal dramas, but Blanche was just a teenager with no thoughts of marriage or divorce during the Pollock saga. Besides, the lawsuits that served as sequels to South Dakota decrees were rarely about setting legal precedent. Most cases were personal struggles over money and reputation. Ellen had not challenged the right of South Dakota courts to issue divorces to those who met its residency requirements; she merely charged that Edward had lied about his reasons for coming to Sioux Falls and his intention to live there.

Blanche had not lied when asked about her plans, and that very forthrightness was the basis on which Roland's lawyers could challenge her efforts to end the marriage.

⎯⎯⎯⎯⎯ ◈ ⎯⎯⎯⎯⎯

BLANCHE SPENT THANKSGIVING alone. At the request of her lawyers, a holiday meal for one—breaded turkey, sweet potatoes, and cranberry jelly—was delivered to her room at the Cataract. Someone stole the check with her signature and tried to sell it to a reporter for $100. Elsewhere in the hotel, champagne corks popped, and revelers chattered.

Blanche's social standing was no better by Christmas. A few days prior, hotel guests had witnessed an unknown man entering Blanche's room late on a Saturday night. A few moments later, the man began yelling. Blanche shouted back. The argument went on for some time. The words were unintelligible to those in nearby rooms, but the vitriol of the exchange came through loud and clear, and that was enough to make the headlines. Some speculated that the stranger was a friend of Roland's sent from New York to intimidate Blanche into abandoning her planned divorce suit; others presumed he was another forsaken lover.

Finally, in early 1903, as Blanche entered the third month of her wait, her fortunes appeared to be improving somewhat. The newspaper reporters, weary of day after day spent waiting for a glimpse of a woman who rarely left her room, had decamped, and Blanche could now take long walks through the city. She had set herself to learning the ways of the colony, and each day that passed without another breach of its opaque etiquette made her less of a target for scorn. Still, Blanche remained an outcast. When it was reported that one Mary Knapp of Baltimore had befriended Blanche, Mary immediately wrote to her hometown paper to deny the account. She had spoken to Blanche once in a Sioux Falls department store, she said, and only by accident. The sorority of divorce seekers determined to ostracize Blanche did not realize that the true threat to the colony's continued existence had arrived in—and departed— Sioux Falls long before she had. His name was Charles Andrews.

Charles had been a fixture of the early days of the divorce colony, an embodiment of everything the city had quickly come to hate about its temporary residents. He was young, brash, and certain that his father's money could buy him anything he wanted. Worst of all, Charles's father owned the *Boston Herald*, and many suspected Charles of sending reports of the colony's antics back east. He "engaged in a good deal of pleasure, but not any business that I ever knew of," one Sioux Falls lawyer remembered, but he was among the few who recalled "the dude of the colony" a decade after his departure. Charles's stay had been short, and though he had been frequently in the company of Edward Pollock and Elliott Zborowski, his story had none of the drama that had etched their tales in Sioux Falls' memories. His wife, Kate, had not come to Sioux Falls from Boston; although she hired a lawyer, she ultimately agreed to the divorce without filing an appearance with the court. (A $2,050 payment—certainly illegal under South Dakota's collusion laws—aided her decision.) There was no trial, just a decree, signed in Judge Aikens's shaky cursive, issued on the grounds of abandonment.

But on Monday, January 19, 1903, the name Charles Andrews was the talk of Sioux Falls. The Supreme Court of the United States had handed down its decision in *Andrews v. Andrews*. The parties in the case were not Charles and Kate but Kate and Charles's second wife, Annie, whom he married eight months after the divorce. Charles had died of consumption in 1897 at the age of thirty-one. His wives had been battling ever since over his estate and the legitimacy of the two young children Annie had borne. For those in Sioux Falls and all the colonists who came before them, the stakes seemed higher still: in choosing between Charles's wives, the court could decide if other states were required to honor any South Dakota divorce.

The case had begun when Kate appealed a probate court decision making Annie the administratrix of Charles's estate. Kate, who had not remarried, claimed that she was Charles's lawful widow. His Sioux Falls divorce, she said, was invalid.

The Supreme Judicial Court of Massachusetts found that Charles had been a bona fide resident of South Dakota under the state's laws in 1891 and 1892. He had lived in Sioux Falls for more than ninety days and voted in the state election in the spring of 1892. That's where most inquiries into the validity of a South Dakota divorce ended. But things were different in Massachusetts. An 1835 law decreed, "When any inhabitant of this state shall go into any other state or country, in order to obtain a divorce for any cause, which had occurred here, and whilst the parties resided here, or for any cause, which would not authorize a divorce, by the laws of this state, a divorce so obtained shall be of no force or effect in this state." Charles's divorce thus was ruled to be of "no force or effect."

Annie appealed the decision to the US Supreme Court, claiming that Massachusetts was bound to recognize another state's divorce under the "full faith and credit" provision of the Constitution. The Supreme Court disagreed. It found Massachusetts had the right to dictate the terms of marriage and its dissolution among its residents. Charles's brief stay in Sioux Falls, though sufficient for South Dakota's courts, did not change his Massachusetts residency. To strike down the Massachusetts statute would have dangerous consequences, the court wrote. If a resident of Massachusetts could freely go to South Dakota, obtain a divorce, and require Massachusetts to recognize it, that state—and therefore every state—would lose all power to legislate divorce. "This would be but to declare that, in a necessary aspect, government had been destroyed by the adoption of the Constitution," Justice Edward Douglass White Jr. claimed.

Charles's divorce from Kate was deemed invalid. His second marriage to Annie was bigamous. His children were bastards. And a Sioux Falls decree, it seemed, was not worth the paper it was printed on.

Bishop Hare, who was visiting family in Philadelphia, certainly thought so. He wrote to a fellow opponent of divorce, "The decision of the U.S. Supreme Ct published this a.m. declaring null divorces granted in S. Dakota to residents of other states who take up a 6 months residence in S.D. is reassuring."

In Sioux Falls, would-be divorcees rushed to see their lawyers: "What's going to become of us?" In one law office, an attorney ran his fingers through his hair in distress and asked his clients to wait outside. For half an hour, he waded through his law books. Then he called the divorce colonists back in. "Things are not so bad as they seem," he told them, with a smile that may have been a bit forced. He went on to explain that the Supreme Court had been perfectly right in its decision; Charles Andrews had not been a bona fide resident. He had lived in the state for only three months—the law at the time. "But the Supreme Court's decision cannot possibly apply to divorce applicants who have established a bona-fide residence by remaining within the boundaries of the state for the six months required by the state law," he said.

Though few current or former divorce colonists, many of whom traveled frequently, could meet that standard—and it was wholly unsupported by the Supreme Court opinion, which offered no guidance on how long a stay was required to change residences—the clients seemed calmed by the attorney's hasty legal analysis.

"Just keep a stiff upper lip, serve your time, and you will get what you came here for," he said.

Chapter Fourteen

TO BE LEFT ALONE

B LANCHE WAS nervous as she sat in one of the lavishly decorated parlors at the Murray Hill Hotel at Fortieth Street and Park Avenue in Manhattan. It had been almost ten months since she'd last climbed the hotel's marble staircase. That was a lifetime ago. She had been settled into Room 503, just steps from Grand Central Depot, on November 11, 1902, when one of Roland's lawyers knocked at her door. She would never forget that conversation. Roland had been acquitted, the man told her, and the lawyer had come to take her back to the Molineux home in Brooklyn, where she would be reunited with her husband. The lawyer even had an armful of roses for Blanche to present to Roland. Blanche did not want to go. "Their son is returned to them. They have him. They don't need me any longer," she protested. "Oh, can't I have my own life now? Or what's left of it?" That remained an open question.

On this September 1903 evening, Blanche looked like a Victorian widow emerging from a long period of mourning. She was dressed in an expensive black silk gown with a wide-brimmed black hat adorned with ebony ostrich feathers, but she had a healthy glow that had not been in evidence when she'd left New York. Her right hand sparkled with three hulking diamonds. On her left, where she had once worn Roland's *mizpah* ring, were two shimmering Tahitian pearls. Blanche faced the gathered reporters, but she did not address them herself.

"Mrs. Blanche Chesebrough, as she now wishes to be known, makes this statement simply to set at rest all rumors regarding her case," Alexander C. Young began. Blanche had hired this attorney on her arrival in New York just the day before. He seemed a strange choice for a woman desperate for a little respectability. Young himself had been divorced twice on charges of adultery, most recently from Louise McAllister, niece of the late social arbiter Ward McAllister. Young made the headlines again that summer when he'd kidnapped his own daughter in a custody dispute. It was at least the third time he had done so, and the consequences of those rash acts were still pending in the courts as Young spoke to reporters on Blanche's behalf. "To settle this matter once and for all, we will say right here that she got her divorce about a month ago and is now absolutely free of her former husband, Roland Burnham Molineux."

The reporters were far from satisfied with this brief announcement. They lobbed questions at Blanche, who referred each one to the attorney, though she could be heard repeatedly whispering to him, "Oh, don't say that." On what grounds was the divorce granted? No one "will ever know any of the details of the case," Young answered. Would Blanche receive alimony? "Absolutely none." Would she marry again soon? "The idea is ridiculous." Where would she live? "She expects to return in a few days to Sioux Falls, which town, she says, will be her future home."

Only one question caught the attorney off guard. Had Blanche read her former husband's books? Since his acquittal, Roland had returned to work at his father's paint company, but he had also fashioned himself as a writer. He published a memoir, *The Room with the Little Door*, about his time in prison, and a local vaudeville theater produced a short play that he had penned while in Sing Sing. Roland's success in these artistic endeavors hinged almost entirely on his infamy. Hearing the news of Blanche's return to New York, his publisher rushed to release excerpts of Roland's upcoming novel, a historical romance called *The Vice Admiral of the Blue*. It was impossible to read the words without thinking of Blanche and Roland. "The husband who has ceased to be a lover soon finds his wife no longer a sweetheart," he had written. "When years have passed since the woman looked upon her husband's face, whether the cause be warfare in distant lands or misery behind a prison's bars, the result is all but inevitable."

Blanche's attorney demurred. He could not say if she had seen Roland's description of a woman who had once been "all devotion, anxiety and love, plunged in loneliness and sorrow." In time, Roland wrote, "the memory of the man becomes to her a shadow. He seems as one dead, or, if anything more real, a living barrier against happiness." Some read Roland's lines as forgiveness. "When such a moment comes into the life of a woman, she is but honest, even if cruel when she frankly says: 'It's over. I love another.'" Others read the words as dangerous jealousy of an unnamed lover and of what Roland saw as a woman's freedom to do as she pleased. "A man, of course, may speak no such words," he concluded. "The bit of chivalry that remains in us forbids." Blanche had not read Roland's words at all. As her attorney diplomatically skirted the question about his client's literary habits, Blanche threw her head back in laughter.

The press corps hurried off to send frantic telegrams to South Dakota. Young claimed to have a copy of Blanche's divorce decree in his possession, but he refused to show it to the reporters, leaving many skeptical that it had been issued at all. Blanche's declaration that she had gone to Sioux Falls for the purpose of getting a divorce should have prevented her from receiving one under the state's laws. The US Supreme Court's decision in *Andrews* seemed to guarantee that. But South Dakota's "bona fide" residency requirement had been construed liberally for years. And *Andrews* was not the immediate threat to the divorce colony that Bishop Hare had hoped it would be.

The *Andrews* decision reversed the effect of only one divorce: that of Charles Andrews. It did raise the possibility that other South Dakota decrees granted to those who had traveled to the state from Massachusetts—as

well as Maine and Delaware, which had similar statutes—could be overturned on the same grounds, but ultimately the number of such cases was
small. And the courts would never hear them if neither former husband nor
former wife complained. The truth was, for all the attention paid to *Pollock
v. Pollock* or *De Stuers v. De Stuers* or *Blaine v. Blaine*, most divorces that
took place in South Dakota were at least grudgingly mutual. The real surprise of the *Andrews* case had been not the Supreme Court's decision but
Kate's. She had broken the unwritten contract she had reached with her late
husband to divorce. In the face of dozens of different state and territorial
laws governing the dissolution of a marriage and the uncertainty that the
Constitution's "full faith and credit" clause would be applied, those infor-
mal agreements were as essential as a judge's decree.

That's why Blanche was in New York. A judge in South Dakota had
declared her free. Now she needed to persuade Roland to accept that
decision as final. The decree she carried from Sioux Falls might hold up
if Roland chose to challenge it in a New York court, but it might not,
and Blanche hardly had the funds for a long fight. On her arrival in New
York City, she had gone directly to the Molineux family lawyer—the
same man who had unknowingly funded her escape to Sioux Falls—
to begin the negotiations. She then hired Alexander Young to improve
her bargaining position. He looked like a dandy, but he was a brawler,
known for his less conventional methods. The lawyer was drawing up an
unusual suit seeking $100,000 from the Molineux family for the mental
anguish Blanche endured during the years she stood by Roland. "The
real Molineux story has never been told," Young announced to the press
a few days later. "It will only come out when this case is brought to trial."
That was the leverage Blanche needed to keep her divorce legal.

⚮

JUDGE JOSEPH JONES, whose autograph adorned countless divorces
issued in recent years, had not signed Blanche's decree. In Sioux Falls and

in each of the other courthouses in the Second Circuit, the clerk denied the claim that he had. Brady Beck, clerk of courts in Canton, was asked about it a dozen times or more. Always, his answer was no. The clerks in the First Circuit, to the west of Sioux Falls, likewise distanced themselves from *Molineux v. Molineux* and the ceaseless attentions of the press. Each maintained that the decree had not been issued in his courthouse. Judge Charles Whiting, who presided over the Ninth Circuit to the northwest, went on record himself. "I know nothing of the case," he insisted. By early October, all nine circuit judges in the state had issued statements on the matter. "Somebody has lied," wrote one South Dakota newspaper.

"There is no doubt about Mrs. Molineux's divorce," Alexander Young repeated when he read the news in a telegram. "I had in my possession for several days a duly certified copy of the decree granting her an absolute divorce from Roland B. Molineux." As to the lawsuit Blanche had threatened against the Molineux family, he added, it had been "settled to her entire satisfaction and is closed." The not-so-subtle threats had worked. Blanche, cornered at breakfast beneath the ornately stenciled ceilings and crystal chandeliers of the Murray Hill Hotel dining room, laughed at a reporter's accusations that she was still married to Roland. "That's the funniest thing I've heard in a long time," she said between giggles. "Pardon me for laughing but"—she began chuckling again—"it's just so funny."

Blanche knew she held a South Dakota decree, one that would not be challenged in the courts, and while she was in New York, her attorney, Wallace Scott, had undertaken one last effort on behalf of his client. Scott's trip from Sioux Falls to Canton would not have drawn attention. The young attorney could often be seen coming and going from his parents' home there. This time, though, his destination was clerk of courts Beck's office. The clerk had been honest: Judge Jones had not given Blanche her freedom; Judge Ellison G. Smith of the First Circuit had signed orders in Canton in Jones's stead that day. The clerks of the First Circuit had been honest too: the Lincoln County courthouse in Canton was in the Second Circuit. They were not responsible for what went on there. With Scott's help, Blanche, once so ignorant of the workings of the divorce colony, had played the system perfectly. Scott withdrew the paperwork—the potentially revealing pleadings and testimony and the final decree of divorce—from the court record, ensuring that no one would ever be privy to the particulars of the case. The only thing left was a single page with the note "Papers taken by attorney."

Frustrated in their efforts to suss out the details of Blanche's case, newspapers turned their attention to another topic. Though many in both Sioux Falls and New York were certain that Blanche would always legally be Mrs. Molineux, those same people seemed equally certain Blanche would soon take a new husband. Widespread speculation had started in May, just before Blanche gained residency in South Dakota. Dressmakers were seen visiting Blanche's rooms at the Cataract. The divorce colonists who still refused to associate with the woman counted fifteen new frocks—a wedding trousseau, to be sure.

As to who the groom might be: from Brooklyn came word that he was a Wall Street man, age thirty-five and never married. According to the whispers this unnamed man had courted Blanche when she first lived at the Murray Hill Hotel; since her departure they had communicated clandestinely via a cashier at a Sioux Falls bank. A dispatch from Duluth, Minnesota, asserted that Blanche would instead wed the actor Chauncey Olcott. The source was a Bell Telephone employee who claimed to have eavesdropped on the couple's declarations of love. Both Olcott and his in-laws quickly called for a correction. The *Boston Herald* was somewhat sure Blanche would marry her lawyer Alexander Young, but it was, the paper noted, "a report that lacks official confirmation or denial."

"Have I not endured enough without still being flaunted before the public?" Blanche demanded of a *Boston Globe* reporter who went to the Murray Hill Hotel seeking to get confirmation that she would become Mrs. Young. "I am living alone and quietly at this hotel. All I desire is to be left alone. I am not engaged nor am I contemplating matrimony." She was exhausted by the attention she had once craved. "I have been so misunderstood, that I shrink at the mention of my name in print. This is the last time I will make any statement to the press." Her last words: "I desire simply to be left alone."

But the *Boston Herald* report had been more accurate than Blanche was willing to admit. She was planning to marry her lawyer—not her New York counsel, Alexander Young, but her Sioux Falls representative, Wallace Scott.

On the first of November 1903, Blanche boarded a train from New York and Wallace, one from Sioux Falls. The couple met the next day in Chicago at the Auditorium Annex, a posh lakefront hotel, and they were married that afternoon—proof, finally, that Blanche had, in fact, been divorced from Roland. Wallace was on record requesting a marriage license. The diminutive, white-bearded county clerk, Morris Salmonson, was used to out-of-towners; in recent years, after Wisconsin made it more difficult to marry on a whim, Chicago had seen an increase in elopements. Still Salmonson gasped when he spotted the names on this application. The next day, though, reporters could not find evidence that the license had been filed. Blanche and Wallace had again outwitted the press, temporarily, by delaying in submitting the final paperwork. The ruse would not ultimately spare the newlyweds exactly what Wallace had predicted a year earlier. They would surely "get more advertisement out of" the marriage than would please either one of them.

❧

BLANCHE WAS COMING back to Sioux Falls. No one in the city had anticipated that. For years, most who opposed the divorce colony had maintained that their objection was not to divorce itself but to the abuse of the laws. Their quibble was not with desperate spouses who sought escape but with those who would swear to their residency, receive a decree for frivolous causes, and leave on the next train. The new Mrs. Scott threatened to put the lie to those claims.

For a few weeks after her marriage to Wallace, as the couple honeymooned in Chicago, it looked like Blanche would hew to the expected path for a South Dakota divorcee and forsake the state. She'd already given up the Sioux Falls cottage she'd moved into after months at the Cataract. Then came the announcement that she would join a vaudeville show at Proctor's Theatre in New York. The venue was not known for its highbrow entertainment—it was the same theater that had staged Roland's play earlier that year—but it had long been an acceptable destination for the society women Blanche admired. Plus, the role paid nearly $1,000 a week; the last time Blanche had sung in the city, she'd made $10 a week. Blanche went east for rehearsals, and her new husband returned to Sioux Falls. She expected Wallace would join her when he'd settled his affairs in the city, but in just a few days, it became apparent that his work at Kittredge, Winans & Scott and his second term as state's attorney would delay him indefinitely. Blanche abandoned her plans to appear on stage and boarded a train west. Wallace explained her decision to the press: when she realized what it meant to face an audience as a singer, Blanche's courage failed her. His wife, he said, had instead decided to become "a good South Dakota girl."

Wallace was used to making such pronouncements and having Sioux Falls society accept his judgment. The twenty-eight-year-old lawyer was a popular figure in the city. He had first moved there with his parents in 1894 and returned to practice law in 1898 after completing his studies at the University of Michigan. His long, thin face, with arched eyebrows and a prematurely receding hairline, was seen at nearly every lawn party and gala. He was a charter member of the bowling club and the founder of the Young Men's Republican Club. He was a regular on the baseball diamond, often taking the mound as the starting pitcher, and a favorite partner at gatherings of the Patriarch's Dancing Club, one of the city's most exclusive social organizations. But now the Patriarchs were in a quandary. Would they accept Blanche into their ranks? Some among them insisted that she be received as Wallace's wife. Others threatened to renounce their membership if she was invited. It was "social war," one South Dakota newspaper observed.

Blanche and Wallace presented a predicament the city had not been forced to consider before. It was unusual for a divorce colonist to marry a Sioux Falls man and unheard of for the couple to settle in the city afterward. The pattern had been set in 1891, when Mima Hubbard—abandoned by her husband and evicted by her father-in-law, who owned their New Jersey home—fell in love with Clark W. Brown, a clerk at William Van Epp's dry goods store just off Phillips Avenue. Clark's scandalized employer delivered an ultimatum: give up the woman or resign his position. Mima and Clark promptly left town. The rarity of lasting romance between the city's temporary residents and its permanent ones was the only explanation for the shock Wallace's friends felt at his nuptials.

Wallace had made it known he wished to marry. In fact, he was the president of the Matrimonial Club. The idea had been born of a February 1903 evening of cards, ping-pong, and cigars at the home of newlywed friends. The membership was limited to ten Sioux Falls bachelors, each of whom would pay dues of $1 per month. The funds would provide for a lavish banquet in celebration of any of them who married. The groom would be thereafter an honorary member of the club, forever feasting on the tab of the unwed. The first such dinner took place in October at the Cataract House to mark the upcoming nuptials of William J. Alexander, a clerk at a local men's clothing shop, and Emma Gillespie, who worked at the city post office. The table was set with roses and carnations. An orchestra had been hired, and Wallace and his friends appeared in evening dress for the seven-course meal.

That night, the men teased each other about their marriage prospects. It was generally agreed that Charles Symms, who had been taking a lot of mysterious trips out of town, would be the next to wed. Had Wallace's efforts to woo Blanche really gone unnoticed? The courtship, which had started soon after Blanche's arrival, lacked the panache she had known in New York. There were no evenings at the theater and no late dinners at Delmonico's. There were no yachts and no Tiffany diamonds, but for months Wallace had been a regular caller at Blanche's cottage; indeed, he had been her only caller. The pair had spent long afternoons in the summer of 1903 picnicking along the banks of the Big Sioux River. Wallace had even been spotted mowing the lawn outside the cottage, a "vulgar" and "plebeian" activity. At the end of the Matrimonial Club's inaugural dinner, a new member, Cataract manager John Emmke, was inducted into its ranks. But John did not pay to publicly toast Wallace when he returned to Sioux Falls with his unwelcome bride; the Matrimonial Club was never mentioned again.

There was, however, a least one in the city who despaired over the match, not for Wallace's sake but for Blanche's. Flora Bigelow Dodge, who arrived in Sioux Falls for a divorce in the weeks after the *Andrews* decision, had never been properly introduced to "the murderer's wife," as she continued to think of Blanche. But Flora couldn't help but see something of herself in the woman she knew from the newspapers. They had once shared a boundless optimism for the new century and a certainty of finding their places in a changing world.

Blanche seemed to have given up on all that now. It had not been her lover's death in 1898 that disillusioned her; she had grieved for Barney but not for her future. It had not been the marriage she entered into a few weeks later without love; at the time, she believed Roland would give her the life she wanted. It had not even been her husband's arrest and the public indictment of her own behavior. Until Blanche arrived in Sioux Falls, she had maintained the poise of the independent woman she wanted to be. "I desire my freedom above all else in the world and I am justified in seeking it," she announced shortly after settling in the city.

It was when she realized that she was nearly alone in this conviction— that neither the law nor her fellow divorce colonists were certain she deserved release from a man who many still believed to be a murderer—that Blanche seemed to break. The woman who had for years protested vocally against her mistreatment at the hands of the courts, the press, and the public fell silent.

Certainly, Flora thought, Blanche must harbor regrets about her "frisky past," but the penance society exacted for those indiscretions seemed too harsh. Blanche "took the most dreary possible way of burying her sins," Flora wrote to her father from Sioux Falls. Flora did not share the high opinion most held of Wallace; according to her, Blanche had "married a dreadful little man just to be virtuous for the first time."

···• PART FOUR •···

FLORA

Chapter Fifteen

HAPPINESS WILL
FOLLOW THEE

F LORA BIGELOW DODGE had not traveled to Sioux Falls in 1903 for the same reason so many women of her acquaintance had. She did not do anything for the same reason other women did—at least not if you believed the newspapers. In their pages, Flora was the "most daring, most original, cleverest woman in New York society." She was a wonderful musician, a graceful dancer, an expert horsewoman, and a captivating storyteller. She was "both courageous and imaginative." She was witty, ambitious, generous, and beautiful, a woman of "unusual individuality" with a retinue of admirers. It was a lot to live up to.

Flora was voluble and vivacious, most of the time. She'd been born to it. Her father, John, had been a lawyer, a journalist, and, through the Civil War, a diplomat in France. By the time Flora, the youngest of his eight children, was born in 1868, John was fifty, an elder statesman who read voraciously, wrote voluminously, and cultivated a wide circle of well-spoken friends. John was an attentive father, and his children were welcome in the impromptu salons of The Squirrels, the family's modest country home overlooking the Hudson River. At the age of five, Flora counted among her playmates British novelist Wilkie Collins, American politician John Hay, and much of the German royal family. Flora's mother, Jane Poultney, had played no small part in building the family's social reputation. The man she married in 1850 had been serious and subdued, but Jenny, as she was known to most, was bubbly, unpredictable, and irresistible. "Mon Dieu! Qu'elle est vive!" Prince Napoléon had declared of her. "How alive she is!"

Flora, now thirty-four, had inherited her mother's spirit and her sparkling blue eyes. John remembered his wife, who passed away in 1889, to be "as near the perfection of womanly beauty as any woman I had ever seen," and Flora was just as admired. It was generally agreed that only Flora's long dark lashes, her creamy skin, her rosy cheeks, and her golden hair kept her from being dismissed as "eccentric." Her true allure lay in her lack of pretension. She was known for simple frocks that lacked the embellishments then in vogue, and she eschewed the unnatural silhouettes formed of crinoline and corsets that had been so popular for decades. What one saw when looking at Flora was Flora herself. She was similarly unaffected in her manners. She would admit into her society anyone who would welcome her as an equal.

Flora had been on every guest list since the age of eighteen. She dined with the Astors, danced with the Rhinelander Stewarts, and celebrated Christmas with the Pierpont Morgans. She took in the opera with Nikola Tesla and the horse show with the Whitneys. Sometimes she was accompanied by her husband, Charlie Dodge, but oftentimes she was not.

Charlie had not been with her in the summer of 1893 when she had been among the guests at Point d'Acadie in Bar Harbor. George Vanderbilt had purchased the thirty-plus-acre estate a few years earlier, even as he had begun construction on the magnificent Biltmore in North Carolina. Frederick Law Olmsted, the landscape architect who had reimagined Biltmore's endless forests and formal gardens, also designed Point d'Acadie's seaside saltwater pool. On that warm July day, the party was dressed in bathing clothes—the most stylish women weighed down by bathing dresses and bathing hats and bathing shoes and bathing cloaks. George, usually introverted, was entertaining those gathered with dives into the pool's depths. But despite his sudden bravado, their host could not swim well. He came up sputtering and shouting for help. It was Flora who leapt into the ten-foot-deep water to rescue him, a fearless act that made her the talk of the town. In 1896, when a burglar crept into her bedroom at The Squirrels, Flora fought off the intruder and cemented her reputation for derring-do. That she'd almost drowned herself saving George Vanderbilt only magnified her bravery. That, years later, she still quaked at the idea of sleeping alone was a fear she kept to herself.

The gushing praise for Flora's pluck in the face of danger, be it mortal or social, said more about the world in which Flora moved than it did about the doting mother of two. It was so rare for a woman of Flora's position to step out of her expected role—to come to the rescue instead of being rescued, to fight instead of faint—that it made the newspapers when Flora joined a coach run from the Waldorf-Astoria to Woodmansten Inn in Westchester, some thirty miles away, in April 1898. Such outings were an idle hobby of the city's millionaire class, men who played the lowly coachman for an afternoon, ferrying travelers for a tiny fare to show off their horses and four-in-hand driving skills. It was a point of pride among Coaching Club members to make each run on time, and that day's driver, William C. Eustis, was determined not to let a spring blizzard slow him. Yet he had no passengers. "Mrs. Charles Stuart Dodge was the heroine of the occasion," the *Philadelphia Inquirer* reported. Flora took a seat next to the driver and rode into the gale without a veil. "Only John Bigelow's daughter would contemplate the drive in the raging storm," said one admiring observer.

It was Flora's pedigree that saved her from the consequences of flouting societal norms, however trivial. Even in the moments when it seemed she'd gone too far—riding astride her horse, appearing for dinner at Sherry's bareheaded and in a décolleté dress—she was not breaking the rules. She was making new ones.

By the time Flora settled into her four-room suite at the Cataract House in January 1903, it was no longer original to travel to Sioux Falls for a divorce, though it was still daring to imagine a life apart from one's husband. Flora had come to the city to end her marriage of sixteen years, but she had no use for a decree that was no more legal than a wink and a nod between lawyers and judges, and she had little respect for those who sought escape through subterfuge. Flora wanted something entirely without precedent: "a legal and dignified Dakota divorce."

⚬◈⚬

SIOUX FALLS WAS certain it had heard Flora's story before. It was Mary's story. In 1886—the same year Mary Nevins met Jamie Blaine—Flora, just seventeen, had engaged herself to the son of a well-known New York family. Charlie Dodge, age twenty-one, was a recent graduate of Yale College, where he rowed varsity crew and was among those few chosen for induction into the Scroll and Key, one of the school's secret societies. The four-decade-old social club counted among its membership corporate leaders and several US congressmen. Charlie, tall and lean with dark wavy hair and a cupid's bow pucker, was expected to join the family business, an international mining and lumber conglomerate.

The extended Bigelow and Dodge families had been acquainted long before Flora and Charlie professed their devotion to one another—New York society was a small world—but Flora's parents had never set eyes on the young man. Now, sixteen years later, her father bemoaned the American courtship customs that permitted such an egregious oversight. "The peril of allowing children to choose their mates without consultation with their parents is greater I think than the opposite extreme favored in Continental Europe to have the mates selected by the parents and then submitted for approval by their children," John wrote in his diary a few days after Flora arrived in Sioux Falls.

But it's doubtful John had hesitated to give his gregarious daughter permission to attend Yale's Junior Promenade in the winter of 1886. She was to be the guest of her schoolmate Ethel Dodge. Ethel's mother would serve as chaperone to the two young women, who had not yet made their debut into society. It was but an afterthought that Ethel's older brother Charlie would also be in attendance.

The promenade was a spectacular annual affair. It had begun in 1861 as a quirky college tradition, a procession that ended with the awarding of a wooden spoon to the year's most popular student, but it had transformed into the highlight of a multiday reunion. In 1886, more than one thousand people crowded Carll's Opera House in New Haven. The room overflowed with flowers, and the long racing shell the varsity crew team had rowed against Harvard during Charlie's senior year hung from the ceiling. The early promenades had forsworn dancing, owing to the faculty's opposition to such frivolity, but by the time Flora and Charlie arrived on the scene, elaborate cotillions were all the rage. Hundreds bowed and spun across the dance floor until well after 2 a.m. A month later, after a family lunch at home on a Saturday afternoon, Flora told her father that Charlie "had confessed to an incurable affection for her" and that she was "suffering badly from the same malady."

John had not rejoiced at the news. He advised his teenage daughter that she and Charlie "both were too young and inexperienced to know whether their affection would wear." He begged Flora to wait, and she obliged, for a few months. After spending part of the summer with her family in East Hampton, Flora traveled to the Hudson Valley for a July visit with Lucretia Schieffelin—Charlie's grandmother. The very next day, a note arrived at the Bigelows' home on Gramercy Park in New York City, addressed to John. Charlie's father wished to speak to him.

In the Dodges' Central Park–side brownstone in the newly fashionable East Seventies, Charles Cleveland Dodge pleaded his eldest son's case. He spoke for the better part of an hour. The family was very fond of Flora, Charles told John, and would "do everything in their power to promote her happiness." Then he got practical. At twenty-one, Charlie was not yet independently wealthy. For the next few years, it would be unwise for him to spend more than $5,000 annually—a significant sum—but he had "improving prospects," and as the Dodges had abundant space in their new home, the couple could live there after the wedding. Charles's accounting was less persuasive than he might have thought. The Bigelows lived well, but John had never valued wealth for its own sake. He did, however, value Flora's happiness.

John could have denied Charles's petition. Flora did not need to marry for money or a position in society. She did not need to marry at all. At thirty-three, her eldest sister, Grace, was unwed and a society darling. But Flora made it clear to her parents that she wanted to be Mrs. Charlie Dodge. John could delay the marriage and insist that she be introduced into society first, but he knew his willful daughter. She was in love. "If they were to go into society," John realized, "they would see but little of anyone else but each other." He had already decided to acquiesce. There was "no young man to whom I would commit a child with more confidence than to Charlie," he told Charles.

Flora and Charlie's engagement was announced in the last weeks of the summer of 1886. They "will probably be the youngest couple that New York society has seen united in many years," the *Chicago Tribune* noted days before the still younger Mary Nevins and Jamie Blaine's elopement became known. But Flora's youth did not cause the uproar that Jamie's seventeen years would. With the Bigelows' blessing of the union, her tender age became another romantic detail in a society-column love story.

The wedding march echoed through St. George's Church just after noon on Wednesday, December 15, 1886. Hundreds had gathered for the "Baby Wedding," as it was affectionately called, and they all rose to catch a glimpse of the bride as John escorted Flora down the aisle. She wore white satin and tulle and carried not the expected bouquet of orange blossoms but a small bunch of violets and an ivory vellum-bound Bible. Facing her groom that day, Flora cried. Her tears were not an unusual sight; she was extravagant in all her emotions. The excitement of standing before the altar was simply too much, one wedding-goer said. "But when she walked down the aisle afterward with her young husband, the smile came like the sun bursting through April showers." Now those who remembered her sobs wondered if Flora—always inclined to the superstitious—had experienced a premonition of her future.

⸎

A CROWD OF nearly twelve hundred—about 10 percent of Sioux Falls' population—sat in expectant silence as Anna Eva Fay retook the stage at the New Theater on Ninth Street in February 1903. In front of the rapt audience, the clairvoyant was blindfolded and draped from head to toe in a white sheet. She looked like an apparition. The evening up until that moment had been a vaudeville revue, filled with laughter and delight. Fay, her hands and feet bound, had been secured in an empty cabinet barely large enough for the slender woman. From inside the box, some- how, bells rang out, unknotted pieces of twine emerged elaborately tied, and a nail was driven through a thick plank without the telltale staccato of a hammer. It was a consummate performance, but it had surely been a trick. What was to come was harder to explain.

Each spectator—Flora among them—was asked to write a question on a blank sheet of paper and then to fold that paper and keep it close, showing no one. On stage, the shrouded clairvoyant appeared to be in a trance, a state she called "somnolency." Suddenly, she shouted out a name: "Thomas Freeman!" The man, a tinsmith with a shop on Main Avenue, raised his hand. He was still clutching the folded piece of paper as Fay revealed its contents. Freeman wanted to know who had stolen his bicycle. It was a man who was well known to Freeman, the clairvoyant told him. A man he called Jocko but who was properly named Johnson. The onlookers were in awe. That was the question Freeman had written down—and there were several John Johnsons in the city, including a rival tinsmith.

Over the course of a week—eight performances, including two matinees reserved for women only, so they could pose any question they would not dare ask in the presence of the "sterner sex"—Anna Eva Fay answered dozens of queries. There were those who went to every show in hopes of discovering the trickery behind Fay's feat, but this brand of spiritualism—more entertainment than religion—held strong sway in the West, and most wanted to believe. Mediums bridged the growing gap between science and faith, providing answers in a turn-of-the-century world filled with uncertainty. Fay generally told people what they hoped to hear, and her predictions were often accurate enough to be accepted as proof of her abilities. And so, when the clairvoyant told an *Argus-Leader* reporter who had asked about the Molineux case that "a cast in the eye"—a misalignment of the gaze, like the one caused by Blanche's glass iris—"means ill-luck invariably for the person associating himself with the possessor of the defect," she provided yet another reason to avoid the divorcee.

The night Flora was in attendance at Anna Eva Fay's show, John Emmke posed the question she might have asked. The manager of the Cataract—who "looks after us all like a mother," Flora said of his kindness toward the divorce colonists—wanted to know if he would find happiness. It didn't take a psychic to divine what the bachelor was really wondering. Fay assured him that he would be happy in love but warned that in the next couple of years, he would not enjoy getting up late at night with a new baby.

Flora had spent a lot of time thinking about happiness over the last decade. A story she had written, published in the July 1893 edition of *Short Stories: A Magazine of Fact and Fiction*, warned against its pursuit. The main character of the allegory was rich, beautiful, and talented.

Those around him were dazzled and could not see what he lacked; the unnamed man searched in vain for happiness. But his true downfall came when he saw it in the distance. "He cried aloud with joy," Flora wrote. "'It is happiness: I see it, I will reach it;' and jumping up he began his terrible pilgrimage. The briars tore his clothes, the excitement made him weak, he left behind his friends, family, work, all." Years passed before the man reached the mountaintop where he thought he saw happiness in the guise of a woman. "Poor humanity!" she murmured. "And who has ever obtained happiness by seeking it?" The figure admonished, "Turn and go back towards duty, and happiness will follow thee."

That advice had not worked for its author. She thought she had found happiness at seventeen, and for the next decade, she and Charlie did their duty as a society couple. The baby bride ushered new debutantes into the world of balls, teas, and charity events, while Charlie worked for the family business. In the summers, the family vacationed at The Squirrels or their own country home in the Somerset hills in northern New Jersey. As years passed, though, Flora began to appear in public alone more often. Her husband, it was said, preferred to be home by the hearth with a cigar. She took long trips to Paris and London unaccompanied by Charlie but worried other people would begin to talk about her absence.

The characters that populated Flora's scripts and short stories had not stopped pursuing happiness. With the debut of the *Smart Set*, a literary magazine for New York's elite owned by the same man who skewered them in *Town Topics*, Flora's writing found a wider readership alongside works by O. Henry and Jack London. Her contributions were gentle comedies of manners, poking fun at the petty grievances, outdated mores, and gossip-fueled misunderstandings of the world she moved in. Flora's play *Mrs. Mack's Example* was a satire, but one character's pronouncement rang true: "Oh, I must be an unnatural woman," moaned Mrs. Elton, bored by marriage and trapped by societal expectations, "but I must live my life just the same and snatch the little scraps of happiness where I find them. Happiness isn't growing on every bush."

The idea that a woman should find happiness in her marriage—not just the support and protection offered by an eighteenth-century union—was an article of faith in the nineteenth and early twentieth centuries. That happiness might require more than a husband with a good income and healthy children was less easily accepted. But Flora wanted more. In the summer of 1902, in the presence of their lawyer, Flora and Charlie agreed to the terms of a separation that Flora, at least, had long been contemplating. They decided Flora would go to Corn Hill, a small resort in Cape Cod, a deliberate parting of ways to show Charlie had "abandoned" her. Then, in the fall, she would go west. She wrote to her father, thanking him for watching their children, twelve-year-old Lucy and eight-year-old Johnny, as she and Charlie made this decision. "I fear my unhappiness of late years has overshadowed them often," she confessed.

If Charlie had done Flora a great wrong that led to the break, she wasn't saying. If Flora had done Charlie grievous harm, he too had chosen to remain silent. It seemed that "the years of misery" that Charlie himself acknowledged could be blamed not on bad behavior or the monetary woes the family suffered when Charlie's business floundered but rather on simple unhappiness. As she waited in Corn Hill, Flora wrote to her father of Charlie, "I can be a better friend to him when I am free." John had been prescient when he cautioned his daughter that youthful affection could wear away. Even those who were perfectly matched at seventeen could be mismated at twice that age. "First let it be said that universally it is conceded that Flora Dodge's husband Charlie is a good chap," acknowledged the *Chicago American* in 1903. "At this the smart set shrugs its shoulders. He is good, but Flora is brilliant."

Anna Eva Fay had not called out Flora's name from the stage at the New Theater, but the clairvoyant made a point of visiting her at the Cataract House before leaving Sioux Falls. Naysayers claimed that Fay's mind reading was an elaborate ruse. Her assistants collected the pads upon which the questions were written and used ash to reveal the impressions left on the waxed pages underneath. But she was a perceptive woman and didn't need sleight of hand to discover what Flora wanted to know. Years spent answering unspoken questions had convinced Fay that there were but four or five topics in the whole world. Flora was easy to read; Fay knew what sadness looked like.

On stage, Anna Eva Fay was a woman of mystery, but face-to-face there was no artifice. The fifty-two-year-old was frank and direct. She told Flora about her own difficult life. Her early years had been "dark and bitter." Her mother died when Fay was ten or eleven. Her father was unable to support the children, and Fay was forced to work for her room and board on an Ohio farm. Within a few years, she had found some fame—and a paycheck—as a spiritualist who could conjure specters, but as she rose in prominence, Fay was betrayed several times by friends who revealed the tricks of her "wonderful phenomena" to the world. But this woman with the quick smile, bright eyes, and packed schedule of performances did not seem to Flora to be scarred by this litany of sorrows. Fay exuded confidence, and by the time she finished her story, Flora was convinced of "how much good unhappiness in life does people if they can climb above it and not be crushed in the battle."

Chapter Sixteen

A TRAMP AND AN EXILE

D ARKNESS HAD settled over Sioux Falls long before the supper dishes were cleared on the evening of March 16, 1903, and a cold rain poured down outside the windows of the Cataract House as Flora began a long letter to her father. For the region's farmers, the rainfall was the first promise of spring after a long and snowy winter. But for Flora, the barren season stretched on. "Dear Papa," she wrote. "I do not regret having come but it is very dreary sometimes."

In the seven weeks since Flora had joined the divorce colony, she had filled scores of pages of the hotel's stationery with her loopy cursive. She wrote almost daily to her father and frequently to her sisters. She wrote to her husband—installed at the Iroquois Hotel in Manhattan—only when absolutely necessary. Charlie kept sending "foolish letters" and money; Flora kept sending them back.

Flora tried to make each letter to her father sound cheerful, but the woman who had earned fame as a short story writer seemed to have lost her skills for fiction. "I am not unhappy or depressed at all, and enjoy everything I see so much," she had promised him in an earlier letter.

Now she confessed her true feelings. "It seems as if I was doomed to being a tramp and an exile."

In truth, Flora did not want to belong in Sioux Falls. It was overrun with gamblers, drunkards, and foulmouthed louts, she wrote—and the divorce colonists were worse. The women seemed foolish, selfish, and wanton to Flora; she did not want anyone to think of her that way. To her sister, Grace, Flora wrote, "The richer women spend their time having what Mrs. Leiter"—a family friend—"would call 'nervous prostitution' in bed with trained nurses." Surely Grace could hear the quotation marks around "trained nurses." "And the others sit in the parlor exchanging their troubles."

Flora tried to steer well clear of all of them. She had been mortified when Margaret Pennington introduced herself. The two authors had mutual acquaintances and would have been friendly under other circumstances, but Flora dared not be seen in her company here. It was no secret that Margaret planned to marry the actor J. R. Mordecai as soon as she was released from her obligations to her first husband, Clapham. Flora did not want to be counted among the ranks of the colonists and was further dismayed when she got a letter from a stranger in Poughkeepsie, New York, asking for her assistance. The woman offered to do laundry work in exchange for Flora's help in obtaining a divorce. "I shall not answer," Flora decided.

"Doomed to being a tramp and an exile," Flora had written, but the thought must have seemed too sad. In a rush of words, she added, "But I shall make the best of it." Flora was used to making the best of it. Her trip to Sioux Falls had come after years of estrangement from and reconciliation with Charlie. Through it all, she'd tried to shield her family—especially her children—from any of what she termed as "unnecessary unhappiness." Lucy and John, along with the family's longtime maid, Delia, had accompanied Flora west. For their part, the children seemed to be overjoyed with their new adventure. Flora was adamant that they sit with her for their school lessons each day, but afterward she let the pair run as free as she had as a child at The Squirrels. Most afternoons would find them skating on a frozen bend of the river or pestering the conductor for a ride on the engine as it was moved from one end of the train to the other to prepare for its return trip east.

Before Flora left New York, she had resigned herself to an absence of eight months, but that timeline changed when the Supreme Court handed down its decision in the *Andrews* case. Now she told her father that her lawyer, C. O. Bailey, demanded that she "give up New York absolutely." She was devastated at the thought, but she agreed to the condition. She planned to write to the *New York Social Register* and have her name removed from its pages. She would not be going home.

❧

MAGGIE ZBOROWSKI HAD not returned to New York either. She had not been welcome there. In the last decade, Flora had dined and danced with the Astors, but Maggie had never been among the guests. She now called Europe home. Maggie, at fifty, and Elliott, at forty-six, had not given up their peripatetic lifestyle. The couple moved between rented houses in London, Paris, and Genoa on a whim. Anywhere but the Netherlands, lest Maggie be convicted of bigamy.

Maggie could be seen as a cautionary tale for Flora and other would-be divorcees. Her decree demanded sacrifice, both during her time in Sioux Falls and in the years since. The financial costs meant little to Maggie, but she had also been forced to give up her family, her home, her health, and her privacy. Flora had to wonder if her freedom was worth this toll.

Maggie's former husband had not accepted the verdict handed down in Sioux Falls in 1892. In its immediate aftermath, the Baron announced that he would ask the South Dakota Supreme Court to overturn the decision. It was "a terrible warning to all young American women who are contemplating matrimonial alliances with titled foreigners," *Town Topics* wrote. "An American husband, under similar circumstances, might be depended upon to retire gracefully." If the supreme court were to reverse Judge Aikens's decision, Maggie and the Baron would again be married, pending the outcome of a new trial. This flummoxed the *Town Topics* writer. "I must, however, confess myself at a loss to imagine just what the Chevalier"—another of the Baron's titles—"will do with her when he gets her back."

A few months later, the Baron changed tactics. He withdrew his appeal in South Dakota and filed his own suit in Holland. He did not seek a divorce, which was available but rare under Dutch law; he wanted a judicial separation. Such an arrangement allowed the parties to live separate lives but did not dissolve a marriage. Maggie would still be committing bigamy. Maggie's Dakota divorce held no sway in the Dutch court, and in the fall of 1892, the court issued the Baron the decree he sought and awarded him custody of his daughter, Margot, still secreted away in a French convent.

Maggie had not seen her daughter in more than two and a half years when the parties came to court yet again in February 1893. This time they were in Paris, where the Baron still lived. Maggie had petitioned the French court to honor her South Dakota decree and reunite her with Margot, but she was not in the courtroom the day the case came up. The ongoing legal battles had taken a toll on Maggie's health, and the first months of her pregnancy added to the strain. Elliott sat in the gallery in her stead, as the lawyers argued not about husband and wife or mother and father but about the Baron's diplomatic status. Maggie's attorneys made the case that Margot was in the custody not of the Baron but of the mother superior of Sacré-Coeur, who said she would abide by a French court ruling. But the judge ultimately found that Margot was legally in her father's custody, and the French government had no jurisdiction over the matter. Maggie was ordered to pay court costs.

Maggie had lost her daughter and, later that same year, her infant son. At his birth in August 1893, doctors had warned Maggie and Elliott that their child was weak and ailing. Martin Ladislus—named for his paternal grandfather—lived less than three weeks, but Maggie mourned him as she did Alida. Years later, she was moved when a seance seemed to bring forth the shadow of a small child and the medium delivered a loving message from "M."

Those first years of marriage had not been the life the newlyweds had envisioned when they left Sioux Falls, but slowly things began to get better. In February 1895, at the age of forty-two, Maggie gave birth to another son, Louis Varrow, with his father's dark hair and protruding ears. The baby thrived and was well spoiled by both his overjoyed parents. For a while, Maggie's health was improved, and the couple began to entertain more often at Coventry House, Elliott's country home in the English town of Melton Mowbray. The property was often described as a hunting lodge; that was classic British understatement. The coveted property included a ballroom that could accommodate at least 150 revelers and stables for more than two dozen horses.

Only now, as Flora began to realize the true costs of a South Dakota divorce, could Maggie honestly say Sioux Falls was, at last, a distant memory. As Maggie awaited her husband in the town of La Turbie on the French Riviera on Wednesday morning, April 1, 1903, the last of the lawsuits stemming from her time in South Dakota had ended; it had taken almost a decade to settle a dispute over the house Maggie had backed out of buying there. Maggie continued to suffer from bouts of nerves and depression, but she had built a life with Elliott and Louis, now eight and at school in England, and she had found a new passion to share with her husband. Once the pair had been favorites among the horsemen of the Quorn, England's most famous fox hunt. Now they were motor car enthusiasts.

Maggie had been doubtful when Elliott first decided to buy a noisy and smelly motor car in 1898, and she'd been shocked when he'd announced two years later that he would sell his horses, which no longer held a fascination for him. He craved the ever-improving speed and agility of an engine. But Elliott's love of the new sport of motor car racing drew her in, and Maggie was now anticipating the delivery of a Mercedes for herself. That bright spring day, Elliott would be speeding up the steep and winding road from Nice to La Turbie in a new, blue sixty-horsepower Mercedes. He'd participated in the race the year before, covering the 9.6 miles in a disappointingly slow twenty-five minutes and twenty-one seconds. This year he hoped to complete the course in a record-breaking fifteen minutes.

Elliott was dressed for the competition in the long, heavy coat and thick goggles of a racer and the white kid gloves and gold cuff links of a gentleman in his parlor. He would be the fifth car in the time trial. "I want to give you a good race today," he told a competitor, and then, at 9:12 a.m., with his mechanic beside him, Elliott hit the gas. He left the starting line faster than any of the other cars, pushing the Mercedes to its top speed of sixty miles per hour. A quarter mile into the race, the road veered left. Elliott did not slow as he approached the turn as the other racers had. Far too late, he applied the brakes and tried to steer the car away from the rock face in front of him. When metal struck stone, the mechanic was thrown into the road. Elliott catapulted over the steering wheel and into the wall.

At the finish line, the first three cars arrived, one covering the distance in just fourteen minutes and twenty-six seconds. A fourth car had been stranded by a mechanical failure. And then nothing. Maggie had not worried as the minutes ticked by; her husband seemed invincible. It was a half an hour later when another car arrived. The driver of the sixth car in the race was Pierre de Caters, a friend to Maggie and Elliott. He drew Maggie away from the crowd of onlookers and told her there had been a terrible accident. He had witnessed Elliott's death. In the chapel where her husband's bloodied body lay, Maggie wept.

In his last days, Elliott had confided in a friend that he had once thrown himself into danger without thought, but now he worried for his wife and son should anything happen to him. The day before the fatal race, Elliott wrote out his will, leaving his property and fortune, estimated at well over $1 million all told, to Maggie and Louis. But the fear would not stop him from racing. It would not even slow him down. After his death, the newspapers called it the Zborowski curse—no man of the family would ever die in bed.

⁂

DIVORCE HAD KILLED Elliott. Of this, Bishop Hare was certain. Through the Lenten season of penitence and absolution, the bishop had been stewing on the consequences to "those who play fast and loose with marriage and its sacred obligations." Such repugnant behavior, he believed, "infects its perpetrators with a contagious poison which debases everything it touches."

The newspaper headlines in Sioux Falls of late affirmed this truth for Hare. First came the story of Alice Hull Burdick of Buffalo, New York. Alice had wed Edwin Burdick in 1886, and sometime after her tenth anniversary, she began a years-long affair with one Arthur Pennell, who was also married. When Edwin first discovered her infidelity, he forgave his wife, but when the relationship continued, he instituted divorce proceedings in New York. Alice admitted that she was glad she would soon be free of Edwin. Arthur planned to head to South Dakota and secure his own divorce so that he and Alice could marry. Now, Edwin, Arthur, and Arthur's wife, Carrie, were all dead, and Alice was on the stand at Edwin's inquest. Her husband had been shot on the divan in his own den; her lover, with his wife beside him, had driven his motor car over the edge of a quarry. It was "the devastating course of lustful sin," the bishop said.

A few days later, Hare read about an incident in New York City. This time, the parties had not been embroiled in a divorce—though perhaps a decree would have forestalled the tragedy. In the middle of the afternoon in an East Harlem apartment building, a jealous and mercurial husband grappled with his wife's former paramour. The wife wailed as her husband wrestled the unwelcome man down the stairs, and as he fled, the man fired his pistol over his shoulder, killing the husband. On hearing the news, the bishop was perhaps most appalled to realize that "the intruder," as Hare thought of him, was "reported to have a wife of his own and two children!"

Hare's dismay was sincere, but he also found the outrageous details useful to his cause. The people of South Dakota had grown blasé about divorce. In Sioux Falls, the colonists rarely provoked outrage anymore. Blanche Molineux's arrival had aroused the town's displeasure, and Hare had been briefly hopeful that the legislature would use the opportunity again to pass a stricter divorce law. He'd been agitating for a still-longer residency requirement since North Dakota had changed its laws in 1899. The effort had attracted little support. In 1903, despite assertions that Blanche's drama would be the "final straw," a bill to require one-year's stay didn't make it out of committee. Curbing divorce no longer had the moral urgency of the 1890s. It was just politics.

In Elliott's death, Bishop Hare saw the opportunity to change that. The day after the crash, he wrote a letter to the editor of the *Argus-Leader*. In it, he dwelled on the illicit love and violent deaths in Buffalo and hinted at the calamity that had occurred in France—and the one that had occurred, in the form of Maggie's divorce decree, in Sioux Falls in 1892. "We need to be shocked," the bishop demanded.

Sioux Falls was stunned just a few days later when news of Louise Ames Van Welk's death reached the city. Six weeks earlier, the thirty-seven-year-old woman had been the Baroness Wolfbauer, a resident for several months at the Cataract House. After receiving her divorce decree, she rechristened herself. Ames was Louise's maiden name; Welk, her first husband's surname; and the "Van," a flourish. Louise loved such adornments as anyone who remembered her elaborate dresses knew. She departed promptly for the East, reserving a suite at the Hotel Washington in Jersey City. And then, just after midnight, in the earliest hours of Sunday, April 5, 1903, Louise raised a pistol to her chest and shot herself through the heart.

Hare had known of the Ames family. Louise's grandfather had been Episcopal bishop Edward Raymond Ames, who, like Hare, spent much of his ministry on American Indian missions. In the days after Louise's death, Hare returned to his writing desk. His message needed to be heard beyond Sioux Falls. "Within the few days last past the daily newspapers have given us the details of several terrible moral catastrophes which have come upon persons who assaulted or trifled with the exclusiveness and sanctity of the marriage relation," he wrote in an open letter to his brethren throughout South Dakota. He detailed Elliott's sins and his demise. He rehashed Louise's transgressions and described "her stiffening corpse." Then he recounted a story he found to be "a greater catastrophe."

A woman had come to South Dakota with her husband and their daughter. The family seemed respectable and had been welcomed into the church. But it was revealed that they had come for a divorce. Husband and wife had mutually agreed to the separation—"with the understanding that after it was accomplished and his wife was married to another man, the first husband was to have the privilege of living with them!!" Living with divorce, it seemed, was a greater tragedy than death.

"I do not presume to be the clerk of the court of heaven, charged with recording the decision of the divine tribunal in any particular case," Bishop Hare avowed. "But certainly there is enough in the awful tragedies attending the horrible cases I have named to startle into activity consciences as inured to stories of divorces and violations of the marriage vow as perhaps ours in Sioux Falls may have come to be."

Chapter Seventeen

STUPID, UNJUST, MONSTROUS, AND FOOLISH

T HE STREET in front of the Cataract House was clogged with people. They stood shoulder to shoulder, pressing closer for a better
view or perhaps a little warmth. It was a cold and wet early Monday
morning in April 1903, and the only respite from the icy drizzle came
when it began to snow. The thousands thronging the intersection—and
the luckier few with suites overlooking the stage built there—were waiting for President Theodore Roosevelt.

Flora was not among the eager onlookers that day. She'd given up her
rooms at the Cataract after two expensive and disillusioning months. She
was now renting a home from a clergyman who had no problem profiting
from divorce seekers. (Flora reported that the woman who occupied the
house before her had "lived with her 'father'—and married him in seven
months!!") She described the family's new home as "a dear little cottage
just out of town." Her son, Johnny, was less charitable. To him, it was "a
bum house without a bathroom, nearly in the country." Flora was sorry
to miss the parties that heralded the president's appearance in Sioux Falls.
She had grown up with the extended Roosevelt clan, and her father and

sister, Grace, were friendly with TR. Any familiar face—except those among the divorce colonists, of course—cheered Flora, but she and the children had been laid low by spring colds, and Flora thought it would be unwise for them to venture out into the weather.

Planning for "Roosevelt Day" had begun weeks earlier when the president's two-month tour through the West was announced. The buildings along Phillips Avenue were festooned with bunting, and thousands of photographs of the president had been distributed to homes and businesses. Special trains—charging a third more than usual—had been arranged to ferry supporters in from north, south, east, and west. Some would make the trip from Sioux City, a full seventy-five miles away. Roosevelt buttons and badges were on sale at Simons' Book Store, and Caldwell's advertised sheet music for "Alice Roosevelt Waltzes," a musical ode to the First Daughter.

The president's itinerary through the city had been scheduled down to the minute, but things went awry even before Roosevelt stepped off the train the morning before. The engine had mistakenly headed for the Great Northern Depot, which had burnt to the ground the previous year. The welcoming committee waited at the Omaha Depot nearby while the train backed up and changed tracks. South Dakota's governor should have been among those greeting the president, but he had been delayed, leaving Senator Alfred Kittredge to take his seat in the first carriage with Roosevelt. The president requested there be no big event to mark his arrival. It was Palm Sunday. Still, supporters lined the streets of Sioux Falls to watch the caravan travel from the depot to the Cataract House, and when Roosevelt disembarked in his black suit, those gathered roared their approval. Roosevelt doffed his silk hat. That day he attended two church services—another scheduling mishap—though to Bishop Hare's displeasure, Roosevelt was not in the pews at St. Augusta.

Bishop Hare and Roosevelt had previously worked together on matters related to the region's reservations. As US Civil Service commissioner, Roosevelt toured South Dakota in the fall of 1892 and attended the Episcopal convocation on the Cheyenne River Reserve in the northwestern part of the state. At the time the bishop had impressed Roosevelt with his advocacy for better schools both on and off the reservations. Now, at Roosevelt's suggestion, Hare joined the presidential party for Sunday lunch at the Cataract. The bishop and Roosevelt walked arm in arm from the president's suite to the hotel dining room.

Roosevelt had not come to Sioux Falls to discuss the state of American marriage, but the issue of divorce had been on his mind. He'd once been accepting of its necessity. In 1891, he counseled his sister-in-law Anna to divorce his brother Elliott. Elliott was a drunkard. "I have no patience with allowing mere dread of scandal or Mrs. Grundy"—slang for a priggish gossip—"to make a person continue a life of degradation," he said. He was, then, resolved to do "as much as I can toward helping her to free herself if she wishes to." Anna did not divorce Elliott; instead the couple agreed to separate without involving the courts. (Both husband and wife died soon after.) Then, in 1895, Roosevelt, now New York City police commissioner, spent months advising his older sister, Bamie, on how to navigate the complicated legal concerns of marrying Will Cowles, a divorcee.

The laws of New York were "stupid and unjust," "monstrous and foolish," Roosevelt had told Bamie. He worried that the state would not recognize Will's divorce and that if Bamie and Will lived as husband and wife within its borders, they would be committing bigamy. Will had married his first wife, Mary, in Washington, DC, and Mary later sought a divorce in California on the grounds of neglect, a cause New York did not recognize. To avoid any trouble, Roosevelt even offered to pass a private bill of divorce for Will, a throwback to the earliest days of legislative release from a marriage. Bamie declined her brother's help. Bamie and Will married in London in 1895, and after a short residence in New York, the couple settled in Connecticut, where neglect was a recognized reason for divorce. (Despite the Roosevelts' concerns, it is unlikely Will would have found himself in any danger as his first wife had sought out the separation.)

Those same "stupid," "unjust," "monstrous," and "foolish" divorce laws drove many to Sioux Falls, but in recent years, the politician's views on the matter had shifted. Roosevelt had entered public life to safeguard "the spirit of public decency." Now he saw moral decay among his own social circle. He believed the upper class had a responsibility to model good behavior for the rest of the country. Instead, they threw lavish parties, gambled with abandon, and married—and divorced—for money, lust, and social status. It was a path to ruin, for American families and for the country. "If the homes are all straight," he believed, "the state will take care of itself."

It was his daughter, Alice, age nineteen, who seemed to have the most influence on these views, though it was quite unintentional. Alice talked freely about the marital tribulations of the family's acquaintances. In the newspapers, these stories were still a scandal, but they did not shock Alice. She accepted the idea that one could marry without the guarantee of a lifelong commitment—or even of children, another topic of much concern for TR. The president did not think that divorce should be outlawed, but he was nearing the conclusion that it was too easy to end a marriage. He had long been convinced that moral suasion would ensure the stability of the family, but in the story of the divorce colony, he could see the shortcomings of that approach. Despite Bishop Hare's best efforts, religious teachings had not stemmed demand for divorce in the city; nor had societal disapproval. At lunch that day at the Cataract House, Roosevelt found himself dining with the angel and devil—the roles assigned depending on one's point of view—of the city's divorce debate: Bishop Hare, ailing, but no less fierce in his commitment to rid Sioux Falls of the reincarnated colony, and Alfred Kittredge, celebrated divorce lawyer. There were no women at the table set for eleven.

Alfred Kittredge introduced the president as he took to the stage in front of the hotel that Monday morning. Famous as a man of few words,

Kittredge upheld that reputation. "Our President," he said, and then he ceded the floor. The president spoke at greater length about labor relations. To the rest of the country, Sioux Falls was synonymous with divorce, but in the city itself, the fate of farmers and factory workers was a far more pressing issue. Roosevelt's true message was one of weathering the "huge and complex problems of our modern industrial life," and he pondered when it was appropriate for the federal government to step in and reshape society for the better.

FLORA HAD NOT been invited to the card party that Mary Bailey organized at her home on Duluth Avenue one early spring day. She had stopped by the Baileys' unannounced that afternoon. In the months since she arrived in Sioux Falls, Flora had grown friendly with the family. C. O. Bailey was her lawyer. She thought the man "clever and interesting." His wife, Mary, was "charming, clever, and capable" in Flora's estimation, though not the equal of her husband as a conversationalist. The couple welcomed Flora and her children into their home, and she was grateful for the gesture. "The people here have very low opinions of the divorcees," Flora told her father. They "will not even rent their horses to them."

Mary confessed that Flora was only the second "Eastern resident" that her husband had allowed her to help. The first, who remained unnamed, was often drunk and had other unmentionable weaknesses. Mary, almost a decade older than Flora, helped Flora find a wash woman and walked with her to St. Augusta on Sundays, about fifteen minutes away. Mary also called at Flora's new cottage and encouraged the friendship between her thirteen-year-old son, Charlie, and nine-year-old Johnny. Her attorney warned Flora "not to have any friends among the 'deserted colony,'" so the Baileys had been almost the entirety of her social circle before that afternoon.

Six-handed euchre was the game of choice for Sioux Falls matrons in the spring of 1903. The competition was friendly. The women were partnered by a cut of the cards, and the stakes were always perfectly civilized: a dainty china syrup pitcher, a painted serving tray, a colorful deck of cards. The winner took home a prize, but so did the day's loser. The conversation, however, was not quite as proper. Tittle-tattle—the more outrageous, the better—was traded over the trump. Did you hear that the former Baroness Wolfbauer killed herself because the man she'd planned to marry after her divorce backed out of the engagement? "'Sioux Society' turns up their nose at New York," Flora complained to her father. "But they know everything that is going on there and everybody by name."

There must have been an empty seat at the card tables when Flora arrived to visit with Mary, because quite "by accident" she found herself in conversation with the very women who were likely to snub her in the Cataract dining room. "I never heard so many personal remarks and such gossip," Flora said. "They all attacked me on what they heard of me—it seems I am supposed to be engaged to Mr. Neily Vanderbilt!" It was a particularly shocking accusation, given that Neily—Cornelius Vanderbilt III—was already married.

Flora withstood the interrogation, and the unexpected introductions became her entrée into social life in the city. Soon after, her landlady took Flora to tea. "*Everybody* was presented to me, and everyone had to say goodbye very carefully and I forgot everybody's names," she later admitted. Flora was wary of her new acquaintances. She still thought Sioux Falls was "wild" and its people were "without any interests except money and gambling. Women, too." But Flora also knew their approval could give her something the courts could not: the respectability she wanted along with her divorce decree.

Flora set out to establish herself as a full-fledged resident of the city, an undertaking she took much more seriously than most eastern arrivals. Flora subscribed to the newspapers and to the church. She did not take personal offense at Bishop Hare's opposition to divorce, but perhaps that was because she could hardly understand him; a painful, malignant growth marring his face affected his speech. "Much of his strength was taken up in holding on to his false teeth," she wrote to her father of his sermons. She had not been impressed by her first visit to his All Saints School—"demoralizing," she thought—but ultimately enrolled Lucy there for the fall. She decided the regular routine of the boarding school would be good for her daughter.

Flora thought even less of the options for Johnny's education. "At the boy's school they learn nothing but toughness," she said. Johnny was a source of some despair for Flora. He had taken to swearing and gambling "because all the boys do." She persuaded C. O. Bailey to let her send her son back east to a boarding school in Massachusetts. Flora's lawyer had nixed every other plan she presented for leaving the city, but he agreed that Flora could accompany Johnny on the long train ride.

Flora's wanderlust was actually rooted in deep loneliness, something her tentative acceptance at Sioux Falls' card parties and afternoon teas could not alleviate. Her lawyer advised that she could have visitors—male or female, he allowed—but she didn't "see any stampede coming this way." Though her father had previously thought a trip west would be too expensive and tiring, John heard the sadness in Flora's letters. After a particularly distressed dispatch in July, he hastily made plans to visit his daughter accompanied by Flora's sister Annie. He was pleased to find that Flora and the children were in "perfect health as never before" but was not cheered by the legal analysis C. O. Bailey offered. After a long chat with the lawyer at his law office, John was convinced that "a divorce in Dakota does not amount to much if anyone has or ever comes to have an interest to contest it."

Throughout her stay in Sioux Falls, Flora had lived as cheaply as she felt a woman of her stature could; she had learned the skill when Charlie had proven—in her father's words—his "incompetence for the management of business of any kind." One of Flora's closest friends,

Daisy Leiter, had insisted on giving her $500 to help her make the trip. Daisy wanted to give her more, but Flora refused. She would not take the money her husband now sent either, and she chaffed at the idea of asking her father for funds, but C. O. Bailey urged Flora to buy property in the city as evidence of her residency. She scrimped the best she could, giving up the rental home after the children went to school and letting the servants go, except Delia, who was more family than employee. To save money, she and Delia boarded for a time with the Paultons, old family friends whom Flora was surprised to discover settled in Sioux Falls, but Flora finally asked her father for a loan of $3,656—to be repaid with interest, she insisted.

With the money, Flora bought a house on the outskirts of town, "almost on the prairies." It was "not a fashionable neighborhood," she admitted, "but respectable and quiet." The house, painted all white, had five bedrooms, a parlor, a dining room, a bathroom, and a kitchen with running water. Flora hung white muslin curtains and papered the parlor with a border of pink roses. She rented a piano and bought chickens for the coop. She named one of the roosters Mr. Bailey and the hen Carrie Nation, in honor of the divorced temperance activist. The house she called Wookiye Tipi. Flora originally bungled the spelling in the language of the Lakotas, but she intended her new home to be "the house of peace."

⚬◈◦

BY JULY 1903, Flora had gained legal residence in South Dakota. It took a few months longer for her to gain social acceptance, but by the time she settled into Wookiye Tipi in the last months of the year, she'd been embraced by those who had scorned so many divorce colonists before her. She went door to door with Mary Bailey taking the city census and hosted a concert at the penitentiary. Flora served as emcee for the event, introducing some of Sioux Falls' leading citizens and playing several catchy songs on her zither, a stringed instrument she had been practicing since childhood. She became a fixture of the local society column, attending dancing parties and hosting guests, among them Lady Rodney—herself a recent divorcee—and her brothers Henry and Lionel Guest. Flora had become friendly with the English family several years earlier, and the trio stopped in Sioux Falls en route to the Rockies, where they would spend several weeks hunting. "They made such a good impression on everyone in the town they had a hard time getting away!" Flora said.

"I have heaps of callers + a 'lady' told me yesterday that I was the *only* divorcee who had ever been *considered a resident* here, or had any social position," Flora reported in December. But still C. O. Bailey would not file her divorce papers. She had reconsidered her initial opinion of the man as the months ticked by. Flora still thought him a clever man, but she had revised her description to include "cautious and slow."

Divorce seekers had been flocking to Sioux Falls for more than a dozen years, but there was still no road map to ensure the legality of a decree. At first, the lawyer planned to initiate the proceedings in the summer, but as the warmer months passed, he told Flora that it would be legally advantageous to remain in the city through the autumn. He again intended to begin the process in October, until news broke of an impending engagement. Allegedly, Flora was to marry Joe Leiter, her friend Daisy's brother. Joe was a Chicago millionaire, known for his risky—and often successful—business gambles and his penchant for matchmaking. But at thirty-four, the "great introducer" had not yet found himself a bride. The newspapers admitted that the information that Chicago's most eligible bachelor would marry was reported on "dubious authority," but that did not keep them from repeating it. "Mrs. Dodge is just the sort of woman that Joe will wed," a friend confided to *Town Topics*. "The ordinary society girl does not interest him. He likes brilliant women."

C. O. Bailey was firm in his denial on behalf of his client. "There is absolutely no truth in the newspaper statements that Mrs. Dodge is engaged to Joe Leiter. She is not engaged to Mr. Leiter or to anyone else and has no matrimonial intentions," he announced. "No divorce proceedings have been instituted by her and none are pending or in immediate contemplation." The lawyer went further in his denial, claiming that it was "within the range of probabilities" that Flora would ask only for a limited divorce.

For his part, Joe responded to the talk with a "killing"—hilarious—"letter about the way he was congratulated for being engaged to me," Flora told her family. The two had been friends for years, and Flora was reasonably certain he had no designs on her. Joe told three different reporters that he was not planning to marry anyone, "but they said they couldn't deny it for the public would be *so* disappointed."

Flora suspected Mamie Fish was to blame for the imagined engagement. The fifty-year-old woman was second only to Lina Astor in her social stature, but where *the* Mrs. Astor was still hosting the exclusive formal balls Flora had attended as a newlywed, Mamie styled herself as the fun-maker of New York and Newport and declared the stuffy Four Hundred to be long dead. Her parties, frequented by the smart set, were never predictable. Mamie was just as likely to be dressed as a fairy queen as she was to promise to introduce her guests to a prince—who would turn out to be a monkey dressed in a tuxedo. She had a wry sense of humor and would have seen little harm in this obvious fiction about her neighbor; the Fishes and the Bigelows lived next door to one another on Gramercy Park. She probably should have known better, as Mamie's words often got her into some trouble, but this time it was Flora who found herself in a predicament.

C. O. Bailey's strong statement had been meant to placate Judge Joseph Jones, who would eventually be asked to rule on Flora's divorce. He didn't want anything to undermine the court's faith in Flora's residency. But Charlie Dodge must have heard a different message in the words of his wife's lawyer. After several months of silence, Charlie began to write to his wife again. Three letters and a box of candy arrived in

Sioux Falls in the two weeks after the statement. Charlie also went to visit his son at school in Massachusetts. Flora worried Johnny would be upset by the sudden appearance of his father. "I very much fear that Charlie is making trouble," she wrote to her father in January 1904, almost a year to the day after arriving in Sioux Falls. "The long delay may have made him think I was giving up divorce. He has that sunny hopeful disposition that often goes with useless people." She was still waiting to file divorce papers.

It did not seem to Flora that it should be this hard for her. When her brother, Poultney, and his wife, Edith, ended their marriage in 1903, there had been comparatively little press. Although his sisters thought him nervous about the separation, Poultney did not seem that way in public. Confronted by the news that his wife would seek a divorce, Poultney called the anticipated suit a "mere trifle." "Politics is my wife," he told reporters, steering conversation back to his writings on that subject. Edith had filed in New York on what the papers politely called "statutory grounds"—that is, she had accused Poultney of adultery but the evidence was not interesting enough to make headlines. The process had taken most of a year, but while the divorce was pending, Poultney had not been banished to a small western city. Instead he undertook a lecture tour through the United States and Europe. There was no question as to the validity of his decree, which was issued so quietly that news did not break for more than a month. It was true that Poultney could not legally remarry in New York, but that did not seem to bother him either. He felt no social or economic pressure to take a wife.

Flora's experience was entirely different. "I feel as if I were being buried alive under the endless prairies with the world throwing stones across my grave," Flora said. She imagined her husband's response to her plight. "And Charlie says with a smile, 'Dear little Wiffles, I advised her not to go to Dakota and have always tried to make her happy.'"

Chapter Eighteen

LIGHT IN THE SKY

E VEN THE old-timers were forced to admit that the first months of 1904 were harsh and unrelenting. The sun shone brightly on Sioux Falls that winter, but in January the temperature rarely reached the freezing mark, and for more than a week, the mercury never registered above zero. February brought little relief, with gales from the north and an average temperature in the single digits. Pneumonia took hold of the city, and each day brought news of another sufferer. Doctors advised pure air and sunlight to prevent the disease. The newspapers advertised celery seed, malt whiskey, cannabis, and cocaine. Flora wouldn't have approved of the latter, but she had no faith in the city's doctors either. One she had met was always drunk, and another was an opium fiend— "though a charming man." Even sober, they could not have helped Flora. Her constant, throbbing headaches, sudden chills, and short temper were not symptoms of pneumonia but evidence of the anxiety that came with prolonged waiting. Flora diagnosed herself and prescribed a strict regimen of "exercise and swearing" for "momentary relief."

Flora felt her anticipation keenly on the sunny and cold morning of Sunday, February 8. As usual, Flora went to church with the Baileys that day. The elderly Reverend J. H. Babcock, not Bishop Hare, was on the pulpit. It's hard to imagine that Flora concentrated on his sermon. C. O. Bailey had finally decided it was time to file Flora's divorce complaint, and she had been waiting for more than a week for the necessary paperwork to arrive from the family attorney in New York. After the service, Flora accompanied her lawyer to the post office nearby. To her relief, the package had arrived.

But her wait was not over; nor was her worry. Flora signed the papers in a deliberately legible script, charging her husband with desertion, and C. O. Bailey filed the suit, as was now the custom, far from Sioux Falls— in Salem, almost fifty miles northwest. Charlie would be served notice of the proceedings in New York, where he was still living. Flora needed her husband to file an appearance, or the delay would be even longer, but she still feared he would put up a fight. The sacrifices she had already made for her divorce weighed on Flora. She wrote to her son, again in school in Massachusetts, to tell him she could not come to hear him do his examinations. Her father had tried to cheer her up with examples of men who had withstood greater loneliness, but that wasn't what she needed. She wrote plaintively to him, "It seems a long time since I have hugged you." And yet, she wrote in the same letter, she was surprised to realize that "in spite of everything, I am happier than in past years."

Two more months passed before Flora's divorce came before the court. By horse, the journey to Salem took three hours, but Flora was too eager on the morning of Monday, April 11, to mind the dusty trip. She and Delia—her "rock"—waited another three hours in the "most awful" hotel parlor before Judge Joseph Jones was ready. It was almost 5 p.m. before C. O. Bailey ushered them into the courtroom. Flora's excitement gave way to fear as she took the stand and looked out at the gallery filled with men. Charlie had offered only a perfunctory denial of Flora's claims, but the judge still needed to question her. "I nearly fainted," Flora admitted, "but I got through somehow."

Judge Jones signed Flora's divorce decree there in the courtroom. "I wanted to hug him," Flora said. The judge did not share her excitement; divorces were routine. On the bench, he yawned. "I am not yet used to it all," she wrote to her father. "I watched the sunset across the endless bleak prairies as we crawled back—and there seemed in the distance a light in the sky which has not been very near before now."

IN THE DAYS after her trip to Salem, something happened that Flora, despite her efforts to become a part of Sioux Falls life, had never expected. As she walked through the city on her daily errands, she was stopped, more than once, by acquaintances who had something to say about her divorce: "Congratulations!" Callers came by; the telephone rang; letters and cables arrived. All expressed the same joy Flora felt. She was "much touched by the real kindness people seem to feel or profess." It all seemed too good to be true to Flora. Bishop Hare even crossed the room to greet her at a church reception. He did not congratulate her—he is "beloved but very bitter about the divorce question," Flora noted—but he did not snub the woman who had tried so hard to earn the respect of the community, and that felt like a victory. She rewarded his tolerance with a dozen fresh eggs the next day.

The divorce decree that had ended Flora's marriage and awarded her custody of Lucy and Johnny came with an unwritten caveat. Flora remained uncertain of her legal status outside South Dakota. She would not leave its borders immediately, and she did not foresee herself leaving forever, as divorce colonists before her had. She had made that decision a long time ago. Despite herself, she'd come to like her home in Sioux Falls, though she still worried about raising her children there, so far from the family and society she had known as a child. But Flora was also uncertain about her social standing outside the city. She felt compelled to go to

London, where she had felt at home during the unhappiest times in her marriage, just for a few weeks. I "want to hold my head up," she said.

The trip would be expensive. She was still paying off her house loan, and C. O. Bailey's $1,000 bill had not yet been settled. But Flora had been making a little money selling chickens and eggs and renting out a horse she had purchased. She'd struck a good deal with the furniture seller who would buy back some of her furnishings, and she thought she could rent out the house for $40 a month. Her bigger worry was the reception she'd receive in the English capital. To be snubbed by strangers as she had been her first months in Sioux Falls was a pinprick compared to the pain that would come with being spurned by ladies and gentlemen she'd known her whole life.

Flora went to London that summer with Lucy and Johnny by her side. At fourteen, her daughter was nearly a debutante, but it was Flora who felt on the verge of entering society. Married at seventeen, Flora had never had that experience. "My divorce debut," she called the trip. At first, Flora was shy and coltish, but she needn't have been. Her rented rooms were soon filled with flowers from friends, and hardly a meal was unspoken for. She dined with lords and ladies and dukes and duchesses, and her confidence in her social acumen restored, Flora called on May Dodge, who was Charlie's aunt, and Edith Jaffrey, her former sister-in-law. She took long walks through the gardens, attended the opera, and went yachting, but she still awoke early every morning thinking she had to feed her chickens.

After nearly three months' absence from Sioux Falls—during which Flora also visited her father at The Squirrels and Johnny and Lucy spent time with Charlie—the family returned home. "People could hardly believe their eyes!" Flora said. John didn't stay long; he was expected back at the Fay School in Boston. Lucy continued her studies at All Saints, and Flora immersed herself in the city's affairs. She was a regular at the Epiphany Guild, a weekly gathering of churchwomen, who met "to sew and abuse their neighbors." ("I skip it once in a while so they have a chance at me!") And she made an appearance at the men's socialist club, where she spoke on the topic of equality to boisterous applause. Her biggest undertaking, however, was to be a charity concert. The rectory at St. Augusta needed a new furnace.

Flora convinced the manager of the New Theater to donate the space and sweet-talked a local printer into producing programs. Tickets were fifty cents apiece and available at some of Sioux Falls' better retailers, or they could be bought from Flora herself. For several days before the show, she hawked them on the street from 8:30 a.m. until dark. Some doubted Flora could raise the $255 necessary to make the improvements at St. Augusta, but she was determined. She sold the boxes for "a fancy price," and the theater was packed when the curtain rose on the evening of October 5, 1904. Flora played the zither, and nearly a dozen other Sioux Falls ladies sang in the program. After the show, Flora was the guest of honor at a dinner at the Cataract House. The event raised far more than was needed for the furnace, and the church accepted the gift with gratitude.

⁕

BISHOP HARE SAW death approaching. The sixty-six-year-old man was in near-constant pain caused by the cancerous growth on his face, which had become more pronounced since Flora first noted his garbled speech more than a year earlier. It now threatened the vision in his right eye. The bishop's heart condition had not improved either. After being stricken in 1895, he had never regained the energy that once earned him the nickname "Zitkano Duzahan"—"swift bird"—and he fell seriously ill again in March 1904. He went east for treatment more willingly this time. He tried to reassure his brethren in South Dakota that the affliction was a temporary one, but he also wrote to the presiding bishop to discuss his resignation. The bishop asked him to delay, certain Hare's "days of self-denying heroism are not over."

When Bishop Hare returned to Sioux Falls months later, it was, he said, not as "a well man, but as a convalescent." He had come to put his affairs in order. He wished to ensure the continuation of the missionary efforts and the schools to which he had dedicated his life. "I cannot keep up the struggle," Hare had acknowledged to a friend that spring. Now, in the fall of 1904, he admitted it publicly in his annual address. "The work in South Dakota has reached proportions which put its proper oversight and direction quite beyond my strength," he said.

His illness, did not, however, weaken his rhetoric. Hare used his written address to again denounce divorce to his brethren. He spoke of the colony as if it were the cancer eating away at him: it was a "disease"—and Hare sought yet another remedy. A dozen years earlier, dismayed with the inability of religious edict to sway divorce seekers to abandon their quests, Hare had turned to the legislature, but South Dakota's stricter laws had not had the effect Hare desired, and his efforts to make the laws even more stringent had faltered. The courts had long failed him too. He despaired at the alacrity with which South Dakota judges continued to dispense decrees, and though he still professed the belief that the US Supreme Court's decision to nullify Charles Andrews's 1892 divorce would invalidate all decrees awarded to the divorce colony, it had had no noticeable effect in the nine months since the opinion had been handed down. So Hare returned to his fellow clergy. He needed their help.

South Dakota's ministers must teach young people the "reverent and right view of marriage as constituting a sacred and indissoluble bond," Bishop Hare argued, for "insuring health is more important than curing disease." But religious leaders also had more powerful tools of persuasion at hand. The Episcopal Church already had restrictions on remarriage: the innocent party in a divorce granted for adultery or a divorced couple intent on reuniting could rewed; all others could not be married in the eyes of the church until the former spouse had died. But Hare thought even this narrow exception was too generous. It seemed too easy to him for a sympathetic divorcee to convince a minister that her former husband had committed the sin of adultery but that she had sought a divorce for another offense to avoid embarrassment. And, Hare pointed out, the courts only examined the alleged wrongdoing. A divorce decree awarded to a wife on grounds of adultery was a declaration of her husband's guilt, but it was not evidence of her innocence. The clergy "should by no means think that they are helpless to discourage the divorce evil," Hare said, reminding them they could withhold the rites of holy matrimony. "Do not solemnize the marriage of any person whatsoever who has a husband or wife still living," he exhorted.

Bishop Hare hoped to find allies for this plan in Boston, where the Episcopal Church was holding its annual general convention. Travel was difficult for Hare, but he had missed only one of these meetings in his life in the church—when he was ill in 1895—and he was determined to attend. The general convention would be debating the canons on marriage and divorce.

This was far from the first time the body had considered rewriting the canon on divorce—Hare had himself been advocating for change for nearly a decade—but revising canons was always a slow process. Those who feared for the sanctity of marriage believed that this would be the year they succeeded in their endeavor. For hours over four days in October 1904, the Episcopal House of Deputies, a body made up of elected clergy and lay people, debated the question of remarriage after divorce in the nave of Emmanuel Church on Newbury Street. The pews not occupied by the deputies were filled with spectators, who did not hesitate to applaud an impassioned argument or laugh at a burst of wit or when the gavel came down sharply on the man who could not limit his opinions to just ten minutes. Among the speakers, many, like Hare, believed in denying the sacrament to all who separated from their spouses. "There is no way the church can have so much influence as by closing the prayerbooks to the divorcee," declared a representative from Pennsylvania. Others advocated for the status quo, worried that eliminating the exception for those wronged by an adulterous partner or those who sought reconciliation would violate scripture. The words of Matthew, Mark, and Luke rang out.

But a few among the deputies—lay people all—begged for practicality. "It is easy to pass canons and make rules," one from the Territory of

New Mexico cautioned, "but what is needed is the consideration of the concrete example of saddened human nature. Shall a woman, who has been betrayed by a false husband and left poor and possibly with a child, be forbidden to marry a noble man who comes into her life and who offers to care for her and to do what he can to make her happy, be refused the service of the church?" For another, from Louisiana, "The strongest argument made in favor of the proposed canon is that it will stop the evil." But this man planned to vote nay "because I feel sure that it will not stop it."

Perhaps owing to his illness, Bishop Hare did not make himself heard publicly on the issue in Boston. His contribution to the convention was a report on his missionary work among the Sioux and a plea for a bishop to be sent to assist him; in this matter, the general convention obliged. On the question of divorce, the conclusion it reached was not as satisfactory.

The new canon enacted by the church should have been a victory for Hare and those who shared his goals. It put the church "out of the divorce business," explained one such minister. The new rules made it more difficult for even the wronged spouse who obtained a divorce for adultery to remarry, establishing a one-year waiting period between the end of one marriage and the start of the next and requiring that the legal decree, along with evidence of the facts of the case, be evaluated by the minister. Even presented with these documents, any minister could, at his discretion, decline to bless a second marriage. But the new canon was still not as far-reaching as Hare had hoped, and the process of adopting it had been a messy public one. Even religious leaders would not take the most drastic measures to curb divorce; even the church had to compromise.

⌘

IN THE THIRTEEN YEARS between Maggie Zborowski's arrival at the Cataract House and Flora's divorce debut, the question of who could end a marriage had made its way from the pews of St. Augusta to the Episcopal general convention. There had been heated debates over access to divorce on the floor of the South Dakota legislature and in the committee rooms of the United States Congress. Judges from Sioux Falls to the US Supreme Court had ruled repeatedly—and often contradictorily—on the issue. By early 1905, another major decision on divorce and domicile, *Haddock v. Haddock*, awaited the country's highest court, and President Theodore Roosevelt could no longer avoid the matter.

The divorce question had bedeviled the president since his visit to Sioux Falls almost two years earlier. That was Colonel James Jewell's fault. James was a relative of former president Grover Cleveland and had been appointed to the US Board of General Appraisers by Cleveland's successor, Benjamin Harrison. The board reviewed the value of imported goods and the minutia of tariff laws. Their decisions were often controversial, but when they made news, the subject was typically the proper classification of silk ribbons or the duty on the brine needed to preserve herring and mackerel. James, however, ended up in the headlines after he abandoned his wife, Caroline, and their son. Caroline might have let him leave without a fuss, but when James failed to pay the family's bills and the house was on the verge of foreclosure, she took him to court in New York. "It is merely a marital disagreement," James's lawyer said, but the dispute quickly made its way to the West Wing.

Speculation that Roosevelt would demand James's resignation or simply fire the absent husband only increased when James sued his wife for divorce in the summer of 1903, charging her with adultery. Caroline fired back with accusations that he had wooed one of their household servants. The president asked the attorney general if he should wait for the court to determine guilt in the divorce proceedings, but he had already selected James's replacement. "I feel that Mr. Jewell's usefulness in the department is at an end," TR wrote to a confidant. Roosevelt was particularly angered by James's cavalier attitude toward his marriage. He had traveled frequently, and publicly, with the woman he was accused of having an affair with, claiming her to be his nurse. "If he is so much of an invalid that it is necessary," the president grumbled sarcastically, "I do not think he is in fit physical condition to hold his present office." By the fall, James was relieved of his government duties.

The Jewell case was still winding its way through the courts when President Roosevelt decided to take a stronger stand on divorce. He invited the committee of the Inter-Church Conference on Marriage and Divorce—representatives of Protestant denominations—to the White House on the afternoon of January 26, 1905, to announce his intentions. The matters that typically held a president's attention were, he told those gathered, of "importance, but a wholly ephemeral importance." "Questions like the tariff and the currency are literally of no consequence whatsoever, compared with the vital question of having the unit of our social life, the home, preserved," TR said. "If we have solved every other problem in the wisest possible way, it shall profit us nothing if we have lost our own national soul."

In his remarks to the Inter-Church Conference, the president professed that he did not know how to assist the men in their crusade, but a few days later, TR instructed Congress to again compile data on the country's marriages and divorces, a follow-up to the 1889 report that had sparked the initial panic. "Divorce laws are dangerously lax and indifferently administered in some of the states," he wrote. The statistics would help states enact uniform divorce laws "containing all possible safeguards for the security of the family."

Privately, TR wasn't against divorce entirely. "It is mere foolishness" for a woman "who has been deeply wronged to refuse to get a divorce and marry again," he wrote to the author Robert Grant, whose latest novel, *The Undercurrent*, told the story of just such a woman. But "it is another thing to do as 'the Four Hundred' does and show an atavistic return to the system of promiscuity." TR had had enough of what he called "easy divorces" and bemoaned hearing young girls who were about to marry "calmly speculating on about how long it will be before they get divorces."

Publicly, though, the president berated all women who "deliberately forego" the blessings of family. "The existence of women of this type forms one of the most unpleasant and unwholesome features of modern life," he told the National Congress of Mothers, an organization that advocated for traditional roles for women in the face of the rapid societal changes of the turn of the century. More than three thousand people had packed into the Metropolitan M. E. Church in Washington, DC, on the evening of March 13, 1905, to hear the president praise "the woman who is a good wife, a good mother." She is "entitled to our respect as is no one else, but she is entitled to it only because, and so long as, she is worthy of it," he told the approving crowd. That not all are so worthy, he continued, is made evident "by the census statistics as to divorce, which are fairly appalling; for easy divorce is now, as it ever has been, a bane to any nation, a curse to society, a menace to the home, an incitement to married unhappiness and to immorality, an evil thing for men and a still more hideous evil for women."

Chapter Nineteen

HEART

"I AM SO MUCH HAPPIER, Papa, and I feel more each day the wisdom of the step I have taken," Flora had written to her father in November 1904. Freedom suited Flora. She spent the winter months traveling, visiting New York, Boston, Washington, DC, London, and Montreal, and she returned to Sioux Falls with the spring. It had been a year since the judge had signed her decree, and Flora still saw that light in the sky. She worried about money, her children's education, and her family's health, but she had risked everything to chase happiness, and she had caught it.

The long and lonely wait for a divorce and the joy Flora found when she accomplished her mission in South Dakota seemed to soften her toward other women seeking the same escape. At first Flora had refused to count herself among the divorce colonists or associate with them, but she made an exception to lunch with Blanche Scott, and when Flora had traveled to London in the summer of 1904, she rented her house to a divorce seeker. Wookiye Tipi had been a haven for Flora as she waited out the final days of her marriage. Now it would be refuge for others in the same predicament. Just before she left for the winter of 1904, Flora again rented the house to an unhappy wife, one Ethel Coles.

Twenty-three-year-old Ethel had traveled from her home in Somerset, England, for a divorce from her husband, Henry. In an English court, Ethel accused the man she married in 1899 of violent abuse. He had struck her repeatedly and tried to strangle her, she said. He had even threatened the life of their infant son. It was unsafe to continue to live with him, she told the court. The allegations of adultery she also leveled were almost an afterthought. But the English court system moved slowly. Sioux Falls' "easy divorces" had beckoned.

An ocean away from the husband she feared, Ethel charged Henry with the lesser crimes of desertion and nonsupport. Such an ordinary petition would attract little attention from the press, and the outcome was the same. Just before Flora's return in May 1905, Ethel received her decree, and two weeks later, Flora, Lucy, and Delia looked on as Ethel wed Walter Phelps Dodge. Flora and Ethel had been strangers when Walter wrote to Flora and asked her to look after the Englishwoman who had recently arrived in Sioux Falls, but now they would be family, of sorts. Walter was a cousin of Flora's ex-husband and an uncle to her children.

The next resident of Wookiye Tipi was to be Annie M. Stewart, a friend of Flora's. The wife of William Rhinelander Stewart, Annie was a doyenne of New York society, but her husband had little interest in entertaining; as with Flora and Charlie, there was speculation that difference in temperament had caused the couple's split. Annie tried to obscure her reasons for traveling to Sioux Falls—something fewer divorce colonists bothered with these days—but her thirty-five trunks gave away her true intentions. Annie had plans to renovate Flora's home to better accommodate all her belongings. But first, the "house of peace" would serve as a backdrop for a celebration: Flora was getting married.

FLORA AWOKE BEFORE dawn on the morning of July 4, 1905. She blamed her inability to sleep on her neighbors, who had been up since the night before celebrating Independence Day, but it may have been nerves. Lionel—Flora's beloved fiancé—would arrive by train in just a few hours.

Flora's engagement to the Honorable Lionel George William Guest, the fourth son of Lord and Lady Wimborne and first cousin of Winston Churchill, had been announced, in proper fashion, six weeks earlier in the *Times. Town Topics*, which had delighted in skewering a decade's worth of South Dakota divorcees, heartily approved of this match and predicted that Flora's would be "the quaintest"—most out of the ordinary—"wedding the Dakotas ever knew."

Her marriage would be as "legal and dignified" as her divorce. To ensure its legality, her lawyers insisted on some unusual wedding preparations. Flora wrote a lengthy statement documenting her first marriage and collected all the receipts she could find from her time in Sioux Falls as evidence of her residency. The package was sealed, to be opened only if her divorce faced legal trouble; otherwise, it was to be burned upon her death. Meanwhile, the press helped to ensure the union was deemed dignified, spinning a romantic tale of the moment that Lionel fell in love with Flora.

Although Flora had known the Guest family for a decade, Lionel had "first conceived of his fascination for this brilliant American woman" just six months earlier in the grand music room of the Leiter mansion in Washington, DC, the *Washington Times* reported. Flora's dear friend Daisy Leiter had been preparing to marry Henry Howard, Earl of Suffolk and Berkshire. Flora chaperoned the couple in New York in the weeks leading up to their December 1904 wedding and took charge of the flowers for the small affair. She festooned the mansion with white blossoms and delicate green foliage. Lionel was to be Henry's best man, and Joe Leiter, Daisy's brother, would give the bride away to her groom. Joe, whose name had long been linked with Flora's, was still often asked if the two were involved, but those watching closely saw Lionel's attentiveness to the divorcee and wondered if there would be a double wedding in the mansion on Dupont Circle that Christmas.

No one in Sioux Falls was surprised to see Flora's name linked with Lionel's. Lionel had come to visit her—appropriately accompanied by his sister and brother—in the city in 1903, and all seemed to approve of the tall, slender young man with light hair and blue eyes. Though he was only twenty-four, twelve years Flora's junior, he had established himself as a successful civil engineer in Montreal and had recently organized Canada's first appraisal company. More importantly, he and his bride-to-be had been suitably patient. "Many 'colonists' walk from the divorce courts to the remarriage altar with scarcely an hour's interval between being relieved of former matrimonial bonds and assuming new ones," the *Argus-Leader* wrote. In waiting a year, Flora had "established a new precedent," one the city celebrated.

Would Sioux Falls have embraced the couple if anyone had known their association went back much further? Lionel had been a frequent companion of Flora's for at least five years and had been steadfast throughout the dissolution of her marriage. She had quickly come to rely on him. He was a friendly face when she ventured alone into unfamiliar drawing rooms, her husband happier to remain at home. He was her confidant and her editor. She already thought of him as family, and she confessed that she slept better when he was visiting. His support had given her the strength to imagine life after her divorce.

That intimacy would likely have drawn disapproval in South Dakota. But it was, for Flora, the very reason she was willing to marry again. At age seventeen, she'd fallen for Charlie in a sudden rush of emotion. It had taken her parents' pleading to delay the wedding by mere months. But at age thirty-six, Flora seemed to recall her father's decades-old caution that affection could quickly wear away. Lionel had wooed Flora with his constancy. He was a man who "loves me enough to work for me." "I am convinced that the love grown from a friendship highly tested is a safe marriage," she told her father.

Flora's only regret would be leaving Sioux Falls. "I will always love it and never forget my happiness here," she wrote to her father in the early dawn light the morning Lionel was to arrive. The wedding was just two days away, and Flora's cottage was filled with wedding gifts. Emily Hammond—a Vanderbilt—had sent amethyst studs and cuff links for the groom, and Annie Stewart had found room in her traveling trunks for two evening petticoats for the bride. Joe Leiter shipped a solid silver coffee set, and his sister Nannie picked out a silver candelabra. The Baileys gave the couple a mantle clock. Crafted from South Dakota's petrified wood, it would be a memento of the city for Flora. Hours after her wedding, she would leave for her new home on a small island near Montreal.

If Flora and Lionel had married in New York or London, there would have been a long church aisle, a booming organ playing the wedding march, and a crush of guests. In Sioux Falls, there was only Flora's parlor, filled with flowers—the gossamer petals of pastel snap peas, the wide-open blooms of pale pink wild roses, and the crimson ruffles of American Beauties, the "million-dollar rose"—and Flora's closest friends. The guest list was limited to Annie Stewart, Joe Leiter, the Baileys, the Paultons, Alfred Kittredge, and a few of Lucy and Johnny's companions, among them the teenage son of the *Argus-Leader* editor. Flora had asked her father, now eighty-seven, not to make the difficult trip west. He sent his blessing. At noon on Thursday, July 6, 1905, Flora, in a white chiffon gown painted with apple blossoms, and Lionel, in a frock coat and high hat, stood before a Presbyterian minister, who uttered a few simple words. Then wife and husband kissed.

It had been a long journey to that blissful moment, but Flora thought it had been a necessary one. "Were I a younger woman," she said of Lionel, "I could not appreciate him."

⤙❦⤚

OUTSIDE THE OPEN window, Flora could hear the cheering of thousands of people. Maybe it was millions of people, she thought. John Bigelow's daughter was no stranger to the pageantry of royalty, but she was surprised to find herself in the Queen's Drawing Room at Buckingham Palace on this gray February 1906 day, watching for King Edward VII's procession from the ceremonial opening of Parliament. Since Flora and Lionel had arrived in London a week earlier, they had been inundated with invitations. Today, they'd received two dueling requests. William Onslow had asked them to sit with him in the House of Lords for Edward's speech. But the couple instead chose to join Horace Faquhar and Alice Kepple—the king's confidant and the king's mistress—to observe the goings-on from the palace. The only place in London that Flora and Lionel were not welcome, it seemed, was among her new in-laws, the Guests.

Flora was awestruck the first time she met the family in 1896. Friends had invited Flora and Charlie to a ball the Guests were hosting at their home. "I never imagined anything so wonderful," she told her father at the time. ("Charlie's impressions of the ball were not as enthusiastic as mine," she added.) She remembered being embarrassed when, overwhelmed by her surroundings, she had forgotten to address the host by his noble title. Ivor Bertie Guest was the family patriarch, a Welsh industrialist who had been elevated to the peerage as Baron Wimborne. His wife, Lady Wimborne, was Cornelia Spencer-Churchill, Winston's doting aunt and mother to the nine Guest children. Flora had been friendly with Ivor, the eldest son, for several years before she met Lionel, and the family had embraced her on her earlier visits to England and theirs to America. But there had always been something a little uncouth about the Guest clan.

Baron Wimborne was considered by many to be a snob and a ceaseless social climber, dismissed as "the paying Guest." Ivor was considered to be far worse. Ivor was a good friend to Churchill, but Winston's wife, Clementine, did not like the man, and behind his back he was called a bounder and a cad. By 1906, Flora would not have been even that kind. Any fondness she once had for Lionel's brother had given way to disgust after a fiery dispute between the two in the months after her divorce. Flora was characteristically discrete about the details of the disagreement, but she could not forgive him for—in her words—behaving "like a rotten coward"; nor could she be persuaded to apologize for her harsh response. The animosity between Flora and Ivor caused a rift in the family that had not yet fully healed. Lionel had been quick to side with Flora, but his parents had allied with Ivor.

It was this squabble—and not propriety—that had been the true cause of the yearlong delay between Flora's divorce and her wedding. She had accepted Lionel's marriage proposal in early 1905, but Lord and Lady Wimborne withheld their blessing. Though Flora's marital status had not been an issue before her trouble with Ivor, afterward Lady Wimborne accused Flora of using her younger son. Maybe Flora had never cared for Lionel at all. Maybe she only wanted his social backing. And no wonder: a divorced woman should not be able to hold her head up in English society without such distinguished support, Lady Wimborne declared. The Guests eventually gave their grudging permission for Lionel to wed, but in shunning the couple on their first visit to England as newlyweds, they made clear what they thought about having this divorcee as a daughter-in-law.

It was a bit of a shock to be thrust back into a debate over her first marriage. Flora's divorce seemed to be in the past. The newlyweds had settled happily into their home in Quebec, where Flora's arrival merited a letter of greeting from the Canadian prime minister and an invitation to stay at Government House as the guests of the governor-general and his wife. Final issues over the custody of the children had been settled, with Charlie agreeing to pay support. Johnny was still enrolled at the Fay School, where he had been chosen as captain of the eleventh-grade football team, and Lucy was attending Royal Victoria College. ("We are free just like men!" Lucy exclaimed to her grandfather.) Flora's father and her sister, Grace, had visited the family in Quebec, and Flora and Lionel had visited them in New York before sailing to London. Just before the couple departed, Flora was granted the only approval of her life choices she still desired. She wrote to her father of a "wonderful dream about mama." In her sleep Flora had found a large paper box with her mother's ashes inside. When she opened it, she saw dust and the edges of an Indian shawl. Then the specter of her mother rose up and hugged Flora. As Flora cried, her mother told her, "I wanted to put my arms around you and feel your happiness, Flora, and tell you I rejoice in yours and Lionel's happiness."

The roar of the crowd signaled the king's return. From the second-floor window, Flora had an unparalleled view of the parade as it crossed the palace grounds. The king rode in the ornate final carriage, pulled by eight cream-colored horses. It was a moving sight, Flora thought, and the day was not yet over. Horace toured the couple through the palace's galleries and then delivered a surprising request: King Edward wished to meet them.

Lionel had been introduced to the monarch once before, when he was just a child. Before Bertie—as he was then known—assumed the throne, he had visited Canford, the Guest family estate in Dorset. Flora could think of only one reason the king would ask to see them now. He was choosing sides in the family feud. "He has heard of the row Lionel has had with his family and feels the injustice done to me," she thought.

Flora and Lionel descended to the entrance hall where King Edward waited in his regalia. Flora, dressed in black in mourning for Lionel's aunt, who had recently passed away, made a deep curtsey. Lionel made a joke. "Have I not done well to bring you another American subject?" he asked the king. Edward laughed, and though he had been forced to lean heavily on his cane to move about that day, he stood chatting with the couple for several minutes. Flora later wrote to her friends in Sioux Falls and to her father about the exchange. "None of his pictures do him justice," she said. "One must see him speak to appreciate his heart and real kindness."

That brief conversation had been a gift to the divorcee and her new husband. "This is a hint which Lord and Lady Wimborne cannot fail to take," wrote the Associated Press. "It is certain that when Mr. and Mrs. Lionel Guest again visit England, no matter what the new divorce laws may be, they will be received in a very different manner."

A RISING OF IDEALS

Minnehaha County Courthouse, circa 1900.

A S IT DID EVERY MORNING, the Illinois Central from Chicago arrived in Sioux Falls at about 9:45 a.m. Passengers spilled out onto the station's narrow platform, greeted by the surprising warmth of a spring heat wave. On this morning in May 1906—as Sioux Falls had come to expect—there was a well-known lady in the crowd: Mrs. James G. Blaine Jr. had again come to South Dakota. She made her way to the

Cataract House and booked a suite of four rooms for a six-month stay. It had been fifteen years, almost to the day, since Mary had made this trek. Now Martha, Jamie Blaine's second wife, followed in her footsteps.

Martha Hichborn married Jamie in June 1901. But by 1904, before her third anniversary, Martha had left her husband and returned to her parents' home in Washington, DC. Though she did not fault Jamie's mother for the separation—Harriet had died in 1903—Martha's story of marital woe sounded much like Mary's. In the years after his first divorce, Jamie continued to bounce between professions. He tried law and then journalism again and then joined the military, appointed by President William McKinley as an assistant adjutant general. Despite two stays at the Keeley Institute, which guaranteed to cure the afflicted of a craving for alcohol through regular injections of gold, Jamie was still drinking, and when he drank, he fought. Not long after he was nearly involved in a duel in San Francisco in the summer of 1898, he was discharged from his four-month career in the army. His next stint, as a stockbroker, was no more successful. By the time of his mother's death, Jamie was in debt to her for more than $40,000.

Despite his very public shortcomings, Jamie had been linked to at least three different women before he wooed Martha, all hailing from prominent families, but each relationship fizzled before it reached the altar. Martha's father, Rear Admiral Philip Hichborn, had hoped for the same outcome for his daughter. But Martha was a tolerant and forgiving soul, right up until the moment her alcohol-addled husband punched her dinner companion at Delmonico's on Fifth Avenue in 1904. If there was any surprise at all in Martha's trip to South Dakota, it was that she waited two more years to make the couple's separation official.

When Martha finally joined the divorce colony, the newspapermen hoped for a feud between the first Mrs. Blaine and the second. A rumor circulated that instead of seeking her own divorce, Martha intended to challenge Mary's, a legal maneuver the US Supreme Court seemed to invite with its most recent decision on the subject. *Haddock v. Haddock* pitted

Harriet Haddock against her husband, John. In 1881, John had moved from the home he shared with his wife in New York to seek a divorce in Connecticut. The court found that John had properly established a domicile in his new state and fell under the jurisdiction of its courts—unlike the finding in the *Andrews* case—but that, nonetheless, New York was not obligated to give full faith and credit to the Connecticut decree because the Connecticut court did not also have jurisdiction over Harriet. The baffling result of the case was a couple who was simultaneously married in New York and divorced in Connecticut. Writing in dissent, Justice Oliver Wendell Holmes worried the decision was "likely to cause considerable disaster to innocent persons." Under the ruling, Mary's divorce from Jamie Blaine might be void, the newspapers opined, in which case his second marriage would be nullified and Martha would be free.

Mary declined to comment on the furor. She had left Sioux Falls behind in 1892 and never looked back. With William Bull, she found the stable society life she might have expected when she married into the Blaine family. The Bulls had money and social standing. Mary had become a leading hostess in Newport, entertaining at Dudley Place, the historic mansion with wide, sloping lawns gifted to the couple by William's father. She was now a mother of two: Jamie III, eighteen, who had inherited his mother's love for the stage and his father's rakish looks, and William Tillinghast Bull Jr., eleven. In Mary's place, her husband issued a statement to the press, defending Mary's divorce and attacking Martha for causing a stir. The couple wanted nothing to do with the proceedings. "Mrs. Bull and myself are content with life now and I am glad to say that Mrs. Bull seems happy with her second matrimonial venture," William said.

Despite reports to the contrary, Martha planned to get her divorce in the usual way. In most respects, Martha's time among the colonists would have been as familiar to Mary as her marriage to Jamie was. At the Cataract House, Martha found herself in society-column company, which included millionaire Alfred Dupont, of the Wilmington Duponts. As was the case in 1892, a legal threat—the repercussions of *Haddock*—loomed over each decree. In Philadelphia, the National Congress on Uniform Divorce Laws convened in an effort to abolish migratory divorce. And the issue of marriage and its end was again the subject of a proposed constitutional amendment. This time the push came from President Theodore Roosevelt himself, in his annual message to Congress in December 1906. "At present the wide differences in the laws of the different States on this subject result in scandals and abuses; and surely there is nothing so vitally essential to the welfare of the nation, nothing around which the nation should so bend itself to throw every safeguard, as the home life of the average citizen," the president warned.

But unlike earlier divorce colonists, Martha had no fear of these threats. Those who had come before her had proven that a woman could get a divorce. She did not have to relinquish her reputation or her future prospects to rid herself of a husband she did not love. A divorcee could find a place in society, a religious community that would accept her, and at least a reasonable degree of legal certainty in her independence. (The colony, having already weathered the *Andrews* decision and other court challenges, hardly paused to acknowledge the ruling in *Haddock*.)

Martha had undertaken her trip to Sioux Falls with little fanfare. At twenty-four, she had entered into a bad marriage—her friends described it simply as "Martha's bad luck"—and at twenty-nine, she would remedy that mistake. There was no commotion when she told the *Washington Post* of her plans even before she left for South Dakota. "I leave Washington for Sioux Falls where I will remain till I obtain my decree," she acknowledged. "I am very anxious to spend as short a while in the west as possible," she told another paper.

And she did. Three days before Christmas 1906—seven months and one week after Martha had arrived—her case came before a judge in Yankton. A snowstorm had delayed the hearing, and it was after 7 p.m. on a Saturday when Martha began to tell the story of her marriage in Judge Ellison Smith's chambers. She spoke for just a few minutes, charging her husband with nonsupport, cruelty, and desertion—though she had left him—before her lawyer asked if the judge had heard enough. He had. He granted the decree immediately.

A carriage waited outside the courthouse for Martha—once again Miss Hichborn. It sped to the train station a half mile away, and Martha boarded just before the conductor's final call. She hoped to be with her parents in Washington in time for Christmas dinner but missed the meal by two hours. Nevertheless, Martha's mother, Jennie, overjoyed by her daughter's release, thought it "the first Christmas I have had for years."

MARTHA HICHBORN REPRESENTED everything Bishop Hare had reviled about the divorce colony since Maggie married Elliott Zborowski in 1892. Martha had taken advantage of South Dakota's laws, coming to the state for the sole purpose of a divorce. She had charged her husband with offenses Hare did not believe violated the marital vows. She sought—and received—the speediest end to her marriage the state would allow. And she had done so, without shame or consequence, for the purpose of committing "consecutive polygamy."

Less than three weeks after her return to the East, Martha married Paul Pearsall, a well-to-do New Yorker who had been a lieutenant in Teddy Roosevelt's Rough Riders during the Spanish-American War. The ceremony was a small one, attended by the couple's families and a few friends, but it took place under a canopy of palms and roses at the Bellevue-Stratford Hotel, one of Philadelphia's best addresses. The bride—long known as Washington's "heliotrope belle" for the color she dressed in to stand out in a crowded ballroom—wore a hat of soft brown chiffon velvet adorned with striking plumes in her unmistakable signature purple. Martha had nothing to hide.

Destroying the divorce colony had become Bishop Hare's life's work—and the man still lived. News of the second ex-Mrs. Jamie Blaine and her rapid remarriage reached him in Atlantic City, where he was convalescing in the sea air. Despite the crippling ailments that baffled his New York doctors, Bishop Hare determined that he would again mount a fight against the divorce colony. He must have known it would be his last stand—and that he would not have the overwhelming support for stricter laws he had enjoyed in the previous century.

President Roosevelt had called for a constitutional amendment governing marriage and divorce, but even in his statement Roosevelt acknowledged the futility of such a request, and there had been no progress toward that goal. And after more than a decade of work to codify statutes at the state level by the Uniform Law Commission, the special National Congress on Uniform Divorce Laws produced model legislation in 1906 that included a complete ban on migratory divorce but also included six standardized causes for divorce to be made available in every state. There was little chance such a law would pass in more than a few places. "States which have strict laws will hardly relax them," predicted the *New York Tribune*, and "easy Western states will hardly see any reason for making their laws more severe." There would be no sweeping changes to save "our national soul." Bishop Hare, though, had always been more concerned about South Dakota's soul.

"I am intensely jealous regarding the sweetness, purity and happiness of the home life in our state," the bishop wrote to the South Dakota legislature in February 1907. "What is called 'Migratory Divorce' is striking a terrible blow to that dear domestic sanctuary." From his sick bed in Atlantic City, Hare described the money the divorce seekers spent in Sioux Falls as a bribe that corrupted the state's residents and led them to overlook or even condone the colonists' behavior. "The divorce which they procure, though it is a horrible consummation of many antecedent follies and sins, comes to appear to our people—to our boys and girls, alas, as well as to others—not as a painful catastrophe, but as quite an ordinary event in married life!"

Hare wanted the South Dakota legislature to pass a radical overhaul of the law: a two-year residency requirement before seeking a divorce and a further one-year residency after the decree was granted before it went into effect. But the bill that was introduced had weaker restrictions than Bishop Hare advocated—a one-year residency requirement and several provisions to prevent "secret" divorces—and even that faced fierce opposition. This time there were divorce supporters willing to voice their objections to any law that would limit access. After weeks of debate and parliamentary maneuvering, the bill passed in March 1907. But before Hare and his allies could celebrate, the divorce supporters revealed their final gambit: they were already collecting signatures to demand a public referendum on the issue.

This would be the first time that voters—all men—would be asked to pass judgment on divorce. At first, Bishop Hare hoped to prevent the vote from taking place. Those who supported divorce needed thousands of South Dakotans to put their names on a petition to force the referendum. Hare, who had returned from New Jersey just in time for Easter, announced his intention to publicly shame those who signed it. It would be "a roll of dishonor." But he had not yet followed through on the threat when his illness forced him to travel back to New York to undergo dangerous surgery to remove his right eye. When the petition was submitted in May, 6,135 people had signed, some 65 percent more than the law required.

Divorce would be on the ballot eighteen months later. In the meantime, colonists continued to arrive, get their decrees, and depart. After Annie Stewart got her divorce and returned to New York to marry the city's most eligible bachelor, James Henry Smith, Emma Dresser moved into Flora Guest's former home to bide her time before filing suit for freedom from her husband, Daniel, a financier who had lost his fortune—and his wife's. Emma enrolled in typewriting and shorthand classes at the Sioux Falls Business College. At the Cataract House, guests gossiped about Sarah Brewster, who had come to Sioux Falls chaperoned by her twenty-three-year-old son Franklin. It was widely believed that Sarah wanted to escape her millionaire husband in order to marry an attaché to the king of Greece, but it was Franklin who was wed a few months later. During his mother's stay, he had fallen in love with a woman named Helen Baker, who was residing at the hotel while she awaited a decree of her own.

Such events were the "nasty importations of the divorce traffic," the bishop and his allies groused. Shortly before the vote he signed a strident missive to voters: "There are two signs which persons stick up on their town lots. One is, 'Dirt Wanted.' The other, 'Dump No Rubbish Here.' The question now is, which of these signs shall South Dakota present to persons who purpose bringing hither from other states their hateful conjugal follies and sins. Is it, 'Dirt Wanted! Come!' or is it, 'Dump No Rubbish Here! Keep Off!'"

Bishop Hare sounded like a desperate man in a losing battle, but there was never any real doubt that those who opposed divorce would win the referendum. In November 1908, the state's residents voted 60,211 to 38,794 in favor of the yearlong residency requirement, a wait as long as that of most states; the law went into effect immediately upon the official announcement of the results. The Sioux Falls divorce colony was shuttered.

⬥

THROUGHOUT THE NEARLY two years South Dakota debated its new divorce law, the Census Bureau counted. As representatives of the Bureau of Labor had in the 1880s, special agents of the newly formed Census Division of the Department of Commerce and Labor crisscrossed the country collecting vital statistics on marriage and divorce. This time, however, the public interest was so intense that the director of the census was forced to confirm that the agents in question were equally divided between married and single men and women so that no prejudice would color the bureau's conclusions. Feeling the urgency of its task, the Census Bureau did not wait until it had completed a lengthy analysis of the data before releasing the results of its canvass. Just a few weeks after Hare claimed victory in South Dakota, the government announced its initial findings. In this nationwide tally, Hare had lost.

Between 1887 and 1906, there had been 945,625 divorces in the United States, nearly three times as many as the already shocking number recorded between 1867 and 1886. The country's population had grown through those decades, but not nearly enough to account for the increase. In 1870, there was an average of eighty-one divorces per fifty thousand married couples; by 1900, that number had risen to two hundred divorces per fifty thousand married couples.

To explain the boom, statistician Joseph Hill wrote on behalf of the Census Bureau, "It is perhaps natural to look first of all to the figures for the state of South Dakota." They did not show what divorce opponents hoped. The numbers revealed that the much-reviled divorce colony had been significantly smaller than the public imagined. During the twenty-year period in question, the state had issued just 7,108 divorce decrees; of these 380 had been signed in 1900, for an average of 270 divorces per fifty thousand married couples. The state that had until days earlier been home to the country's laxest divorce laws had a rate higher than the national average—but still lower than that of seventeen other states with stricter provisions. For those who hoped to curb divorce through legislation, the South Dakota figures were a defeat.

Nearly two decades of religious, judicial, and social pressure had also been ineffective. Bishop Hare had preached against trifling with marriage, courts had questioned the validity of migratory divorces, and Sioux Falls society had shamed those seeking their freedom; yet the number of decrees issued in South Dakota increased in eleven out of the sixteen years between the earliest days of the colony and the conclusion of the Census Bureau's study. In the same period, the divorce rate increased nationally in all but two years, 1894 and 1902, periods of intense economic crisis. As had been the case in the first report on marriage and divorce released in 1889, more women than men had sought a legal exit from their marriage in the prior twenty years, though the disparities in the number were far higher in the North and West than in the South. The data on the Black community was too sparse to reach any statistically relevant conclusions, but Hill had an easy explanation for why fewer white women in the South sought their freedom. "In general, white women in the Northern states have a greater degree of economic independence than their southern sisters," he wrote. "This may influence their attitude towards divorce, by making them less dependent upon their husbands for support and more ready to dissolve the marriage tie when it becomes a cause of unhappiness or suffering." Nothing but a lack of money, it seemed, could thwart those determined to end their marriages.

"The statistics given out by the Census Bureau are simply shocking," said Cardinal James Gibbons, the archbishop of Baltimore and a respected voice in the American Catholic Church. For Gibbons and others opposed to divorce, these revelations in late November 1908 were, as they had been twenty years earlier, "nothing less than appalling" and a call to further action, lest the institution of marriage be destroyed completely. Gibbons urged the same strategies that had failed to curb divorce over the previous decades: stricter religious teachings, more severe laws, and harsher social consequences. "In former times, a woman who was divorced was shunned," he said. "Now this is not the case. If divorce is to be checked, let the divorced person be shunned."

Statisticians who further analyzed the data produced even more dramatic numbers for newspaper headlines. In 1906, there had been one divorce for every twelve new marriages, and if the trends continued, there would be one divorce for every two new marriages by the end of the century. But that did not alarm Cornell University professor Walter Willcox, who had, over the previous twenty years, become a leading authority on American marriage and divorce. He was heartened by the story the numbers told. "We are slowly awakening to a new ideal of the family based not upon the subordination of the wife in all phases of family life," Willcox told his students. "The increase of divorce in this country may be due rather to a rising of ideals than to a decay in family life."

⌒∞⌒

IT TOOK DECADES before the country's laws reflected the awakening Willcox had calculated. With the Sioux Falls divorce colony closed, Reno, Nevada, became the prime destination for unhappy spouses. In 1909, the residency requirement in the state was still six months, and Reno, like Sioux Falls circa 1891, was one of the more convenient municipalities for travel from out of state. With one brief exception—when the residency requirement was increased to one year between 1913 and 1915—Reno embraced the divorce seekers who flocked there, and by the 1930s, one could file for divorce in Nevada after a six-week stay in a local motel. If the defendant in the case was amenable to the proceedings, the plaintiff could have a decree one day later.

Elsewhere, though, the laws changed even more slowly. Lillie Hendrix and Otis Williams learned that the hard way. In 1940, the two North Carolina residents each sought a divorce in Las Vegas. Both charged their spouses with cruelty, and Lillie also alleged nonsupport; neither was grounds for an absolute divorce in their home state. Lillie and Otis married in Las Vegas the day Lillie's decree was awarded, and they returned east to live in Pineola, North Carolina, where they were easily accepted by the community and the local Baptist church—until they were arrested for bigamous cohabitation at the urging of Carrie Williams, Otis's first wife. Under North Carolina law, Otis was still married to Carrie and Lillie to her first husband, Thomas.

Over the next five years, Lillie and Otis's divorces and marriage would come before the courts six times, including two hearings in front of the US Supreme Court on the same issues that had confronted some Sioux Falls colonists: domicile and full faith and credit. In its first ruling in 1942, the Supreme Court overturned *Haddock*, finding that migratory divorce decrees issued to plaintiffs who had achieved bona fide domicile were to be given full faith and credit under the Constitution. But in its second ruling in 1945, the court found that the full faith and credit clause did not prevent the state from questioning—and ultimately finding lacking—the bona fide residency of the divorce plaintiffs. Though Thomas had since divorced Lillie in North Carolina courts and remarried, and Carrie had died, it seemed that Lillie and Otis would have to serve their prison terms—eight months to two years for Lillie and one to three years for Otis—until the state governor stepped in. It would not look good to imprison the couple for their marriage.

Social barriers to divorce had fallen with the influx of divorce seekers in Sioux Falls at the turn of the century. In 1908, when some 60 percent of those who voted on the South Dakota referendum wanted to make it harder to obtain a divorce, almost 40 percent had cast a ballot against stricter regulation, a far larger coalition than ever could have been imagined when the divorce colony first took root. Now, divorce seekers had crumbled legal barriers too. Like the colonists decades earlier, Lillie and Otis traveled to Nevada for nothing but their own freedom. But their case set a precedent: a divorce obtained legally anywhere in the United States was legal everywhere in the United States—even in New York and South Carolina.

Following the *Williams* decisions, South Carolina, which had no provisions for divorce prior to the Civil War and had enshrined the prohibition in its constitution in 1895, began the process of amending that document to reflect modern realties. The legislator who introduced the bill to repeal the ban used the arguments of those who opposed divorce in the nineteenth century to press for its acceptance now. "The sanctity of marriage, the legitimacy of children, and the possession of property are hanging in the balance," he said. Couples were finding ways to divorce; the state could not afford to pretend otherwise. A change to the constitution required a public referendum, and in 1948 the issue came before South Carolina voters—men and women now, though many Black citizens were still disenfranchised. The amendment passed easily; nearly 60 percent of those who voiced an opinion on the ballot question approved of making divorce accessible in the state.

It would take New York another two decades to expand its grounds for divorce beyond adultery, a limitation that sent so many to Sioux Falls, but the delay was mostly inertia. New York residents had long ago figured out ways around the state's laws—migratory divorces, fraudulent annulments, and even a cottage industry of actresses willing to play the role of the other woman for couples who wanted a divorce on the grounds of adultery without actually committing it. According to one calculation, the state with the strictest divorce law saw marriages among its residents end at a rate higher than the national average. The absurdity of it all became clear to the public in the 1960s when a court case brought attention to New Yorkers traveling to Mexico for divorces, which could be obtained in some Mexican states in just one day. In 1966, after some political wrangling but little public outrage, New York governor Nelson Rockefeller—whose wife, Mary, had divorced him in 1962 after six weeks in Reno—signed into law a bill recognizing five grounds for divorce in New York, including cruelty and abandonment.

Three years later, California governor Ronald Reagan, also a divorcee, signed the first no-fault divorce law, allowing spouses to separate without a finding of guilt—and without the lies and collusion that had been rampant in the divorce colony and the legal jeopardy that came with them. Originally conceived in yet another effort to limit decrees, the law eliminated all statutory grounds for divorce, giving the courts unilateral control over a couple's fate. That was a responsibility the courts did not want: in the years following the enactment of the new law, not a single divorce petition was denied. This real-world version of no-fault divorce spread quickly across the nation. Once opponents had championed uniform laws as a way to limit divorce. Now, that same tactic was used to bring statutes into line with practice and began to democratize access. By 1977, all but three states had such an option. (New York was the last, in 2010, to institute a no-fault statute.) The newspapers called it the "divorce revolution."

In asking for their own freedom, Maggie, Mary, Blanche, Flora, and their fellow colonists in Sioux Falls had been among the first rebels of this revolution. Collectively, they had, quite unintentionally, set the country down a winding path toward the acceptance and accessibility of divorce. They had rising ideals and a new vision for marriage, and for each of them, divorce was a declaration of independence.

That's what Maggie Zborowski tried to tell a reporter in 1891, before her divorce from the Baron: "I made up my mind to leave my husband to save myself."

Acknowledgments

T HE IDEA FOR *The Divorce Colony* started with Jean Harold Edward St. Cyr—or maybe it was Jack Thompson. Jean was a Frenchman, a well-to-do dandy dressed in pink and blue silks, a man of no particular profession who frequented the grand hotels of the East Coast in the 1900s wooing wealthy women. Jack was a Texan, a newsboy, a haberdasher's clerk, and a Broadway bit player. And I'm nearly certain they were the same person. (They even had identical Russian wolfhounds. Jean's dog was named Watlands Klondyke. Jack's dog was named Ripper.)

I was following this likely con man through newspaper archives: his surprise wedding to the recently widowed Caroline Redfield, more than three decades his senior; their lavish lifestyle; her death; his inheritance; and just a few months later, his marriage to another aging heiress, Annie Smith. There could be a story here, I thought, as reporters hounded Jean about his true identity. It was an audacious tale of reinvention set in a vanishing sliver of the world where the Gilded Age had yet to tarnish.

I was *almost* right. This was a story of bold self-transformation, but it wasn't Jean's or even Jack's. It was Annie's. In June 1905, Annie—then known as Mrs. Stewart—traveled to Sioux Falls for a divorce from her first husband. She was my introduction to the sorority of unhappy wives who revolutionized our understanding of marriage. As soon as I saw the words "the divorce colony," I forgot all about Jean/Jack's deception.

My research into the lives of the divorce seekers who undertook the journey to Sioux Falls in the late 1800s and early 1900s spanned continents and centuries. It would not have been possible—especially during a pandemic—without the assistance of so many archivists, both official and accidental.

In South Dakota: collections assistant Shelly Sjovold, volunteer Greg Olsen, and their colleagues at the Siouxland Heritage Museums, which makes its home in the former Minnehaha County Courthouse where Maggie's divorce trial took place; clerk of courts Angelia Gries and clerk of courts liaison Tara Hicks and their colleagues at the (new) Minnehaha County Courthouse; collections assistant Elizabeth Cisar and her colleagues at Augustana University's Center for Western Studies; Reverend Ward H. Simpson at Calvary Cathedral (once known as St. Augusta Cathedral); the staff of the Siouxland Libraries; Deadwood city archivist Michael Runge; the staff of the Deadwood History Inc.'s Homestake Adams Research and Cultural Center; Ken Stewart, now retired, and his colleagues at the South Dakota State Archives; librarian Samuel Hurley at the University of South Dakota; and the clerk of courts offices in nearly every county in eastern and southwestern South Dakota.

Elsewhere: the staffs of the Library of Congress Manuscript Division; the Center for Legislative Archives at the National Archives and Records Administration; the Archive Center at the Smithsonian Institution's National Museum of American History; the New-York Historical Society; Columbia University's Rare Book & Manuscript Library; Harvard University's Schlesinger, Houghton, and Fine Arts Libraries; Harvard Business School's Baker Library; the Boston Public Library; the Susan C. Cleveland Library at Colby-Sawyer College; Union College's Schaffer Library Archives and Special Collections; the Syracuse University Special Collections Research Center; the Franklin D. Roosevelt Presidential Library & Museum; Yale University's Beinecke Rare Book & Manuscript Library; the Hagley Museum and Library; Rutgers University's Archibald S. Alexander Library Special Collections Archives (and the Skillman Family Association, which digitized a portion of its collection); the Frances Willard House Museum and Archives; the North

Acknowledgments

Dakota State University Archives; the West Virginia & Regional History Center at West Virginia University; the National Archives of the United Kingdom; the Paris Archives; and the countless anonymous individuals who have digitized invaluable books, newspapers, and vital records for public, academic, and commercial databases. I would be remiss not to make special mention of the New York Public Library's Manuscripts and Archives Division—home to the Bigelow Family Papers—which supported this book through the library's short-term fellowship program. Of all the benefits of the fellowship, none was more valuable than the assistance of reference archivist Tal Nadan.

I first told Maggie De Stuers's story in the *Atavist Magazine*; my gratitude to Evan Ratliff and Katia Bachko for the opportunity. The full sweep of the divorce colony later became the subject of my master's thesis. I am so thankful to professor Meghan Healy-Clancy, now at Bridgewater State University, who first urged me to pursue this topic for my thesis, and to Harvard University professor Nancy F. Cott, who served as my thesis director; her contributions to our understanding of the history of marriage are essential to a better understanding of the history of divorce.

The path toward turning this story into the book you hold in your hands was a long and winding one, with some unexpected pitfalls. For their advice on the weird, weird world of publishing, I am grateful to Kevin Birmingham, Michael Callahan, Andrew Carroll, Carolyn Gleason, Robert Huber, Sona Movsesian, Megan Kate Nelson, Ben Wallace, Larry Weissman, and Simon Winchester. Particular thanks to Clare Pelino of ProLiterary, my cookbook agent and good friend who agreed to pitch in on this project at a challenging moment, despite the book's appalling lack of recipes, to Matthew Pearl—who is unfailingly generous with his time and insight—and to Suzanne Gluck and the people who introduced to me to Andrea Blatt of WME Books. I cannot imagine a better agent and champion for this book than Andrea.

Working with Carrie Napolitano of Hachette Books—and discovering our shared fascination with the forgotten people and places that have shaped our history—has been a delight. I am also grateful for the efforts and enthusiasm of the whole Hachette team, including Mary Ann Naples, Michelle Aielli, Michael Barrs, Monica Oluwek, Michael Clark, Jen Kelland, Amanda Kain, Sara Wood, Marie Mundaca, Lauren Rosenthal, and Ashley Kiedrowski.

Special thanks are due to Meredith Goff for her tireless fact-checking efforts; any errors that remain are my own.

I discovered my love of archival research many years ago working on book and magazine projects for Michael Capuzzo, Sabrina Rubin Erdely, Edward O'Donnell, Gary Pomerantz, and Duane Swierczynski. I couldn't have asked for better training for this undertaking. But I could not have realized my ambition of writing a book of my own without the support of my colleagues at *Smithsonian Magazine* and *Atlas Obscura* and my ever-encouraging friends and family, among them my mom and dad, Joan and John White; my sister, Amy Allen, her husband, Stew, and my nephew, Logan; my aunt and uncle, Diane and Jim Gloriant; my nana, Beverly Malpass; Becky and Al Sniezevage; Michael McCormick; Vicki Glembocki; Christy Speer Lejeune; Rich Rys; Roxanne Patel Shepelavy; Emma and Mike Boyle; Todd Wilson; Mike and Shannon Oscar; Renee and Sebastian Stojek; Jen Neuhoff; Paul, Lena, and Kieran Flannery; Dan Morrell; Julia Hanna; Janice Adams; Alicia Fortier; Aimee Hutchinson; Jessica Moore Wilson; Jen Myers; Michelle Johnston-Fleece; Jennie Rothenberg Gritz; and Arik Gabbai. Thank you all. I owe an even greater debt of gratitude to dear friends who also agreed to be the book's first readers. For their friendship, hard work, and kind criticism, thank you to Aaron Mettey, Courtney Foley, Anna Altman, and especially Sasha Issenberg, who gets the first draft of just about everything.

I knew I had found the story I wanted to tell almost as soon as I stumbled upon the divorce colony. Still, it wasn't until I traveled to Sioux Falls myself that I fully grasped the importance of this history. On my first visit—nearly a decade ago—the welcoming staff of the Minnehaha County clerk of courts office pulled out the massive leather-

Acknowledgments

bound docket books dating back more than a century and pointed me to a small desk near the counter where the office accepted legal paperwork from judges, attorneys, and the general public. As I sat there reading case captions, I tried not to eavesdrop on conversation after conversation about protection orders, divorce petitions, and custody battles. Many of the people who walked through the doors of the courthouse that morning reminded me of the women I was discovering in the aged pages of the docket books. They each found themselves in difficult personal circumstances and needed to avail themselves of the protections promised by the law to improve their situation. The nineteenth-century women I was researching helped ensure that we have that option in twenty-first-century America. For that, I am forever grateful to the divorce colonists.

Notes

T HIS IS A WORK OF NONFICTION. Every detail and quotation here was drawn from letters, diaries, photographs, court filings, vital records, countless newspapers and magazines, and other historical sources. The *Sioux Falls Argus-Leader, Sioux Falls Press*, and *Sioux Falls Gazette* provided a particularly valuable peek into life in the city. These notes, though not comprehensive, include citations for all quotations in the book as well as scholarly works and other resources of note. Dedicated endnote readers (like me) will also find a few Easter eggs.

Epigraph

vii "Three centuries ago": [Charles Elmer Holmes], "Pilgrims," *From Court to Court: A Collection of Verses Touching upon the Ancient, Popular and Sacred Rite of Divorce* (Sioux Falls, SD: Press of Will A. Beach, 1905), 22.

Prologue: Is Marriage a Failure?

xi The North Shore Limited departed: On the New York and Chicago Limited and the North Shore Limited: Albro Martin, *Railroads Triumphant* (New York: Oxford University Press, 1992).

xii A swirl of steam: On Grand Central Depot: Jeff Brown, "The Heart of New York: Grand Central Terminal," *Civil Engineering* (March 2013): 38–41; Tom Miller, "The Lost 1871 Grand Central Depot—42nd Street," *Daytonian in Manhattan*, February 4, 2013, http://daytoninmanhattan.blogspot .com; Kurt C. Schlichting, *Grand Central's Engineer* (Baltimore: Johns Hopkins University Press, 2012).

xii   The well-to-do: On Wagner Palace Cars: John H. White Jr., *The American Railroad Passenger Car* (Baltimore: Johns Hopkins University Press, 1978).

xii   A woman of means: On women traveling by train: Rebecca Jumper Matheson, "Ways of Comfort," *Dress* 43, no. 1 (2017): 23–43; R. David McCall, "'Every Thing in Its Place': Gender and Space on America's Railroads, 1830–1899" (master's thesis, Virginia Polytechnic Institute and State University, 1999).

xii   As the sun rose: On the International Suspension Bridge and the Underground Railroad: Judith Wellman, *Niagara Falls Underground Railroad Heritage Area Management Plan Appendix C: Survey of Site Relating to the Underground, Abolitionism, and African American Life in Niagara Falls and Surrounding Area, 1820–1880* (Niagara Falls, NY: Niagara Falls Underground Railroad Heritage Area Commission, 2012), 160–169.

xiii   "in ample time": "No. 4," *Salina (Kansas) Herald*, November 12, 1891.

xiv   Such was the story: On the history of divorce in early America: Roderick Phillips, *Untying the Knot* (Cambridge: Cambridge University Press, 1991); Norma Basch, *Framing American Divorce: From the Revolutionary Generation to the Victorians* (Berkeley: University of California Press, 1999); Nancy F. Cott, *Public Vows: A History of Marriage and the Nation* (Cambridge, MA: Harvard University Press, 2000); Stephanie Coontz, "The Origins of Modern Divorce," *Family Process* 46 (2007): 7–16.

xiv   South Carolina had no provisions: On South Carolina's divorce laws: Janet Hudson, "From Constitution to Constitution, 1868–1895: South Carolina's Unique Stance on Divorce," *South Carolina Historical Magazine* 98, no. 1 (January 1997): 75–96.

xv   The most permissive divorce statutes: On earlier divorce destinations: Nelson M. Blake, *Road to Reno* (New York: MacMillan, 1962); William O'Neill, *Divorce in the Progressive Era* (New York: Franklin Watts, 1973).

xv   In 1889, the newly formed: US Bureau of Labor, *Report on Marriage and Divorce in the United States, 1867–1886* (Washington, DC: Government Printing Office, 1889), 16.

xv   Even more alarming: US Bureau of Labor, *Report on Marriage and Divorce in the United States, 1867–1886*, 142.

xv   "Is Marriage a Failure?": For example, *Seattle Post-Intelligencer*, February 21, 1889; *Kansas City Star*, February 21, 1889; *Scranton (PA) Republican*, February 21, 1889.

xv   They had few champions: US Bureau of Labor, *Report on Marriage and Divorce in the United States, 1867–1906* (Washington, DC: Government Printing Office, 1909), 24.

xvi   When the Bureau of Labor: US Bureau of Labor, *Report on Marriage and Divorce in the United States, 1867–1886,* 142.

xvii The challenges those without: On the history of marriage and divorce in the Black community: Tara W. Hunter, *Bound in Wedlock: Slave and Free Black Marriage in the Nineteenth Century* (Cambridge, MA: Harvard University Press, 2017).

PART I: MAGGIE

Chapter 1: A Thriving and Interesting Place

1   Photo: George Grantham Bain Collection, LC-DIG-ggbain-37705, Prints & Photographs Division, Library of Congress, Washington, DC.

4   "in point of elegance": "Club and Society Gossip," *New York Daily Graphic,* April 24, 1875.

4   It was newly fashionable: On marrying a title: Richard W. Davis, "'We Are All Americans Now!' Anglo-American Marriages in the Later Nineteenth Century," *Proceedings of the American Philosophical Society* 135, no. 2 (June 1991): 140–199.

4   She was already American royalty: On the early history of the Astors: David Sinclair, *Dynasty: The Astors and Their Times* (New York: Beaufort Books, 1984); Axel Madsen, *John Jacob Astor: America's First Multimillionaire* (New York: John Wiley & Sons, Inc., 2007); Harvey O'Connor, *The Astors* (New York: Alfred A. Knopf, 1941).

4   "lit up any room": "Dakota's Wilds," *Boston Globe,* July 14, 1891.

4   Her high spirits: "Dakota's Wilds," *Boston Globe,* July 14, 1891; "Tales of His Cruelty," *Chicago Tribune,* February 9, 1892; "Mme. De Stuers Here," *Chicago Tribune,* November 7, 1891.

4   "the nicest foreigner": Clara and Hardy Steeholm, *The House at Hyde Park* (New York: Viking Press, 1950), 29.

4   Sallie was one of Maggie's cousins: Rita Halle Kleeman, *Gracious Lady: The Life of Sara Delano Roosevelt* (New York: D. Appleton-Century Incorporated, 1935), 68–70, 90–91.

6   Dow had built: On Wallace L. Dow: Jennifer Dumke, *W. L. Dow: The Architect Who Shaped Sioux Falls* (Charleston, SC: History Press, 2013).

6   For more than a century prior: On the history of Sioux Falls and its early residents: Dana Reed Bailey, *History of Minnehaha County, South Dakota* (Sioux Falls, SD: Brown & Saenger, 1899); George W. Kingsbury, *History of Dakota Territory,* Vols. 1–5 (Chicago: S. J. Clarke Pub. Co., 1915);

R. E. Bragstad, *Sioux Falls in Retrospect* (Sioux Falls, SD, 1967); Wayne Fanebust, *Where the Sioux River Bends* (Freeman, SD: Pine Hill Press, 1984); Gary D. Olson and Erik L. Olson, *Sioux Falls, South Dakota: A Pictorial History* (Norfolk, VA: Donning Company, 1985); Gary D. Olson, "A Dakota Boomtown: Sioux Falls, 1877–1880," *Great Plains Quarterly* 24 (winter 2004): 17–30.

6   "great and picturesque": Fanebust, *Where the Sioux River Bends*, 15.

7   "This gave me": "Baroness De Stuers' Story," *Boston Herald*, February 14, 1892.

7   "thriving and interesting place": "A Savage American," *Argus-Leader*, February 8, 1892.

8   Maggie's destination: On the history of the Cataract House: Olson and Olson, *Sioux Falls, South Dakota*.

8   The hotel—in various incarnations: On South Dakota's railroads: Mark Hufsteter and Michael Bedeau, *South Dakota's Railroads* (Pierre: South Dakota State Historic Preservation Office, 2007).

8   "the great rendezvous": "The Future City," *Argus-Leader*, July 12, 1889.

8   The Cataract was: On American hotels of the era: A. K. Sandoval-Strausz, *Hotel: An American History* (New Haven, CT: Yale University Press, 2007).

9   "of good family, but bad habits": [Henry Austin], "The Sioux Falls Divorce Colony and Some Noted Colonists," *The Arena*, 1891, 696–708.

9   Maggie and her maid: It is likely no surprise that the names of the household servants who played a role in this story have been largely forgotten. Maggie's maid was not spared this fate. Of all names reported for her, Mary Van den Heuvel, copied from the court record, is the most likely to be accurate. Nothing else is known about her life.

Chapter 2: In Good Faith

11   and other "wickedness": US Bureau of Labor, *Report on Marriage and Divorce in the United States, 1867–1886*, 108.

11   *The* Mrs. Astor: On Ward McAllister and Caroline "Lina" Astor's reign over New York society: Eric Homberger, *Mrs. Astor's New York: Money and Social Power in a Gilded Age* (New Haven, CT: Yale University Press, 2002). On Newport's mansions: James L. Yarnall, *Newport Through Its Architecture* (Hanover, NH: University Press of New England, 2005).

12   "It is my opinion": "She Had American Spunk," *New York World*, February 10, 1892.

12 Neurasthenia was the disease: On neurasthenia and the rest cure: Anson Rabinbach, *The Human Motor: Energy, Fatigue and the Origins of Modernity* (New York: Basic Books, 1990); Anne Stiles, "The Rest Cure, 1873–1925," BRANCH: Britain, Representation, and Nineteenth-Century History, October 2012, www.branchcollective.org/?ps_articles=anne-stiles-the-rest-cure-1873-1925.

12 "that there always had been an eccentric streak": "Is Also in Sioux Falls," *New York World*, July 14, 1891.

12 "Thousands and thousands": "Baron Stuers's Defense," *Philadelphia Inquirer*, March 20, 1892.

13 The distinction of being the first: A small slice of Magdalen Astor's life can be found in the New-York Historical Society archives: Bentzon Family, box 1, folder 13; Bristed Family, box 3, folder 5, Astor Family Papers, New-York Historical Society, New York, New York.

13 When Maggie's grandfather: Sinclair, *Dynasty*, 97.

14 "vindicated her reputation": "The Chatter of Society," *New York World*, April 13, 1890.

14 "when it shall be made fully": *General and Private Laws, Memorials and Resolutions of the Territory of Dakota* (Yankton, Dakota: G. W. Kingsbury, 1864), 20–21.

14 "Now that a niece": *Philadelphia Record* quoted in "City Briefs," *Argus-Leader*, July 22, 1891.

15 Benjamin could trace: W. W. H. Davis, *History of Doylestown, Old and New* (Doylestown, PA: Intelligencer Print, 1904), 397.

16 "genial dignity": "Judge Aikens," *Mitchell Daily Republican*, February 6, 1890.

16 Benjamin Mann's petition: Portions of many of the divorce cases heard at the Minnehaha County Courthouse at the turn of the century are available on microfilm maintained by the Minnehaha County Clerk of Courts. On Benjamin Mann: *Mann v. Mann*, file no. 3828 (SD 2nd Cir. 1891).

17 As was her style: On the Hotel Orleans: "Hotel Orleans at Spirit Lake," Elia Peattie: An Uncommon Writer, An Uncommon Woman, http://plainshumanities.unl.edu/peattie/ep.owh.oan.0002.html.

18 "in good faith": *The Revised Codes of the Territory of Dakota* (Yankton, Dakota: Bowen & Kingsbury, 1877), 245.

18 "righteous judge": "A Righteous Judge Startles Applicants Infesting Sioux Falls," *Morning Olympian*, August 6, 1891.

19 "the divorce law was not a bad thing": "A Great State for Divorces," *New York Times*, June 26, 1891.

19   Those in the city: On the place of money in the debate over divorce in Sioux Falls: Connie DeVelder Schaffer, "Money Versus Morality: The Divorce Industry of Sioux Falls," *South Dakota History* 20, no. 3 (1990): 207–227. DeVelder Shaffer relies heavily on the observations recorded in *The Divorce Mill: Realistic Sketches of the South Dakota Divorce Colony* (New York: Mascot Publishing, 1895), published under the pseudonym Harry Hazel by divorce colonist Mary Cahill. It's a highly fictionalized account of the colony—and a fun read.

19   As the divorce colony flourished: On Bishop William Hobart Hare: M. A. DeWolfe Howe, *The Life and Labors of Bishop Hare: Apostle to the Sioux* (New York: Sturgis & Walton, 1912); Mary B. Peabody, *Zitkano Duzahan, Swift Bird* (Hartford, CT: Church Missions Publishing Co., 1915); Virginia Driving Hawk Sneve, *That They May Have Life: The Episcopal Church in South Dakota, 1859–1976* (New York: Seabury Press, 1977). A portion of Hare's papers are also collected at the Center for Western Studies, Augustana University, Sioux Falls, South Dakota, and Houghton Library, Harvard University, Cambridge, Massachusetts.

19   "There is no man in Dakota": "Men of Sioux Falls," *Saint Paul Globe*, September 3, 1887.

19   "savage exhibition": Howe, *The Life and Labors of Bishop Hare*, 15.

20   "The notions which prevail": Howe, *The Life and Labors of Bishop Hare*, 355.

21   "Out of this will come": "Ninety Days in South Dakota," *New York Herald*, August 9, 1891.

Chapter 3: Just Another

23   "This will protect": "Hasn't Closed the Divorce Mill," *New York Herald*, August 3, 1891.

24   "ungentlemanly epithets": "The De Stuers Case," *Argus-Leader*, September 29, 1891.

25   "Pardon me, madam": "The Land of Divorcees," *New York World*, November 8, 1891.

26   "I am proud of my sex": "Fannie Palmer Tinker," *Brooklyn Daily Eagle*, September 20, 1891.

26   "It is said the lady": "City Briefs," *Argus-Leader*, October 7, 1891.

27   "manifested the most uneven": "Answer Filed," *Minneapolis Star Tribune*, November 6, 1891.

28   "the art of being agreeable": "Mme. De Stuers Here," *Chicago Tribune*, November 7, 1891.

30   She recognized Charcot: On Jean-Martin Charcot and Hospice de la Salpêtrière: Asti Hustvedt, *Medical Muses: Hysteria in Nineteenth-Century Paris* (New York: W. W. Norton & Company, 2011); Christian Régnier, "Gunpowder, Madness, and Hysteria: The Birth of Neurology in France," *Medicographia* 32 (2010): 310–318; David R. Kumar et al., "Jean-Martin Charcot: The Father of Neurology," *Clinical Medicine & Research* 9, no. 1 (2011): 46–49.

31   "grand asylum of human misery": Hustvedt, *Medical Muses*, 12.

31   "Well, Madame": "Mme. De Stuers Here," *Chicago Tribune*, November 7, 1891.

31   "All will say": "A Savage American," *Argus-Leader*, February 8, 1892.

31   "I saw just how": "Mme. De Stuers Here," *Chicago Tribune*, November 7, 1891.

Chapter 4: Budding Hope and Dead Passions

33   "What a grand phantasmagoria": "The Land of Divorcees," *New York World*, November 8, 1891.

34   Fannie outed one Robert Buchanan: Robert Buchanan did not, unfortunately, get a divorce in Sioux Falls. For unknown reasons, he never filed suit. Instead, he returned to New York and took a path all too common throughout the centuries when a legal end to marriage was not available: On April 23, 1892, he murdered Anna, whom he told friends he had wed only for her money, and a few weeks later, he remarried his first wife. Robert was convicted of Anna's death by poisoning and executed for the crime. On Robert Buchanan's trial: Mark Essig, "Poison Murder and Expert Testimony: Doubting the Physician in Late Nineteenth-Century America," *Yale Journal of Law and the Humanities* 14, no. 1 (January 2002): 177–210.

34   "The article originally sent": "The Write-Up," *Argus-Leader*, November 10, 1891.

34   "Such horrible tales": "Gay and Giddy Life," *Chicago Herald*, January 2, 1892.

35   She was not a widow: I wish I could tell you so much more about Fannie Tinker's divorce, but the records appear to have been destroyed during the Cincinnati courthouse riots of 1884.

35   She had supported herself: More of Fannie Palmer Tinker's story is woven through the Woman's Press Club of New York City records, 1889–1980, Rare Book & Manuscript Library, Columbia University, New York, New York.

35   "matters of current interest": "Local Budget," *Argus-Leader*, November 19, 1889.

35   But a few days before Christmas: On Reverend William J. Skillman: The Reverend William Jones Skillman Collection, Rutgers University, Archibald S. Alexander Library, Special Collections Archives, New

Brunswick, New Jersey, digitized by the Skillman Family Association, skillmanfamily.org.

35 "perfectly stenchful": "Down on Easy Divorces," *South Bend Tribune*, January 4, 1892.

35 "house of questionable character": "Judge Aikens Too Gay," *Chicago Herald*, December 31, 1891.

35 Essie Snyder was said to have leveled: In fact, Essie Snyder's story was even more complicated than was known when she was in Sioux Falls. Her lover, Charles Goodwin, had been killed by Burton Webster, who claimed he had done so in self-defense during an argument over Charles's undue interest in Burton's wife. In the last moments of his life, however, Charles had been writing to Essie. He addressed the letter to his "darling wife," despite the fact Essie was still married to another man. During Webster's trial, unproven but titillating details of Essie's long-standing love affair with Charles were revealed. Essie had been a married woman when she and Charles were introduced in 1883. In the years between the meeting and her trip to Sioux Falls, Essie had borne three children, all fair like Charles; Essie and her husband, Peter, both had dark hair and eyes. When Peter Snyder sought and was granted his own divorce in New York courts in 1894, he declined custody of the children.

36 "If Judge Aikens's hand": "Gay and Giddy Life," *Chicago Herald*, January 2, 1892.

36 "Let us pray": "Standing by Aikens," *St. Paul Daily Globe*, January 1, 1892.

37 The couple had a practical view: All Souls Unitarian would soon confront the issue of divorce directly. In the fall of 1892, Eliza and William Wilkes's twenty-year-old son, Paul, announced his intention to marry Rita Mackay of New York soon after her divorce on the grounds of cruelty. At first, the Wilkes objected, saying Paul was too young to understand the importance of marriage. They advised the couple to wait a year to marry, but the parents soon relented, and the couple was married at All Souls Church with the Wilkes in attendance. Their marriage lasted three years.

Arthur Hastings Grant, too, would divorce. Eliza Wilkes presided over his marriage to Amy Allison of Canton in March 1892, and the couple left Sioux Falls for the East, where Arthur continued his ministry. But Amy was determined to pursue her education. After she moved to the Midwest in 1900 to study at the coeducational University of Chicago, Amy sought a divorce on the grounds of desertion.

37 "It is clear that no remedy": Edward Everett Hale and William H. Lyon, "The Council of the National Conference," *The Unitarian* 6 (1891): 515.

37 In 1878, Hare disciplined: On the dispute between Bishop Hare and Reverend Samuel D. Hinman: Anne Beiser Allen, "A Scandal in Niobrara: The Controversial Career of Rev Samuel D Hinman," *Nebraska History* 90 (2009): 114–129; "Bishop Hare's 'Rehearsal of Facts' in the Case of Samuel D. Hinman, Presbyter. with Mr. Hineman's Reply," September 1879, Bishop Hare Papers, box 5, folder 14, Center for Western Studies, Augustana University; Howe, *The Life and Labors of Bishop Hare*, 161–171.

38 "These charges are the result": "Judge Aikens Makes Denial," *Chicago Herald*, December 31, 1891.

38 "a prohibition crank": "The Other Side," *Minneapolis Star Tribune*, December 30, 1891.

38 "had been known to take a drop": "Judge Aikens Makes Denial," *Chicago Herald*, December 31, 1891.

38 "I have never met": "In Favor of Judge Aikens," *Chicago Herald*, January 6, 1892.

39 "dude of the colony": "Social Misfits," *Brooklyn Daily Eagle*, December 4, 1891.

40 "absolutely and peremptorily": "The Answer," *Argus-Leader*, November 5, 1891.

40 "This case will be fought": "The Baron Is a Fighter," *Argus-Leader*, November 30, 1891.

41 "For the sake of the good name": "The Baron Is Severe," *St. Paul Daily Globe*, January 27, 1892.

42 "so queer in his actions": "Dakota's Divorce Mill," *New York World*, August 2, 1891.

42 "unladylike": "Now the Verdict," *Argus-Leader*, February 9, 1892.

42 "the air of a woman": "Mr. Zborowski's Duchess," *New York Sun*, January 28, 1892.

43 "I had heard from various sources": "The Baron Is Severe," *St. Paul Daily Globe*, January 27, 1892.

43 The man who had been Maggie's: For reasons that will become clear later, Elliott Zborowski would become the subject of two hard-to-find biographies that intertwine the myth and facts of his life: David Paine, *The Zborowski Inheritance* (Cambridge, UK: Victoire Press Ltd, 2008); David Wilson, *The Racing Zborowskis* (Chipping Norton, UK: Vintage Sports-Car Club Limited, 2002).

45 "was among the most admired": "From Our Lady Correspondent," *Sheffield (England) Daily Telegraph*, January 8, 1890.

45 "The strongest count": "In Writing About the De Stuers Matter," *Town Topics*, February 18, 1892.

Chapter 5: A Savage American

48 "dollars and cents": "The Case Is Closed," *Argus-Leader*, January 21, 1892.

48 "What was your husband's treatment": "A Savage American," *Argus-Leader*, February 8, 1892.

49 "When did you come": "A Savage American," *Argus-Leader*, February 8, 1892.

50 "at everything and nothing": "Now the Verdict," *Argus-Leader*, February 9, 1892.

50 "That was the last glimpse": "Tales of His Cruelty," *Chicago Tribune*, February 9, 1892.

50 "never shown much tenderness": "Now the Verdict," *Argus-Leader*, February 9, 1892.

50 "She at first loved me": "Loved Him Not," *Boston Globe*, February 10, 1892.

51 "It is well that I should not care": "Now the Verdict," *Argus-Leader*, February 9, 1892.

52 "This case closes": "A Savage American," *Argus-Leader*, February 8, 1892.

52 "My stenographer": "Baroness De Stuers Made Out a Strong Case," *New York Herald*, February 10, 1892.

52 "the baron's conduct": "A Savage American," *Argus-Leader*, February 8, 1892.

52 "that a false and ignorant": Arthur A. Carey, *New Nerves for Old* (Boston: Little Brown and Company, 1918), 9.

52 "As to the baron's treatment": "Helping Baron De Stuers," *New York Times*, February 12, 1892.

53 "There were positively no traces": "Dr. Stowell's Story," *Chicago Inter Ocean*, March 1, 1892.

53 "acts of extreme cruelty": "She Gets It," *Argus-Leader*, March 7, 1892.

54 "single and unmarried": "Application for Marriage License," March 7, 1892, Minnehaha Country Register of Deeds, Sioux Falls, South Dakota.

55 "bad ways": S. Rep. No. 420, 53rd Cong., 2nd Sess. (1894).

55 "One of the Astor family": When Mark Anthony DeWolfe Howe published this letter in a biography he wrote of Hare, his cousin, in 1913, the names were obscured. As there is no doubt about whom Hare is complaining, I've added them back in here. I have not located the original letters. Howe, *The Life and Labors of Bishop Hare*, 355.

55 "I won't have them": Howe, *The Life and Labors of Bishop Hare*, 356.

56 "abstain, therefore": "The Church and Persons Seeking Divorce," *Church News*, June 1892.

57 "It is by no means safe": Howe, *The Life and Labors of Bishop Hare*, 355.

PART II: MARY
Chapter 6: Ardor and Inexperience

59 Photo: Special Collections, 119.1976.4328, Fine Arts Library, Harvard University, Cambridge, Massachusetts.

63 Nineteen-year-old Mary: Mary's age is a source of some debate. Her gravestone in Newport, Rhode Island, lists her birthdate as October 20, 1867, but the majority of vital records list 1866 as her birth year. This earlier date matches the age on her marriage license.

63 "We may be separated": "Gotham Gossip," *Daily Picayune (New Orleans)*, November 4, 1888.

63 "Mr. and Mrs. James G. Blaine, Jr., Maine": "Blaine's Bride," *Argus-Leader*, September 16, 1886.

64 James's past campaigns: On James G. Blaine's campaigns: Charles Edward Russell, *Blaine of Maine* (New York: Cosmopolitan Book Corporation, 1931); David Saville Muzzey, *James G. Blaine: A Political Idol of Other Days* (Port Washington, NY: Kennikat Press, 1934); Mark Wahlgren Summers, *Rum, Romanism, and Rebellion: The Making of a President, 1884* (Chapel Hill: University of North Carolina Press, 2000); Neil Rolde, *Continental Liar from the State of Maine* (Gardiner, ME: Tilbury House, 2006).

65 "James G. Blaine betrayed": Quoted in Summers, *Rum, Romanism, and Rebellion*, 185.

65 "You can imagine how inexpressibly": "A Statement from Mr. Blaine," *Cincinnati Enquirer*, September 20, 1884.

66 "The young people are very young": "Blaine Jr.'s Runaway Match," *Richmond Dispatch*, September 15, 1889.

67 "quaint little": "The Land of Divorcees," *New York World*, November 8, 1891.

67 "It is too bad": "Mecca for the Mismated," *Pittsburgh Daily Post*, August 3, 1891.

68 "Father saw Jamie's wife": Emmons Blaine to Harriet Stanwood Blaine, October 15, 1886, James Gillespie Blaine Family Papers, Library of Congress, Washington, DC.

68 "lordly and patronizing": "James G. Blaine Jr.," *Herald (Washington, DC)*, March 13, 1887.

68   "worst he had ever seen": "The World of Society," *Pittsburgh Dispatch*, February 28, 1892.

69   "They swung along": Quoted in "Prominent Men's Sons," *Pittsburgh Press*, February 25, 1888.

69   "Wait until my father": "Playing the Old Man," *New York Herald*, October 21, 1888.

70   "Three cheers": "Young Mrs. Blaine," *New York World*, November 6, 1888.

70   "James G. Blaine, Jr. disregarding": Some divorce records that were not maintained at county courthouses have been preserved by the South Dakota State Historical Society. On Mary Nevins Blaine: *Blaine v. Blaine* (SD 8th Ct. 1892).

70   "The fault is with his mother": "Husband Not Blamed," *Pittsburgh Press*, October 24, 1888.

Chapter 7: The Campaigns

71   "looking up the needs": "Busy Senator Kyle," *Queen City Mail (Spearfish, SD)*, May 20, 1891.

71   The Senate chamber in the north wing: On the Capitol Building: Glenn Brown and William Bushong, *Glenn Brown's History of the United States Capitol* (Washington, DC: US GPO, 2007).

72   "It is my belief": US Congress, *Congressional Record*, 52d Cong., 1st sess., 1892, Vol. 23, pt. 1: 790–793.

73   Similar proposals: On previous and subsequent amendments: Edward Stein, "Past and Present Proposed Amendments to the United States Constitution Regarding Marriage," *Washington University Law Review* 82, no. 3 (January 2004): 666–670.

73   "Our laws upon divorce": US Congress, *Congressional Record*, 790–793.

74   "apostle of divorce reform": "The Sioux Falls Press," *Mitchell Capital*, February 12, 1892.

74   "Senator Kyle ought to": "Senator Kyle Ought To," *Mitchell Capital*, February 26, 1892.

74   "Do you know who": For example, "Blaine Jr. Roasted," *Pittsburgh Dispatch*, December 19, 1891.

74   "the most helpless": "Marie Was to Blame," *St. Paul Globe*, February 29, 1892.

75   Harriet believed Mary: On Harriet Stanwood Blaine: Gamaliel Bradford, *Wives* (New York: Harper & Brothers, 1925), 237–270.

75   Mary had not been able: There was rampant speculation that Mary's Catholicism was the cause of the difficulties between her and Harriet, especially after

Jamie III was baptized as a Catholic. It's true that both Harriet and James were skeptical, to put it kindly, of Catholicism. (Though James was likely baptized Catholic, he was a practicing Protestant.) But it seems unlikely religion was the root of the rift. The Blaines' elder daughter, Alice, had married a Catholic man, John Coppinger. Their union had been solemnized by a Catholic priest in an extravagant wedding at the Blaines' Washington home. Alice had converted and was raising her children as Catholics, and there was no public friction between the Coppingers and the Blaines. On the Blaines and Catholicism: Thomas E. Blantz, "James Gillespie Blaine, His Family, and 'Romanism,'" *Catholic Historical Review* 95, no. 4 (October 2008): 659–716.

75 Mary and Jamie remained: On the Blaine house: H. Draper Hunt and George K. Clancey, *The Blaine House: A Brief History and Guide* (Augusta: Maine Historic Preservation Commission, 1986).

75 "the dismal failure": "Marie Was to Blame," *St. Paul Globe*, February 29, 1892.

77 "If you go": "Locked James in a Room," *New York World*, February 20, 1892.

77 "You shall live": "Marie Was to Blame," *St. Paul Globe*, February 29, 1892.

77 That day, as Mary's: *Blaine v. Blaine* (SD 8th Ct. 1892).

78 "We are as happy": "They Are a Happy Couple," *Pittsburgh Daily Post*, September 28, 1888.

78 And Robert Green Ingersoll: On Robert Green Ingersoll: C. H. Cramer, *Royal Bob: The Life of Robert G. Ingersoll* (Indianapolis: Bobbs-Merrill, 1952); Susan Jacoby, *The Great Agnostic: Robert Ingersoll and American Freethought* (New Haven, CT: Yale University Press, 2014).

78 James wrote to him: James G. Blaine to Robert Ingersoll, October 1, 1888, and October 25, 1888, Robert Green Ingersoll Papers, Library of Congress, Washington, DC.

78 "Is it possible to conceive": Henry C. Potter et al., "Is Divorce Wrong?," *North American Review* 149, no. 396 (November 1889): 513–538.

79 "In all cases of trouble": "They Stole Her Husband," *Pittsburgh Daily Post*, October 22, 1888.

79 "Indeed I am so wretched": *Blaine v. Blaine* (SD 8th Ct. 1892).

79 "As your true and faithful wife": "Gotham Gossip," *Daily Picayune (New Orleans)*, December 4, 1888.

79 "I am going to leave": *Blaine v. Blaine* (SD 8th Ct. 1892).

79 "I knew it would hurt": "His Friends Expected It," *New York World*, October 21, 1888.

80 When Mary's lawyers announced: Alienation-of-affection claims have their roots in medieval English common law, which considered a wife the property of her husband. The husband could sue a third party who abducted his wife or induced her to leave the marriage. In the United States in the mid-nineteenth century—when wives were no longer viewed as legal property—alienation-of-affection suits became a legal tool for punishing adultery and, more rarely, in-laws who caused strife in a marriage. However, American courts did not recognize the right of women to sue for alienation of affection until the late nineteenth century, only a few years before Mary Nevins Blaine contemplated such an action. On alienation-of-affection claims at the turn of the century: Robert C. Brown, "The Action for Alienation of Affections," *University of Pennsylvania Law Review* (March 1934): 472–506.

80 "hanging by a thread": "At Death's Door," *Pittsburgh Daily Post*, October 27, 1888.

80 "visibly affected": "James G. Blaine, Jr., Is Sad," *New York World*, October 28, 1888.

81 "the picture of trim simplicity": "Gowns for Summer Days," *Pittsburgh Daily Post*, July 6, 1889.

81 "the entire household": "Jimmie Blaine's Wrecked Home," *New York World*, May 29, 1889.

81 "People send their things": "Mute Evidence of Strife," *New York World*, May 28, 1889.

82 "exquisitely pretty": "Society," *Chicago Tribune*, February 1, 1885.

82 "When I stop to think": "Young Mrs. Blaine's Plans," *New York Sun*, December 5, 1888.

83 "It seems to me": "May Wed Once More," *Pittsburgh Dispatch*, April 12, 1891.

Chapter 8: Undesirable Cattle

85 "to restrain, prohibit and suppress": Watson Parker, *Deadwood: The Golden Years* (Lincoln: University of Nebraska Press, 1981), 190.

86 "The parties to them": "The Sioux Falls Gazette Raises Up Its Voice," *Deadwood Daily Pioneer*, March 22, 1892.

86 "We notice that some": "Jealousy Rampant," *Argus-Leader*, April 20, 1891.

87 "penny-a-liners": "Not long since, Judge Palmer," *Argus-Leader*, September 26, 1887.

88 "We are going to fight": "Mrs. Blaine's Suit for Divorce," *New York Sun*, December 17, 1891.

88 "wholesome atmosphere": "Young Blaine Files His Answer," *Chicago Tribune*, October 7, 1891.

89 "I know you are a detective": "Dogged by Spies," *Pittsburgh Dispatch*, December 18, 1891.

89 "disreputable in its character": "General Principles," January 1, 1878, box 54, folder 1, Pinkerton's National Detective Agency records, Library of Congress, Washington, DC.

89 "new clue": Struble & Stiger to James G. Blaine, October 2, 1891, James Gillespie Blaine Family Papers, Library of Congress, Washington, DC.

89 "The man in this case": "Blaine Jr. Roasted," *Pittsburgh Dispatch*, December 19, 1891.

91 "Not a few of the men": Quoted in "She Gets It," *Argus-Leader*, February 20, 1892.

91 "Mrs. Blaine, I want": "Locked James in a Room," *New York World*, February 20, 1892.

92 "in good faith": *Blaine v. Blaine* (SD 8th Ct. 1892).

Chapter 9: A Personal Statement

94 "I am not afraid": Roy Morris Jr., *Fraud of the Century: Rutherford B. Hayes, Samuel Tilden, and the Stolen Election of 1876* (New York: Simon and Schuster, 2007), 54–55.

95 "My dear sir": "Blaine Not a Candidate," *New York Sun*, February 8, 1892.

95 "disaster is the only": "Marie Was to Blame," *St. Paul Globe*, February 8, 1892.

95 "You know that Blaine suffered": "J. G. Blaine Jr.," *Star-Tribune (Minneapolis–St. Paul)*, January 1, 1892.

96 "what the weather was": *New York Tribune* quoted in Donald Ritchie, *Press Gallery: Congress and the Washington Correspondents* (Cambridge, MA: Harvard University Press, 1991), 138.

96 "To remain silent": "Marie Was to Blame," *St. Paul Globe*, February 29, 1892.

98 "to make no hasty answer": "She Will Answer," *Argus-Leader*, February 29, 1892.

98 "sat by quietly": "Mr. Blaine Repaid in Kind," *New York Times*, March 1, 1892.

98 "instantly flew into a fury": "Blaine's Last Public Letter," *Pittsburgh Dispatch*, March 1, 1892.

99 "The statements of the distinguished": "Judge Thomas Speaks," *New York World*, March 2, 1892.

99 "I acknowledge your well-rendered": "Mrs. Blaine, Jr., Replies," *New York World*, March 2, 1892.

101 "the most sacred relation": House Committee on the Judiciary, Amending Constitution of United States and Providing Uniform Laws on Marriage and Divorce, 52d Cong., 1st sess., 1892, H.rp. 1290, serial 3045.

101 With no hope of action: On the Uniform Law Commission: Robert A. Stein, *Forming a More Perfect Union: A History of the Uniform Law Commission* (Charlottesville, VA: Matthew Bender, 2013); Blake, *Road to Reno*.

102 "Some good in this direction": "Two Reports on a Subject of Growing Interest," *Deadwood Daily Pioneer*, May 15, 1892.

102 "extremely sorry": "James G., Sr., Is Mum," *Sioux Falls Gazette*, March 5, 1892.

102 "Nevertheless, it is true": *St. Louis Republic* quoted in "The Blaine Episode," *Argus-Leader*, March 4, 1892.

102 "You have taken your case": "No Love Letters Yet," *Pittsburgh Dispatch*, March 13, 1892.

103 Ellen announced that she: To be precise, though Florence Cuthbertson had been a prominent member of the divorce colony, she had come to Sioux Falls in search of a legal annulment of her second marriage, on the grounds that she had been wed under duress. She told a harrowing tale: At the age of eighteen, she had married twenty-eight-year-old William Douglas. Four years later, William suspected Florence of being unfaithful. She denied the charges, but he filed for divorce, claiming cruelty and adultery. The judge in the case took testimony from Sydney Cuthbertson, who told the court he had been intimate with Florence. The judge granted the divorce and then threatened Florence with five years in jail. Under Illinois law, adultery was a crime, punishable by a fine not exceeding $500 and up to a year in jail for the first offense, twice that for the second offense, and so on. The only alternative was marriage. And so, under protest, Florence had married Sydney. She left for Sioux Falls six months later.

104 "Will you please state": "Mr. Blaine Writes a Note," *New York World*, June 9, 1892.

104 Neither did the letters: To admit this before now would have given the ending away. None of Mary and Jamie's letters are extant. All of their letters are reprinted from newspaper reports and court filings. Occasionally sources disagree on the exact wording but not on the sentiment.

Chapter 10: Let Not Man Put Asunder

105 "stand fast in his place": "Letter from the Bishop," *Church News* 7, no. 4 (February 1891), William Hobart Hare Papers, Episcopal Diocese of South Dakota archives, Center for Western Studies, Augustana University, Sioux Falls, South Dakota.

106 "Any institution or practice": "National Scandal," *Argus-Leader*, January 2, 1893.

107 "Women should have a voice": *Sioux Falls Press* quoted in "It Seems That the Sioux Falls Press," *Aberdeen Daily News*, February 5, 1890.

107 "all unjust laws": Emma A. Cranmer, "Gains in South Dakota," *Woman's Journal*, August 5, 1893.

108 Months before Bishop Hare: "Minutes of the Fourth Annual Convention of the Woman's Christian Temperance Union of South Dakota," South Dakota State Archives, Pierre, South Dakota.

108 "a disgrace to the state": "There Seems to Be a Determined Effect," *Fresno Weekly Republican*, January 13, 1893.

108 But even within the evangelical group: On the Woman's Christian Temperance Union and social issues, nationally and regionally: Barbara Leslie Epstein, *The Politics of Domesticity* (Middletown, CT: Wesleyan University Press, 1981); Chuck Vollan, "'For God and Home and South Dakota': The South Dakota Woman's Christian Temperance Union's Campaigns for Social Change," Missouri Valley History Conference, Omaha, Nebraska, March 6, 2015.

108 The question of divorce: On disagreements between suffragists: Ellen DuBois, "The Limitations of Sisterhood," in *Woman Suffrage and Women's Rights* (New York: New York University Press, 1998); Blake, *Road to Reno*.

109 "I impulsively urged": Blake, *Road to Reno*, 87.

109 "The States which have liberal": Elizabeth Cady Stanton, "Are Homogeneous Divorce Laws in All the States Desirable?," *North American Review* 170, no. 520 (March 1900): 405–409.

109 "The question of Divorce, like Marriage": Elizabeth Cady Stanton, "Divorce Versus Domestic Warfare," *Arena*, April 1890.

109 A dainty woman: Emma Cranmer's daughter, who later became a notable portrait painter, wrote about—and sketched—her mother in her memoir. Frances Cranmer Greenman, *Higher Than the Sky* (New York: Harper & Brothers, 1954).

110 "Sioux Falls is doomed": "South Dakota Divorces," *New York Sun*, January 1, 1893.

110 "Overdoing the matter": "The Divorce Law," *Argus-Leader*, January 7, 1893.

110 "spoke against the change": "The Divorce Bill," *Argus-Leader*, February 15, 1893.

PART III: BLANCHE

Chapter 11: A Moral Superstition

113 Photo: "Former Mrs. Molineux to Go on Stage," *Chicago Tribune*, August 27, 1905.

115 "Just take my name": "Gems Covered Her Fingers," *Cincinnati Enquirer*, November 18, 1902.

115 "bubbles of champagne": "The 'Woman in the Case,'" *Morning Star (Rockford, IL)*, April 9, 1899.

115 "Mrs. L. C. Johnson": "Gems Covered Her Fingers," *Cincinnati Enquirer*, November 18, 1902.

116 The hotel's newest guest: Three books touch on the life of Mrs. L. C. Johnson—soon to be revealed as Blanche Molineux—before Sioux Falls: Samuel Klaus, ed., *The People Against Molineux* (New York: Alfred A. Knoff, 1929); Jane Pejsa, *The Molineux Affair* (New York: St. Martin's Press, 1983); Harold Schechter, *The Devil's Gentleman* (New York: Ballantine Book, 2008). Blanche also left an unpublished memoir, which *The Molineux Affair* and *The Devil's Gentleman* quote from extensively. Unfortunately, it has since been lost. It is referenced in these notes as "memoir."

116 In Sioux Falls, it seemed: Blanche Molineux was most likely born in early 1874. (Her younger sister, Lora, was born in June 1875.) There is some conflict in the historical record, and her gravestone lists "unknown." I've chosen to echo the majority of sources.

116 If Mrs. L. C. Johnson could reinvent: On the "New Woman": Martha H. Patterson, *Beyond the Gibson Girl: Reimagining the American New Woman, 1895–1915* (Champaign: University of Illinois Press, 2005).

116 "masculine element": Memoir quoted in Schechter, *The Devil's Gentleman*, 42.

116 "that man": "Mrs. Molineux After Divorce," *Boston Herald*, November 18, 1902.

118 "a second Chicago": Between 1970 and 1977, the South Dakota History Project captured the voices of 2,450 state residents (about 750 have been added since), including some from Sioux Falls who distantly remembered the era of the divorce colony. Cynthia Pankow was one of them. Born in 1899, she was only a child when Blanche Molineux joined the divorce colony. In her seventies, Pankow remembered her father, who had arrived in Sioux Falls in 1885, talking about the growth and ambition of Sioux Falls. Of the colony, she recalled, "It put Sioux Falls on the map and I think it did a lot to develop the city in the early days." Oral history interview with

Cynthia Pankow, 1975, South Dakota Oral History Project, University of South Dakota, Vermillion, South Dakota.

119 "If the legislature had": "Bishop W. H. Hare," *Argus-Leader*, April 27, 1893.

119 "It's probably not too late": Howe, *The Life and Labors of Bishop Hare*, 378.

120 It was one of the three windows: The other two windows that Maggie donated to St. Augusta Cathedral remained in the church basement for years. Today they hang in their intended place above the altar at Calvary Cathedral—as the parish was known before the Astor donation and as it is called now—but they do not honor Maggie's family. The memorial panes on the remaining two windows were laboriously scratched out. Still, if you look closely enough, you can see Mary Alida De Stuers's name. On the windows: Susan Pryor Carleton and Robin Burns Reiper, "Calvary Cathedral's Stained-Glass Windows & Religious Symbols," Calvary Cathedral archives, Sioux Falls, South Dakota.

120 There was even the memorable case: The shooter was Rita Mackay, who later married (and then divorced) Sioux Falls resident Paul Wilkes. The incident had been a sensation in the city when it happened, but several years later, it was immortalized for the whole country in *The Divorce Mill*. The book, published in 1895, purported to be a factual sketch of Sioux Falls written by Harry Hazel, a Chicago newspaperman, and S. L. Lewis, a Chicago lawyer. In truth, it was a highly fictionalized account of the colony, written by Mary Cahill, an author who had gotten a divorce in the city in 1894. In this telling, Rita Mackay was Huldah Varker, a "beautiful but frivolous young wife," and her target was a jealous would-be suitor. She's a bad shot in fiction too, but the story ends tragically for Huldah, who is abandoned by her second husband. Impoverished and dying, Huldah begs her first husband for forgiveness. He grants it. "We should have made the best of an unfortunate marriage," he tells her.

121 "The change of the law": "The Bar Association of Codington," *Argus-Leader*, January 9, 1895.

121 "unsavory subject": "Against Divorce," *Argus-Leader*, February 25, 1895.

122 "a tragedy in human existence": "Favors Divorce," *Argus-Leader*, February 25, 1895.

122 "For any man": "Says He Didn't Say It," *Argus-Leader*, February 27, 1895.

122 "biblical causes": "Hare on Divorce," *Argus-Leader*, December 21, 1898.

123 "Many of the lawyers": *Watertown Public Opinion* quoted in "Sioux Falls, S.D., Secures Another Industry," *Argus-Leader*, May 3, 1899.

Chapter 12: Free as Air

125 Blanche Chesebrough first met: The newspapers, other historical documents, and, it seems, her own family could not agree on how to spell Blanche's last name. I've chosen the spelling Blanche used in adulthood.

125 "Bluest of skies": Memoir quoted in Schechter, *The Devil's Gentleman*, 47–48.

126 "That great center": Memoir quoted in Schechter, *The Devil's Gentleman*, 36–37.

127 "ever on their guard": Memoir quoted in Schechter, *The Devil's Gentleman*, 34.

128 "brute masculine force": Memoir quoted in Schechter, *The Devil's Gentleman*, 55.

128 "I wanted passion": Memoir quoted in Schechter, *The Devil's Gentleman*, 43–44.

128 "a narrowing of horizons": Memoir quoted in Schechter, *The Devil's Gentleman*, 46.

128 "half the young married women": "The 'Woman in the Case,'" *Morning Star (Rockford, IL)*, April 9, 1899.

128 "free as air": Memoir quoted in Schechter, *The Devil's Gentleman*, 56.

129 "It was an ecstasy!": Memoir quoted in Schechter, *The Devil's Gentleman*, 47.

129 "Tell Barnet the coast is clear": Schechter, *The Devil's Gentleman*, 70.

131 "lost manhood": Schechter, *The Devil's Gentleman*, 78.

131 "I want so much to see you": Memoir quoted in Schechter, *The Devil's Gentleman*, 91.

132 Blanche married Roland: On the Church of the Heavenly Rest: Tom Miller, "The Lost Church of the Heavenly Rest," *Daytonian in Manhattan*, November 17, 2014, http://daytoninmanhattan.blogspot.com/2014/11/the-lost-church-of-heavenly-rest-551.html.

132 "somehow, all glamour": Memoir quoted in Schechter, *The Devil's Gentleman*, 141.

132 "Police Want Roland": "Police Want Roland Burnham Molineaux [*sic*] in the Poisoning Case," *New York Journal*, January 2, 1899.

133 "You win": Schechter, *The Devil's Gentleman*, 61.

134 "immoral books": Schechter, *The Devil's Gentleman*, 230.

135 "Gentlemen, it is not often": Schechter, *The Devil's Gentleman*, 348.

135 "By George": "Smitten by Sight at Mrs. Molineux," *New York World*, November 5, 1903.

136 "What if she should come": "Mrs. Molineux a Bride Again," *St. Louis Post-Dispatch*, November 3, 1903.

Chapter 13: The Sentence

137 "Thank god my time": "Mrs. Molineux Ill in Sioux Falls," *St. Louis Post-Dispatch*, December 1, 1902.

139 "As I do not go out": "Two Sets of Children," *Seattle Daily Times*, December 21, 1902.

139 "I thought that out here": "Mrs. Molineux Denies Charge That She Sues for Divorce Because She Believes Her Husband Is Guilty," *Salt Lake Telegram*, November 24, 1902.

140 "Will you say to the women": "Defends Mrs. Molineux," *Sioux City Journal*, December 9, 1902.

140 In 1860, at the age of twenty-seven: Mary Walker ultimately divorced Albert in 1861 in New York. She returned home to seek her decree for legal reasons that would quickly become clear to Blanche. On Mary Walker and her divorce: Sharon M. Harris, *Dr. Mary Walker: An American Radical, 1832–1919* (New Brunswick, NJ: Rutgers University Press, 2009); divorce material, 1861–1869, box 2, Mary Edwards Walker Papers, Special Collections Research Center, Syracuse University, Syracuse, New York.

140 "wronged": "Defends Mrs. Molineux," *Sioux City Journal*, December 9, 1902.

140 "to be deprived": Mary Edwards Walker, *A Woman's Thoughts About Love and Marriage, Divorce, Etc.* (New York: Miller, 1871).

140 "Why she desires": "Defends Mrs. Molineux," *Sioux City Journal*, December 9, 1902.

141 "There is really nothing": "Divorce Sequence," *Sioux Falls Press*, November 18, 1902.

141 "more like home": "Molineux in Police Court," *Baltimore Sun*, November 19, 1902.

142 "an embarrassing position": "Out of Misery," *Argus-Leader*, January 6, 1896.

143 "the picture of poverty": "Jurymen Led the Applause," *New York Times*, June 11, 1893.

144 "You abandoned her": "Pollock's Ordeal," *New York World*, June 23, 1893.

146 "engaged in a good deal": Supreme Court of the United States, *Transcript of Record: Annie Andrews, Plaintiff in Error vs. Kate H. Andrews* (Washington, DC: Judd & Detweiler, 1901), 24.

147 "When any inhabitant": *The Revised Statutes of the Commonwealth of Massachusetts* (Boston: Dutton & Wentworth, 1836), 479–484.

147 Annie appealed the decision: On legal decisions, before and after *Andrews*, emerging from migratory divorce cases: Michael J. Hidden, "If You Grant

It, They Will Come: The History and Enduring Legal Legacy of Migratory Divorce," *Utah Law Review* (2021).

147 "This would be but to declare": *Andrews v. Andrews*, 188 U.S. 14 (1903).

148 "The decision of the U.S. Supreme Ct": William Hobart Hare to Samuel Dike, January 21, 1903, box 11, Samuel W. Dike Papers, Library of Congress, Washington, DC.

148 "What's going to become of us?": "Now Hopeful," *Boston Globe*, January 28, 1903.

Chapter 14: To Be Left Alone

149 "Their son is returned": Memoir quoted in Harold Schechter, *The Devil's Gentleman* (New York: Ballantine Book, 2008), 141.

150 "Mrs. Blanche Chesebrough, as she": "No Longer Mrs. Molineux," *Boston Daily Globe*, September 4, 1903.

151 "The husband who has ceased": Roland Burnham Molineux, *The Vice Admiral of the Blue* (Toronto: Copp, Clark, 1903).

152 "The real Molineux story": "Mrs. Molineux Asks $100,000 from Former Husband's Father," *Seattle Daily Times*, September 16, 1903.

153 "I know nothing": "Molineux Suit in Chicago?," *Chicago Tribune*, October 3, 1903.

153 "Somebody has lied": "Somebody Has Lied," *Aberdeen Daily News*, October 8, 1903.

153 "There is no doubt": "Mrs. Molineux's Lawyer in New York Insists She Has Absolute Divorce," *Boston Post*, October 6, 1903.

153 "settled to her entire satisfaction": "Says She Got Divorce," *Union County Courier (Elk Point, SD)*, October 6, 1903.

153 "That's the funniest thing": "Molineux's Wife Laughs at Report," *New York World*, October 3, 1903.

154 "Papers taken by attorney": *Molineux v. Molineux* (SD 1st Ct. 1903).

154 "a report that lacks": "More Than His Client, He Says," *Boston Herald*, September 23, 1903.

154 "Have I not endured": "Not Engaged to Lawyer," *Boston Globe*, September 23, 1903.

156 "a good South Dakota girl": "May Cause Social War," *Mitchell Capital*, November 27, 1903.

157 Mima and Clark promptly: Mima Hubbard and Clark Brown's story did not end there. Though neither was well known before Mima's divorce, the couple made headlines in January 1892 when Clark got cold feet. He jumped

from a moving train outside Sioux City, Iowa, in an attempt to escape Mima. But the pair quickly reconciled. They were married in Rapid City, South Dakota, a month later. Mima and Clark also inspired the characters of Mrs. Taylor and Sam Thompson in the fictionalized *The Divorce Mill*.

158 "vulgar" and "plebeian": "Another Story About Mrs. Roland Molineux," *Omaha World Herald*, October 11, 1903.

158 "the murderer's wife": Flora Bigelow Dodge to John Bigelow, May 9, 1904, Bigelow Family Papers, New York Public Library, New York, New York.

158 "I desire my freedom": "Strange Story of Mrs. Blanche Molineux," *Omaha World Herald*, November 23, 1902.

159 "frisky past": Flora Bigelow Dodge to John Bigelow, May 9, 1904, Bigelow Family Papers.

PART IV: FLORA

Chapter 15: Happiness Will Follow Thee

161 Photo: Cleveland Colby Colgate Photographic Material, MS2001.086, Box 8, Folder 5, Colby-Sawyer College, New London, New Hampshire.

163 "most daring, most original": "Most Daring, Most Original, Cleverest Woman in New York Society Tires of Her Husband," *Chicago American*, [February 1903?].

163 "unusual individuality": "Mrs. Dodge Goes to Sioux Falls," *New York World*, January 28, 1903.

163 She'd been born to it: On the Bigelow family: Margaret Clapp, *Forgotten First Citizen* (Boston: Little Brown, 1947).

164 "Mon Dieu!": William Roscoe Thayer, *The Life and Letters of John Hay* (Boston: Houghton Mifflin Company, 1915), 1:223.

164 "as near the perfection": Clapp, *Forgotten First Citizen*, 84.

164 "eccentric": "Most Daring, Most Original, Cleverest Woman in New York Society Tires of Her Husband," *Chicago American*, [February 1903?].

164 George Vanderbilt had purchased: On George Vanderbilt and his properties: Denise Kiernan, *The Last Castle: The Epic Story of Love, Loss and American Royalty in the Nation's Largest Home* (New York: Atria, 2017).

165 "Mrs. Charles Stuart Dodge was the heroine": "Coaching in the Teeth of a Gale," *Philadelphia Inquirer*, April 10, 1898.

166 "a legal and dignified Dakota divorce": Flora Bigelow Dodge to John Bigelow, April 12, 1904, Bigelow Family Papers.

166 "The peril of allowing": John Bigelow's diary, January 14, 1903, Bigelow Family Papers.

167 "had confessed to an incurable affection": John Bigelow's diary, March 8, 1886, Bigelow Family Papers.

167 "do everything in their power": John Bigelow's diary, July 24, 1886, Bigelow Family Papers.

168 "will probably be the youngest": "The Season's Close," *Chicago Tribune*, September 5, 1886.

169 "But when she walked down": "Society Topics of the Week," *New York Times*, December 19, 1886.

169 A crowd of nearly twelve hundred: On Anna Eva Fay: Barry H. Wiley, *The Indescribable Phenomenon: The Life and Mysteries of Anna Eva Fay* (Seattle, WA: Hermetic Press, 2005).

170 "sterner sex": "Anna Eva Fay," *Argus-Leader*, February 6, 1903.

170 There were those who went to every show: On spiritualism and spectacle: Simone Natale, *Supernatural Entertainments* (University Park: Pennsylvania State University Press, 2016.)

170 "a cast in the eye": "Believes in Omens," *Argus-Leader*, February 12, 1903.

170 "looks after us all": Flora Bigelow Dodge to Grace Bigelow, January 29, 1903, Bigelow Family Papers.

171 "He cried aloud": Flora Bigelow Dodge, "Happiness: An Allegory," *Short Stories: A Magazine of Fact and Fiction* (July 1893): 257–259.

171 "Oh, I must be an unnatural woman": Flora Bigelow Dodge, "Mrs. Mack's Example," *Smart Set* (September 1901): 54.

172 The idea that a woman: On conceptions of happiness in marriage: Stephanie Coontz, *Marriage, a History* (New York: Viking Penguin, 2005).

172 She wrote to her father: Flora's daughter was known to some as Lucie or Luci, but Flora most often referred to her as Lucy.

172 "I fear my unhappiness": Flora Bigelow Dodge to John Bigelow, [1902], Bigelow Family Papers.

172 "the years of misery": Flora Bigelow Dodge to John Bigelow, April 22, 1903, Bigelow Family Papers.

172 "I can be a better friend": Flora Bigelow Dodge to John Bigelow, [1902], Bigelow Family Papers.

172 "First let it be said": "Most Daring, Most Original, Cleverest Woman in New York Society Tires of Her Husband," *Chicago American*, [February 1903?].

173   "dark and bitter": Anna Eva Fay, "Mind Reading," *Chicago Post*, January 5, 1907.

173   "wonderful phenomena": Wiley, *The Indescribable Phenomenon*, 116.

173   "how much good unhappiness": Flora Bigelow Dodge to John Bigelow, February 17, 1903, Bigelow Family Papers.

Chapter 16: A Tramp and an Exile

174   "Dear Papa": Flora Bigelow Dodge to John Bigelow, March 16, 1903, Bigelow Family Papers.

174   "foolish letters": Flora Bigelow Dodge to John Bigelow, February 23, 1903, Bigelow Family Papers.

174   "I am not unhappy": Flora Bigelow Dodge to John Bigelow, February 23, 1903, Bigelow Family Papers.

175   "It seems as if I was doomed": Flora Bigelow Dodge to John Bigelow, March 16, 1903, Bigelow Family Papers.

175   "The richer women spend": Flora Bigelow Dodge to Grace Bigelow, January 29, 1903, Bigelow Family Papers.

175   "I shall not answer": Flora Bigelow Dodge to John Bigelow, February 11, 1903, Bigelow Family Papers.

175   "Doomed to being a tramp": Flora Bigelow Dodge to John Bigelow, March 16, 1903, Bigelow Family Papers.

175   "unnecessary unhappiness": Flora Bigelow Dodge to John Bigelow, [1902?], Bigelow Family Papers.

176   "give up New York absolutely": Flora Bigelow Dodge to John Bigelow, March 16, 1903, Bigelow Family Papers.

176   "a terrible warning": "The Latest Phase of the De Stuers Divorce," *Town Topics*, April 14, 1892.

179   "I want to give you a good race": David Paine, *The Zborowski Inheritance* (Cambridge, UK: Victoire Press Ltd, 2008), 88.

180   "those who play fast": [William Hobart Hare], "From Lover's Arms to Church," *Argus-Leader*, April 2, 1903.

180   First came the story: A sensational look at the Burdick case: Arthur Forrest, *Buffalo's Tragic Mystery* (Baltimore: Phoenix Publishing Company, [1903?]).

180   "the devastating course of lustful sin": [William Hobart Hare], "From Lover's Arms to Church," *Argus-Leader*, April 2, 1903.

181   "the intruder": Open letter from William Hobart Hare, April 7, 1903, William Hobart Hare missions papers, Houghton Library, Harvard University, Cambridge, Massachusetts.

181 "final straw": "Final Straw," *Boston Globe*, November 23, 1902.

181 "We need to be shocked": [William Hobart Hare], "From Lover's Arms to Church," *Argus-Leader*, April 2, 1903.

182 "Within the few days last past": Open letter from William Hobart Hare, April 7, 1903, William Hobart Hare missions papers.

Chapter 17: Stupid, Unjust, Monstrous, and Foolish

183 "lived with her 'father'": Flora Bigelow Dodge to John Bigelow, April 7, 1903, Bigelow Family Papers.

183 "a dear little cottage": Flora Bigelow Dodge to Mildred, March 7, 1903, Bigelow Family Papers.

183 "a bum house": Johnny Bigelow to John Bigelow, [March 1903?], Bigelow Family Papers.

185 In 1891, he counseled: On Elliott Roosevelt: Mason White, "Elliot, the Tragic Roosevelt," *Hudson Valley Regional Review* 5, no. 1 (March 1988): 17–29.

185 "I have no patience": Theodore Roosevelt to Anna Roosevelt Cowles, July 2, 1891, Anna Roosevelt Cowles Papers, Houghton Library, Harvard University, Cambridge, Massachusetts.

185 "stupid and unjust": Theodore Roosevelt to Anna Roosevelt Cowles, July 19 and August 1, 1895, Anna Roosevelt Cowles Papers.

186 "the spirit of public decency": Kathleen Dalton, *Theodore Roosevelt: A Strenuous Life* (New York: Vintage Books, 2002), 301.

186 "If the homes are all straight": Dalton, *Theodore Roosevelt*, 302.

187 "Our President": "More Details of the President's Visit," *Argus-Leader*, April 6, 1908.

187 "huge and complex problems": "Address of President at Sioux Falls This Morning," *Argus-Leader*, April 6, 1903.

187 "clever and interesting": Flora Bigelow Dodge to John Bigelow, February 26, 1903, Bigelow Family Papers.

187 "charming, clever, and capable": Flora Bigelow Dodge to John Bigelow, [March?] 1903, Bigelow Family Papers.

187 "The people here": Flora Bigelow Dodge to John Bigelow, February 26, 1903, Bigelow Family Papers.

187 "Eastern resident": Flora Bigelow Dodge to John Bigelow, February 7, 1903, Bigelow Family Papers.

188 "'Sioux Society' turns up": Flora Bigelow Dodge to John Bigelow, February 7, 1903, Bigelow Family Papers.

188 "by accident": Flora Bigelow Dodge to John Bigelow, April 7, 1903, Bigelow Family Papers.

189 "Much of his strength": Flora Bigelow Dodge to John Bigelow, March 3, 1903, Bigelow Family Papers.

189 "demoralizing," she thought: Flora Bigelow Dodge to John Bigelow, March 16, 1903, Bigelow Family Papers.

189 "because all the boys do": Flora Bigelow Dodge to John Bigelow, April 22, 1903, Bigelow Family Papers.

189 "see any stampede": Flora Bigelow Dodge to John Bigelow, February 7, 1903, Bigelow Family Papers.

189 "perfect health as never before": John Bigelow's diary, July 23, 1903, Bigelow Family Papers.

189 "incompetence for the management": John Bigelow's diary, December 9, 1889, Bigelow Family Papers.

190 "almost on the prairies": Flora Bigelow Dodge to John Bigelow, October 6, 1903, Bigelow Family Papers.

190 "the house of peace": Flora Bigelow Dodge to John Bigelow, October 25, 1903, Bigelow Family Papers.

191 "They made such a good impression": Flora Bigelow Dodge to Grace Bigelow, October 28, 1903, Bigelow Family Papers.

191 "I have heaps of callers": Flora Bigelow Dodge to John Bigelow, December 17, 1903, Bigelow Family Papers.

191 "cautious and slow": Flora Bigelow Dodge to John Bigelow, March 16, 1903, Bigelow Family Papers.

191 "great introducer": "Joe Leiter Wins a Heart," *Erie Times News*, October 3, 1903.

191 "dubious authority": "The Whirl of Society," *Inter Ocean*, October 3, 1903.

191 "Mrs. Dodge is just the sort": "Joe Leiter Remains Convincingly Silent," *Town Topics*, October 8, 1903.

191 "There is absolutely no truth": "Not Engaged to Leiter," *Sioux City Journal*, October 12, 1903.

192 "killing"—hilarious—"letter": Flora Bigelow Dodge to John Bigelow, October 18, 1903, Bigelow Family Papers.

193 "I very much fear": Flora Bigelow Dodge to John Bigelow, January 19, 1904, Bigelow Family Papers.

193 "mere trifle": "Poultney Bigelow Refuses to Discuss His Domestic Troubles," *Cincinnati Enquirer*, March 30, 1902.

193　He felt no social: And when Poultney Bigelow did choose to remarry, he did so in unquestioned defiance of the law. He was wed to Lillian Pritchard in April 1911, almost three decades before his former wife's death.

193　"I feel as if I were being buried": Flora Bigelow Dodge to John Bigelow, February 2, 1904, Bigelow Family Papers.

Chapter 18: Light in the Sky

194　"though a charming man": Flora Bigelow Dodge to John Bigelow, February 10, 1904, Bigelow Family Papers.

194　"exercise and swearing": Flora Bigelow Dodge to John Bigelow, January 19, 1904, Bigelow Family Papers.

195　"It seems a long time": Flora Bigelow Dodge to John Bigelow, March 1, 1904, Bigelow Family Papers.

195　Delia—her "rock": Flora Bigelow Dodge to John Bigelow, April 12, 1904, Bigelow Family Papers.

196　"much touched by the real kindness": Flora Bigelow Dodge to John Bigelow, April 20, 1904, Bigelow Family Papers.

196　"beloved but very bitter": Flora Bigelow Dodge to John Bigelow, May 16, 1904, Bigelow Family Papers.

197　"want to hold my head up": Flora Bigelow Dodge to John Bigelow, April 23, 1904, Bigelow Family Papers.

197　"My divorce debut": Flora Bigelow Dodge to John Bigelow, May 2, 1904, Bigelow Family Papers.

197　"People could hardly believe": Flora Bigelow Dodge to John Bigelow, September 6, 1904, Bigelow Family Papers.

197　"I skip it once in a while": Flora Bigelow Dodge to John Bigelow, May 16, 1904, Bigelow Family Papers.

198　"a fancy price": "The Benefit Concert," *Argus-Leader*, October 10, 1904.

198　"days of self-denying heroism": Howe, *The Life and Labors of Bishop Hare*, 389.

198　"a well man": "Annual Report of Officers and Committees," *Journal of the Convocations Annual Address of the Bishop* (1904): III–IV.

199　"I cannot keep up": Howe, *The Life and Labors of Bishop Hare*, 391.

199　"The work in South Dakota": "Annual Report of Officers and Committees," IV.

199　"reverent and right": "Annual Report of Officers and Committees," XIII–XV.

200　"There is no way the church": "Polygamy That's as Bad as Utah's," *Boston Globe*, October 13, 1904.

201　"out of the divorce business": "The Divorce Compromise," *Argus-Leader*, October 21, 1904.

202 "It is merely a marital disagreement": "Col. Jewell and Wife Part," *New York Sun*, March 12, 1903.

202 "I feel that Mr. Jewell's usefulness": Theodore Roosevelt to Wilson Shannon Bissell, June 26, 1903, Theodore Roosevelt Papers, Library of Congress, Washington, DC.

203 "importance, but a wholly ephemeral importance": Theodore Roosevelt, "Speech to the Committee of the Inter-church Conference on Marriage and Divorce, January 26, 1905," in *A Compilation of the Messages and Speeches of Theodore Roosevelt, 1901–1905*, ed. Alfred Henry Lewis (New York: Bureau of National Literature and Art, 1906), 548.

203 "Divorce laws are dangerously lax": Theodore Roosevelt, "Special Message," January 30, 1905, The American Presidency Project, www.presidency .ucsb.edu/documents/special-message-523.

203 "It is mere foolishness": Theodore Roosevelt to Robert Grant, March 14, 1905, Theodore Roosevelt Collection, Harvard University, Cambridge, Massachusetts.

203 "deliberately forego": Theodore Roosevelt, Remarks Before the Mothers' Congress, March 13, 1905, The American Presidency Project, www .presidency.ucsb.edu/documents/remarks-before-the-mothers-congress.

Chapter 19: Heart

205 "I am so much happier": Flora Bigelow Dodge to John Bigelow, November 8, 1904, Bigelow Family Papers.

207 "the quaintest": "As I predicted," *Town Topics*, May 22, 1905.

207 "first conceived of his fascination": "Society News and Chat of the Week," *Washington Times*, June 18, 1905.

208 "Many 'colonists' walk": "Are Wed at Noon," *Argus-Leader*, July 6, 1905.

208 "loves me enough to work for me": Flora Bigelow Dodge to John Bigelow, [June 1905?], Bigelow Family Papers.

208 "I am convinced that the love": Flora Bigelow Dodge to John Bigelow, May 27, 1905, Bigelow Family Papers.

208 "I will always love it": Flora Bigelow Dodge to John Bigelow, July 4, 1905, Bigelow Family Papers.

209 "Were I a younger woman": Flora Bigelow Dodge to John Bigelow, June 22, 1905, Bigelow Family Papers.

210 "I never imagined anything": Flora Bigelow Dodge to John Bigelow, June 27, 1896, Bigelow Family Papers.

210 Ivor was a good friend: On Churchill and the Guests: David Cannadine, "The Pitfalls of Family Piety," in *Churchill: A Major New Assessment of His*

Life in Peace and War, ed. Robert Blake and William Roger Louis (New York: W. W. Norton, 1993).

211 "like a rotten coward": Flora Bigelow Dodge to John Bigelow, [1905?], Bigelow Family Papers.

211 "We are free": Lucy Bigelow to John Bigelow, September 18, 1905, Bigelow Family Papers.

212 "wonderful dream about mama": Flora Guest to John Bigelow, February 13, 1906, Bigelow Family Papers.

212 "He has heard of the row": Flora Guest to John Bigelow, February 21, 1906, Bigelow Family Papers.

213 "This is a hint": Associated Press quoted in "King Edward Is Gracious," *Argus-Leader*, May 14, 1906.

Epilogue: A Rising of Ideals

217 "likely to cause considerable disaster": *Haddock v. Haddock*, 201 U.S. 562 (1906).

217 "Mrs. Bull and myself are content": "Suit Based on Ruling of US Supreme Court," *Boston Globe*, May 23, 1906.

217 At the Cataract House, Martha found: Letters that Alfred Dupont wrote to Frank L. Connable, general manager of the E. I. Dupont de Nemours Company, from Sioux Falls, primarily focused on business matters, are archived at the Hagley Museum and Library. Alfred I. du Pont–Frank L. Connable correspondence, Eugene du Pont Papers, Hagley Museum and Library, Wilmington, Delaware.

218 "At present the wide differences": Theodore Roosevelt, "Sixth Annual Message," December 3, 1906, The American Presidency Project, www.presidency .ucsb.edu/documents/sixth-annual-message-4.

218 "Martha's bad luck": "The Heliotrope Belle," *Argus-Leader*, May 15, 1906.

218 "I am very anxious to spend": Quoted in "Mrs. James G. II," *Argus-Leader*, May 11, 1906.

219 "the first Christmas": "Mrs. Jas. G. Blaine's Divorce," *New York Sun*, December 24, 1906.

219 "heliotrope belle": "The Heliotrope Belle," *Argus-Leader*, May 15, 1906.

220 "States which have strict laws": "Uniform Divorce Laws," *New York Tribune*, November 16, 1906.

220 "I am intensely jealous": Peabody, *Zitkano Duzahan, Swift Bird*, 62–63.

221 "a roll of dishonor": "They Will be Published," *Argus-Leader*, May 6, 1907.

222 "nasty importations": *The Migratory Divorce Traffic in South Dakota* (Sioux Falls: Will A. Beach Printing, 1908), 7.

222 In November 1908, the state's residents: *South Dakota Legislative Manual 1909* (Pierre: State Publishing Company, 1909), 373.

223 Between 1887 and 1906: Bureau of the Census, *Census Bulletin 96* (Washington, DC: Government Printing Office, 1908).

223 During the twenty-year period: US Bureau of Labor, *Report on Marriage and Divorce, 1867–1906*, 77.

223 The state that had until days earlier: US Bureau of Labor, *Report on Marriage and Divorce, 1867–1906*, 72.

223 Bishop Hare had preached against: US Bureau of Labor, *Report on Marriage and Divorce, 1867–1906*, 54.

223 In the same period: US Bureau of Labor, *Report on Marriage and Divorce, 1867–1906*, 13.

224 "In general, white women": Bureau of the Census, *Census Bulletin*.

224 "The statistics given out": "Gibbons Again on Divorce Evil," *Gazette (York, PA)*, November 30, 1908.

224 In 1906, there had been: "Divorce Statistics," *New York Times*, January 13, 1909.

224 But that did not alarm: I can find no excuse to tell Walter Willcox's full story here, but the statistician's letters circa 1890 are fascinating. They show a young man figuring out what he wants marriage to be as he woos his future wife, Alice Work, and studies the issue of divorce. Walter Francis Willcox papers, Library of Congress, Washington, DC.

224 "We are slowly awakening": "Marriage and Divorce," *Cornell Sun*, November 24, 1909.

225 Elsewhere, though, the laws: On the evolution of divorce laws: Joanna L. Grossman and Lawrence M. Friedman, *Inside the Castle: Law and Family in the 20th Century* (Princeton, NJ: Princeton University Press, 2011).

225 Lillie Hendrix and Otis Williams: On *Williams v. North Carolina*: Hendrik Hartog, *Man and Wife in America* (Cambridge, MA: Harvard University Press, 2000); Herbert Baer, "So Your Client Wants a Divorce," *North Carolina Law Review* 24, no. 1 (1945–1946); William Lewis Parsons, "The Epic of Otis and Lillie," *Massachusetts Law Quarterly* 32, no. 22 (1947); Thomas Reed Powell, "And Repent with Leisure," *Harvard Law Review* 58, no. 7 (September 1945).

226 Following the *Williams* decisions: On South Carolina's twentieth-century divorce laws: Kellen Funk, "'Let No Man Put Asunder': South Carolina's Law of Divorce, 1895–1950," *South Carolina Historical Magazine* 110, no. 3/4 (July–October 2009): 134–153.

226 "The sanctity of marriage": Funk, "Let No Man Put Asunder," 60.

227 It would take New York: On New York's twentieth-century divorce laws: J. Herbie DiFonzo and Ruth C. Stern, "Addicted to Fault: Why Divorce Reform Has Lagged in New York," *Pace Law Review* 27 (2007): 559–603.

227 New York residents had long ago: One such "unkissed professional $10-a-raid co-respondent" was Sara Ellis, a petite, twenty-year-old brunette. By 1948, Sara, who was married with three children, had appeared as the other women in about thirty-five New York divorce cases—sometimes posing as the "unknown woman," conveniently spotted in a hotel room with a man who wished a divorce, and other times appearing on the stand to falsely admit to an affair. (In preparation for her testimony, she would be coached by the couple seeking their freedom.) Sara exposed the "divorce racket," as the newspapers called it, to authorities when the private investigator who employed her fell behind in her payments. An eighteen-month investigation snared at least ten actresses, PIs, and lawyers involved in the scheme. Sara pled guilty to charges of perjury and received a suspended sentence for her cooperation. According to one lawyer, who described Sara and her accomplices as "benefactors of humanity," Sara simply wanted "to be of service to the depressed and incompatible couples of New York." Norma Abrams and Henry Lee, "Hired-Girlie Divorce Probe to Sift 9,000," *New York Daily News*, December 1, 1948.

227 The absurdity of it all: On mid-twentieth-century understanding of Mexican divorces: Hilery Silverman, "Effect of Mexican Divorces in United States," *University of Miami Law Review* 9 (1955): 186–201.

227 Three years later, California governor: On the evolution of no-fault divorce: J. Herbie Di Fonzo, *Beneath the Fault Line: The Popular Culture of Divorce in Twentieth-Century America* (Charlottesville: University of Virginia Press, 1997).

228 "divorce revolution": For example, Bob Rose, "Divorce Revolution in California," *Chicago Tribune*, October 3, 1969.

228 "I made up my mind": "Mme. De Stuers Here," *Chicago Tribune*, November 7, 1891.

Index

Index

clergy (*Cont.*)
  limiting access to divorce, xiii
  ongoing legislative fight over
    divorce laws, 121–123
  See also Hare, William Hobart
Cleveland, Grover, 64–65, 80, 90,
  202
Coaching Club, 165
Coles, Ethel, 206
Coles, Henry, 206
collusion
  Andrews divorce, 39–40
  Blaine divorce, 87–90
  Maggie De Stuers's attempt to buy
    her freedom, 39
  Pollock divorce, 143
Congress, US
  control over marriage and divorce,
    100–102
  proposed constitutional
    amendment for control of
    marriage and divorce, 72–74,
    100–102, 132, 218, 220
Connecticut: *Haddock v. Haddock*,
  217
Constitution, U.S.: proposed
  amendment for control of
  marriage and divorce, 72–74,
  100–102, 132, 218, 220
Cook, Charles Smith, 120
Coppinger, Alice, 95
Cornell, Billy, 120–121
Cornish, Harry, 133–134
Corrigan, Archbishop Michael,
  66–67, 99
Corson, Harry, 8, 36, 118
Corson, Henry, 8, 36, 118

Cowles, Will, 185–186
Cranmer, Emma, 107–110
Cruzan, John A., 21, 54
Cuthbertson, Florence, 9, 34, 103
cyanide poisoning, 133–134

Dakota Territory
  divorce laws, 14
  divorce statistics, xiv
  establishment of, 6
  See also North Dakota; South
    Dakota
Dakota War (1862), 6
De Stuers, Alida "May," 51, 55
De Stuers, Alphonse Lambert
    Eugene, Baron
  accusations of adultery against
    Maggie, 40–45, 49, 51–52
  accusations of spousal cruelty
    during the trial, 48–51
  attempt to institutionalize Maggie,
    30–32, 53
  background and character, 4–5
  challenging Maggie's divorce,
    28–29, 176–177
  controlling nature, 29–31
  Maggie's attempts to leave, 10–11
  Maggie's petition for divorce,
    11–13, 23–25
  marital cruelty, 48–51, 74
  marriage of, 3–5
  reconciliation negotiation,
    13–14
  trial outcome, 53
  trial testimony, 52
De Stuers, Bertie, 51
De Stuers, John, 51